The Subsidized Muse

The Twentieth Century Fund

The Twentieth Century Fund is an independent research foundation that undertakes policy studies of economic, political, and social institutions and issues. The Fund was founded in 1919 and endowed by Edward A. Filene.

The Subsidized Muse

Public Support for the Arts
in the United States

Dick Netzer

Dean and Professor of Economics
Graduate School of Public Administration
New York University

A Twentieth Century Fund Study

CAMBRIDGE UNIVERSITY PRESS
CAMBRIDGE
LONDON · NEW YORK · MELBOURNE

Published by the Syndics of the Cambridge University Press
The Pitt Building, Trumpington Street, Cambridge CB2 1RP
Bentley House, 200 Euston Road, London NW1 2DB
32 East 57th Street, New York, NY 10022, USA
296 Beaconsfield Parade, Middle Park, Melbourne 3206, Australia

First published 1978

Printed in the United States of America
Typeset by Huron Valley Graphics, Ann Arbor, Michigan
Printed and bound by Vail-Ballou Press, Inc.,
Binghamton, New York

Library of Congress Cataloging in Publication Data
Netzer, Dick, 1928–
The subsidized muse.
"A Twentieth Century Fund study."
Bibliography: p.
1.   Federal aid to the arts – United States.   2.   Arts – Scholarships, fel-
lowships, etc. – United States.   3.   National Endowment for the
Arts.   4.   Art commissions – United States.   I.   Title.
NX730.N4   338.4′7′700973   77–25441
ISBN 0 521 21966 3

Contents

Foreword

In the last decade, government has become a major – and increasingly generous – direct patron of the arts. From 1965 to 1974, the appropriations for the National Endowment for the Arts rose from $8 million to $74 million. State and local support for the arts also increased substantially. Much of this expansion was the result of the efforts of various spokesmen for the arts, as well as the findings of a pioneering Twentieth Century Fund Study, *Performing Arts: The Economic Dilemma,* by William J. Baumol and William G. Bowen, published in 1967. The Baumol-Bowen study, which indicated that the performing arts would face increasingly severe financial straits in the absence of significant increases in funding from sources other than the market, strongly influenced public policy toward the arts at a time when the National Endowment for the Arts was just getting under way.

In this formative period, little critical analysis of the government's role was produced. But a few years ago, the trustees of the Twentieth Century Fund recognized that this expansion of funding could not continue indefinitely and that the need for an independent assessment of direct government support of the arts created a fresh opportunity for the Fund to contribute to public debate on this subject. Accordingly, the Fund has mounted a series of projects dealing with public policy toward the arts. None of these projects addresses the immediate concerns of those in this field more directly than the evaluation of the National Endowment for the Arts and the state arts agencies that Dick Netzer, Dean of the Graduate School of Public Administration of New York University, agreed to undertake.

As an economist, Netzer began with the proposition that a state of affairs in which artistic creation outstrips available funding is not inherently undesirable, that creative individuals will always be able to conceive of more artistic productions than can be financed, no matter how much money is available to them. With that point in mind, he

vii

proceeded to identify the conditions under which public support generally is justified and the objectives such support should have.

Netzer also sought to determine the criteria that the agencies through which public support for the arts is channeled have used in making grants. One product of this effort is a detailed statistical presentation that clearly illustrates the economic effects and general orientation of public support for the arts in the past decade.

Until fairly recently, rapid increases in funding have given government arts agencies the luxury of distributing grants to worthy applicants without considering such questions as the relative merits of new applicants as opposed to past grant recipients, who have become somewhat dependent on government subsidy. Competing claims on public resources for purposes other than sustaining the arts are eliminating this luxury. So arts agencies now confront the need to make hard choices.

To assist them in making these choices, Netzer has developed recommendations designed to guide arts agencies in using the funds available to them in the public interest. The Fund is grateful to him for his lively and provocative treatment of a subject that has too often suffered from rhetorical excess or bureaucratic insensitivity.

M. J. Rossant, *Director*
The Twentieth Century Fund
October 1977

Preface

The history of the research project that led to this book begins with an article I wrote in the quarterly journal I edit, *New York Affairs*. The article was a skeptical review of the case for public subsidy of the arts and the skepticism was exaggerated, in order to elicit discussion in the pages of the journal. In the event, the only reaction came from the Twentieth Century Fund; the Fund invited a research proposal and ultimately accepted the proposal.

I began with some knowledge of government and government subsidies to private-sector institutions and activities, but only an ordinary consumer's knowledge of the arts (no doubt this will be all too clear to the informed reader). Thus, the help of my informants, associates and critics was invaluable. I am especially indebted to Geraldine L. Katz, who prepared the appendixes, generally assisted me with the research, did much of the interviewing for the case studies reported in Chapter 5, and wrote numerous research memoranda incorporated in the text of the book. I also am grateful for the many substantive criticisms and suggestions made by Walter Klein, M. J. Rossant, and John Booth of the Twentieth Century Fund; three anonymous reviewers retained by the Fund; and my New York University colleagues, Leanna Stiefel and Ralph Kaminsky. The original manuscript was faultlessly typed by Beth Blaskey.

D. N.

1

The Open Questions

Since the end of World War II, artistic and cultural activities have proliferated in the United States. Arts institutions and professional artists have become much more numerous; new forms of both "high" and "mass" art have been developed; amateur participation in the arts has grown greatly; and the audiences for most art forms have vastly expanded. Cultural events are no longer confined to New York and a small number of other cities; instead, like the performing arts centers and art museums that have sprouted all over the country, they are now widely available.

This flowering of artistic activity is in part the result of increases in real incomes and population and a substantial rise in educational levels. It also is traceable to important technological changes: television, long-playing records, even the advent of jet airplanes, which have facilitated touring for artists and art groups.

A by-product of this boom in artistic activity is heightened public concern about such issues as the financing, organization, social functions, and future directions of the arts. Some of these issues are essentially aesthetic and, as such, are beyond the scope of this book. But others involve decisions about how to allocate the limited time, energy, and money that arts organizations, artists, foundations, private donors, and government officials and agencies have at their disposal. Such issues, being essentially social and economic, are the main concern of this book.

Among the most difficult of these issues are those that arise from the ancient conflict between the old, established, and traditional arts and the new, unconventional, and nonestablished (or even antiestablishment) arts. The major existing arts institutions, particularly in the live performing arts and in the world of museums, tend to be concentrated geographically, and they directly serve only a relatively small part of the total population. But these organizations are in a very real sense the carriers of the best of the high culture that has developed in the Western world since the Renaissance. It is appropriate to ask where we as a society should place our emphasis: on strengthening these institutions, on promoting the geographical diffusion of artistic activities and the development of new audiences, or on encouraging new efforts in these artistic media. We also must decide whether to support amateur participation in the arts (however the arts are defined), or to devote the resources available for fostering the arts entirely to professional artistic activity. In either case, we must define the criteria that distinguish professional from amateur.

This list by no means exhausts the open questions confronting policy making in the arts. For example, in the short run, at least, the concerns of individual artists and arts institutions are not identical; how much attention should we pay to the art forms, such as literature and the visual arts, in which individual writers, painters, or sculptors, rather than arts institutions, predominate? Even within the art forms, such as the various performing arts, that are dominated by institutionalized production, individual artists may have needs that are not met by the support and encouragement that may be available to institutions.

Aside from live, high-culture music, dance, and opera, the arts in America are produced both for profit and on a nonprofit basis. Should the commercial sector (for example, the Broadway stage, trade publishers, commercial art galleries, Hollywood) be left to fend for itself, or should it have some degree of public support? Should the earnings of the commercial sector be tapped for the nonprofit sector, which often feeds the commercial with experienced artists and previously tested works?

In all Western countries, the average earnings of professional artists and performers are notoriously low. Is this state of affairs a matter for public concern? If so, how much emphasis should there be on raising the earnings of artists compared to, say, increasing the number of professional artists, expanding audiences, or improving the physical conditions in which the arts are presented? More broadly, what social role should the artist play: should he be entertainer, educator, verbal and nonverbal philosopher, or ultimate product of civilization? Each of these conceivably desirable roles calls for quite different organizational and financial arrangements. These issues are not new, but until quite recently concern with them was confined to arts producers, critics, private supporters of the arts, and consumers – although all of us were affected by their decisions. Today we confront the issues as taxpayers providing sizable cash appropriations from tax revenue in direct governmental support of the arts.

Arts Policy as Public Policy

Direct public support of the arts is a very new thing in the United States. For a good many years, cosmopolitan Americans viewed as evidence of cultural barbarism the failure of the United States to provide as much public support of the arts and cultural institutions as a number of much poorer European countries. American parsimony has been contrasted with public maintenance of opera in even small Italian cities; the generous support provided by the nationwide British Arts Council and municipal tax rates in Britain; and the lavish and loving reconstruction of war-damaged opera houses, theaters, and museums in continental European countries east and west of the Iron Curtain.

From this perspective, we have joined the ranks of the civilized nations only in the last ten years or so. In the early 1960s, a few cities and even fewer state governments provided direct financial support for a small number of performing arts organizations, art museums, and buildings housing artistic activities. As late as 1965, this support amounted to only about $20 million (see Table 1-1).

Table 1-1. *Estimated Direct Government Support of the Arts in the United States, Calendar Years 1975, 1970, and 1965 (in Millions of Dollars)*

Level of Government	1975	1970	1965
Federal	157	27	5
National Endowment for the Arts	87	12	—
Other federal agencies[a]	70	15	5
State and local	125	58	16
State arts councils	55	18	1
Other state and local agencies[b]	70	40	15
Total	282	85	21

[a] Includes the arts activities of the National Endowment for the Humanities and the Corporation for Public Broadcasting (in 1975 and 1970), the Smithsonian's art museums, and grants expended to employ artists under the Comprehensive Employment and Training Act (in 1975). [b] Includes appropriations for government-run museums, line-item subventions to specified arts organizations, public subsidy for the construction and operation of arts buildings (especially important in New York City), and the subsidy from state university funds for performances by touring arts organizations.
Source: Based upon the data shown in Tables 4-1, 4-10, 4-15, and 4-17 and the text discussion in Chapter 4. Estimates for 1970 and 1965, particularly the latter, are crude ones, and even the 1975 estimate for local governments is a crude one.

But by 1970, direct public support of the arts had reached an estimated $85 million. This fourfold increase was due to the creation of the National Endowment for the Arts, the National Endowment for the Humanities, and the Corporation for Public Broadcasting; to the establishment of state arts councils and a vast expansion in the funding of the New York State Council on the Arts (which dates from 1961); and to expanded local government support, particularly by New York City. In the early 1970s, the appropriations for the federal agencies that support the arts and for state arts councils, along with other forms of state and local government support, again rose significantly. By calendar 1975, total direct public support of the arts reached an estimated $282 million, a more than *thirteenfold* increase within only a decade.[1]

Although direct government support of the arts on a substantial scale is a phenomenon of the 1970s, all levels of government in the United States have provided significant financial assistance to the arts since the inception of federal taxation of income and estates in 1913. The deductibility from taxable income and estates of contributions to nonprofit artistic organizations provided a powerful incentive for such contributions, an incentive that no other country provides to the same extent. I estimate that the "indirect subsidy" provided by deductible gifts to the arts from federal, state, and local income and death taxes – the reduction in tax liability enjoyed by donors because of their gifts – amounted to at least $400 million in 1974.[2]

Direct government appropriations require public agencies to make hard choices among activities and recipients. Although at current levels indirect subsidies to the arts exceed direct subsidies, they do not compel governments to make these difficult decisions. Government does not even determine the total amount of the support it provides through the tax deduction. Instead, the aggregate is determined by thousands of decisions on the part of individual donors. Nor does government have to choose among beneficiaries. These decisions, too, are made by individual donors within the broad policy guideline that virtually all noncommercial artistic activities merit support to the extent that they can sell themselves to individual donors.[3] Until relatively recently, the objectives and design of government direct subsidy programs were not a subject of serious concern because the subsidies were too small to have more than marginal effects on the state of the arts. More recently, when the rate of increase in direct public support was climbing rapidly, there was still no real cause for concern because the new money flowing in seemed sufficient to assist all reasonable claimants. But that rapid rate of increase is not continuing. As of the mid-1970s, direct public support for the arts seems to be leveling off.

Nevertheless, the many groups, organizations, and articulate individuals who comprise what can justifiably be called the "arts lobby" are currently pushing for a new and substantial increase in public support, especially at the federal level. Some arts lobbyists talk in terms of expanding the appropriations of the National Endowment for the Arts from the $80–90 million level of the mid-1970s to $250 million by 1980. That target seems overly ambitious, but even if it is achieved and other sources of public support increase by as much as 50 percent in the next few years (a supposition that seems highly improbable, given the parlous fiscal circumstances of those state and local governments that are now the most important financial patrons of the arts), public support for the arts will merely double. Such a growth rate, far below the thirteenfold increase from 1965 to 1975, is unlikely to accommodate all or even most of the worthy arts claimants for public support.

The rapid increase in availability of public funds for the arts has led to the establishment of a large number of new artistic production and service organizations; these groups are now claimants. The availability of government funds also has accelerated the increase in the costs of production in the arts. Moreover, the finances of arts organizations are not healthy, either currently or prospectively. An intensive study of 165 major performing-arts organizations, conducted by the Ford Foundation and discussed in detail in the next chapter, projects that these organizations, which raised $62 million from private and government gifts and grants in 1970–71, will require $285 million from these sources by 1980–81, even if the rate of inflation over the decade averages only a modest 4.5 percent annually. As of midway through the decade, these organizations were doing marginally better financially than they had been expected to but not well enough to reduce significantly their claims for prospective public support.

Thus, even if the national economy performs more vigorously in the second half of the 1970s than in the first (that is, with less inflation to ravage the finances of artistic organizations and more growth in real incomes to permit high levels of private giving), available public funds are still likely to be anything but abundant. And the competition for these funds will be fierce. The long-standing conflicts – among art forms, between established and new organizations, between professional and nonprofessional artistic activities, between aid for organizations and aid for individual artists, between support for national and regional islands of excellence and the desire to promote the arts in the farthest reaches of the country – will become more, not less intense than ever before.

When private funds are involved, it is only right that national priorities should emerge as a consequence of hundreds of thousands of individual, decentralized decisions. But when governments are disbursing funds that they have collected by involuntary exactions from citizens, the appropriate way to set national priorities in a democratic society is by open decisions on general policies. When public support was trivial, such policy decisions were avoided. When government subsidies were rising rapidly, ill-defined, bromidic, or contradictory statements on general objectives were adequate as substitutes for sound policy formulation. These conditions no longer prevail. Willy-nilly, government agencies now confront hard choices among claimants and will have to establish priorities, either existentially, as the net (and barely conscious) result of hundreds of individual approvals and rejections, or explicitly, on the basis of forthright policy decisions made in advance.

Public Subsidy in Perspective

Most people in the world of the arts agree that the roughly $300 million that government now provides as direct public subsidy of the arts is a very small – even scandalously small – amount. Compared to public spending for other purposes, such as the $85 billion spent for education in fiscal 1975; the $3 billion or so spent for space research and technology, prisons, and the postal deficit; or even the $1 billion price tag of a single aircraft carrier, public support of the arts is indeed minimal. It also fares ill when compared with consumer spending for purposes that are certainly less noble or exalting – the $40 billion spent for alcoholic beverages and tobacco, the $18 billion spent for toys and sport supplies and equipment, the $4 billion spent in barbershops and beauty parlors, or the $2 billion net spent for government-sponsored gambling at racetracks and in lotteries in 1975. And of course those in the arts are constantly making unfavorable comparisons of the extent of public support here with that abroad.

It may be more significant to measure the level of public support against the total size of the "arts sector" in the American economy. Unfortunately, reliable statistics on this sector are extraordinarily hard to find. No definitive information is available about such matters as the total number of dollars expended or received as income or the number of persons employed for the arts as a whole. Conventional sources of statistics are not very helpful, partly because the arts sector is not a well-defined concept. The boundaries between art and "mere entertainment," between art and other cultural activities, and between art for art's sake and art as an instrument for other ends – education, therapy, or commerce – are far from clear. And artistic activities show up in many different forms of economic organization – in commercial enterprises, in nonprofit organizations, within public agencies, and as the efforts of self-employed individuals – that are separately and distinctly treated in government statistical reporting systems.

Because, at least until recently, the arts sector was thought to be relatively small, government statisticians have not tried to assemble coherent and comprehensive data on the arts, as they have, for example, on the automobile industry, public utilities, or agriculture. And because the arts sector is comprised of so many enterprises, individuals, and entities that have been poorly financed and often indifferently managed, the arts "industry" itself has not generated such data.

To fill in the many gaps and to separate the arts data from those of other activities with which the arts are associated in the statistics, I have had to piece together fragmentary evidence from a variety of sources, freely using guesses and sometimes arbitrary estimates. My concern is with artistic activities carried on for their own sake rather than as means to other ends. Thus, I have attempted to exclude, for example, the very considerable volume of art education activities in the nation's schools and higher education systems as well as the work of visual and literary artists in advertising and analogous commercial pursuits.

I have sought to measure first the arts sector as a whole and then those elements of it that are eligible for or are receiving public subsidy. In measuring the arts sector as a whole, I include both commercial and nonprofit artistic activities (especially in the performing arts), both high culture and mass culture, both those who perform in nightclubs and those who perform on the stage of the Metropolitan Opera House. This inclusiveness reflects not a judgment of inherent worth but the limitations of the available data. In fact, many artists work in a variety of settings, some of which are higher in culture than others, and some artistic activities are mixtures of commercial and nonprofit ventures and of high culture and mass culture.

Table 1-2. *Professionals in the Arts in the 1970* Census of Population *(in Thousands)*

I. Artistic professionals by class of worker	
Total experienced labor force	450
Unemployed	25
Employed	425
Wage and salary workers	337
Private	309
Employee of own corporation	10
Federal government	12
State and local governments	16
Self-employed	86
Unpaid family workers	2
Not in the labor force, 1970, but worked at some time between 1960 and 1970[a]	103
II. Artistic professionals by industry in which employed	
Total accounted for	420[b]
Employed by:	
Performing arts, entertainment, and cultural activities[c]	169
Educational, religious, and other nonprofit organizations	41
Publishing and advertising firms	37
Manufacturing firms	84
All other commercial firms and general government	89

[a]Most of these people are probably retirees and women who have temporarily withdrawn from the labor force. [b]The discrepancy between this number and the 425,000 recorded above is a result of the different census samples used for the reports on occupation. [c]Includes these industry categories: broadcasting; entertainment and recreation services; museums and art galleries; eating and drinking places; hotels (that is entertainers and musicians working in hotels and night-clubs); and self-employed artists within the "other professional services" category.

Source: The basic data sources are U.S. Bureau of the Census, *Census of Population: 1970, Subject Reports, Final Report PC(2)–7A. Occupational Characteristics,* and *Final Report PC(2)–7C, Occupation by Industry.* For the present purposes professionals in the arts are considered to be the census category "Writers, artists, and entertainers," excluding these subcategories: editors and reporters; athletes; photographers; and public-relations persons and publicity writers. Clearly, some photographers and editors are very much in the mainstream of the arts (although excluded here), while some authors, designers, and others included here have little to do with the arts.

I begin with estimates of the numbers of people employed in the arts. The 1970 *Census of Population* asked its respondents to identify their principal occupations; 450,000 people classified themselves as professionals in the arts and culture. The census questionnaire also asked respondents to classify the businesses of their employers, if any. As the upper part of Table 1-2 shows, roughly 25,000 of the 450,000 self-classified artistic professionals were unemployed, 86,000 were self-employed, 28,000 worked for government agencies, and nearly all the rest worked for wages and salaries in the private sector. As the lower part of Table 1-2 shows, most of the employed professionals did not work directly in the arts or for cultural institutions. It is quite possible – and, indeed, common in the arts – for a respondent to report correctly as his or her principal occupation something different from the nature of the actual job held. Presumably, a large proportion of those classified in the table as employed in "performing arts, entertainment, and cultural activities" were in fact working at jobs related to their occupational specialties, and a fair number of those working for educational, religious, or other nonprofit organizations also were doing so. Most of those working in other sectors of the economy probably were doing things that few would consider as involving the arts.

In addition to the 200,000 or so artistic professionals working in the arts,[4] the arts sector employs substantial nonprofessional supporting staff. Table 1-3 presents some rough estimates suggesting that as of 1972 (the most recent year in which the Census Bureau conducted its quinquennial economic census), more than 700,000 people were working in the broadly defined arts sector of the economy, well over half of them in activities connected with the performing arts. It is clear that the bulk of this employment was in the co.nmercial entertainment and mass culture side of the arts rather than in the nonprofit high culture side.

The sources of Table 1-3, combined with the estimating methods used to allocate fractions of employment to the arts sector in that table, suggest that the income from wages, salaries, and self-employment of the people working in the arts sector totaled $6 billion in 1972. Similar sources and methods produce an estimate of total expenditures by the arts sector (excluding payments internal to the sector, such as publishers' royalty payments to self-employed authors) of roughly $11.5 billion in that year (see Table 1-4). These estimates of employment, earnings, and total expenditures indicate that the arts sector in 1972 constituted about 1 percent of the U.S. nonfarm economy.

Table 1-3. *Estimated Arts Employment in the United States, 1972 (in Thousands)*

Employment by organizations centrally concerned with the arts	
Motion picture production, distribution, exhibition	196[a]
Live performing arts producers and organizations	107[a]
Art museums	12[b]
Manufacture of phonograph records and tapes	20
Total	**335**
Estimated artistic share of employment by organizations only partly concerned with the arts[c]	
Broadcasting	73
Book publishing, printing, and distribution	42
Periodicals and newspapers	25
Manufacture and sale of music and musical instruments	28
Total	**168**
Estimated employment of artistic professionals and supporting staff in other fields in which the arts are a peripheral factor	
Hotels, nightclubs, educational, religious, and nonprofit organizations[d]	145
Self-employed artistic professionals[d]	86
Total arts employment	**734**

[a]Includes self-employed proprietors of organizations without paid employees. [b]From National Endowment for the Arts, *Museums USA* (1974). [c]Assumed fractions of total employment for the industries listed, ranging from one-half for broadcasting and one-third for book publishing and so forth, to 5 percent for newspapers. [d]Based on data from 1970 *Census of Population* on artistic professionals (see Table 1-2).
Source: The basic data sources, unless otherwise indicated, are the following U.S. Census Bureau publications: *County Business Patterns, 1972, U.S. Summary CBP–72–1; Census of Selected Service Industries, 1972, Area Series, United States, SC 72–A–52; Census of Retail Trade, 1972, Area Series, United States, RC 72–4–52;* and *Census of Manufactures, 1972,* Vol. 1, *Summary and Subject Statistics.*

The data also confirm that the average earnings of those employed in the arts are relatively low. My estimate is that average earnings in the broadly defined arts sector that year were $8,200, compared to an average of $8,630 for the entire U.S. nonfarm

Table 1-4. *Estimated Dollar Magnitude of the Arts Sector in the United States, 1972 (in Millions of Dollars)*

Type	Total income and expenditures[a]	Financed by "earned income"[b]	Other sources[c]
Performing arts[d]	6,900	6,650	250
Visual arts[e]	300	150	150
Literary arts[f]	3,100	3,050	50
Other and unallocable[g]	1,200	200	1,000
Total	11,500	10,050	1,450

Note: These are crude estimates, utilizing the allocation methods and data sources employed for Table 1-3, plus a variety of more or less arbitrary estimates and allocations by the author. Data on advertising revenue are from the Statistical Abstract of the United States; relevant National Income Accounts data are from *Survey of Current Business,* July 1974. [a]An effort has been made to avoid transactions within the arts sector, by utilizing, wherever possible, data on final purchases of the artistic services involved. Thus, for motion pictures, the figure included is personal consumption expenditures for movie admissions, rather than receipts of the motion picture industry, which includes receipts from sales to the television industry as well as transaction among producers, distributors, and exhibitors. [b]Admissions, sales of products and services to consumers, and – for broadcasting and periodicals publishing – advertising revenue. [c]In some cases, this is simply a residual. In concept, the category includes government support, gifts and contributions by businesses and individuals, investment earnings, and funds provided for purposes other than the arts as such (for example, appropriations for educational institutions). [d]Motion pictures, live performing arts, broadcasting, and phonograph record production and distribution. [e]Art museums and self-employed visual artists. [f]Book and periodical publishing and distribution. [g]Service organizations and the work of artistic professionals in educational, religious, and other nonprofit organizations.

economy.[5] This disparity is in reality greater than it seems, for about 30 percent of the people working in the arts sector are professionals, while only about 15 percent of the total nonfarm employed labor force is classified as "professional and kindred workers." In general, the expectation is that workers in an industry or sector that employs a high proportion of professionals will have earnings well above, rather than below, average. Moreover, the $8,200 figure is inflated by the relatively high earnings of celebrities and those with steady jobs in the entertainment and commercial sides of the broadly defined arts sector and in those organizations (such as educational organizations) that provide relatively steady year-round employment; the figure does not reflect the typical earnings of artists in high-culture work, which are almost certainly much lower. But given that the average includes all sorts of high-paid employment, it is all the more strikingly below the average for the entire economy.

As Table 1-4 indicates, the broadly defined arts sector is overwhelmingly commercial in origin, organization, and objective. It is estimated that more than 85 percent of the financing of the arts sector comes from admissions, sales of products and services to consumers, and – for broadcasting and periodical publishing – advertising revenue. Performing-arts activities in this country are dominated by movies, broadcasting, recording, the commercial stage, and other live performances under commercial auspices (ranging from rock festivals to piano bars). Although such activities may strike the reader as largely irrelevant to issues of public policy toward the arts, they employ most of the actors, singers, dancers, and musicians who earn their livings as such in this country.

Similarly, the literary arts are dominated by commercial profit-oriented publishing activities, not by nonprofit literary ventures. Noncommercial activities are relatively more important for the visual arts, largely because of the high costs that art museums incur and the very low sales earnings of visual artists. No doubt, most visual artists, like most writers, dislike having to worry about selling their output and would welcome public or private patronage that would permit them to ignore commerce and focus on art. In the absence of such patronage, they are and will continue to be in the commercial part of the arts sector.

The adequacy of public support must be judged not in relation to total arts expenditure but in relation to the components of the arts sector for which public support is intended – support of noncommercial organizations, particularly those concerned with high culture rather than mass culture, and support of individual artists – poets, sculptors, painters working in art forms for which commercial viability is especially difficult. In 1972, these components of the arts sector almost surely had total expenditures of less than $1 billion, well under a tenth of the total recorded in Table 1-4.[6] Direct government support of the arts in 1972 was roughly $150 million; thus, government sources were providing some 15 percent of the financing of the organizations and activities for which public support programs are intended.

Analyzing Public Support Policy

If public opinion surveys (such as those conducted by the National Research Center of the Arts, Inc.) are to be trusted, most Americans believe that direct government support of the arts at present is too niggardly. The arts today constitute one of the few areas of public policy about which there is general agreement that more of a good thing is better. But unless this widespread sympathy causes the subsidy for the arts to increase at an implausibly rapid rate, the sources of funds will still confront a host of difficult choices among deserving applicants for public support.

The arts are unique, and decisions about government support of the arts should not, and will not, be cast in precisely the same terms as those for other public expenditures. But in some respects, public support of the arts poses the same policy questions as public support of other sectors of American society that are primarily, but not wholly, commercial, such as housing, transportation, energy, and agriculture. On what ground should governments intervene to allocate more resources than commercial processes provide? Should governments intervene to alter the detailed allocation of resources within the particular sector? Should governments intervene to assure that different people, notably those with lower incomes or those living in remote locations, benefit more than other potential recipients from the activities of the sector? What are the hazards of government intervention to achieve meritorious objectives? How can policy be designed to achieve the objectives and avoid the hazards?

Governments may choose from a range of policy instruments to provide financial support, and the countries that preceded ours in providing large-scale support of the arts have used a variety of approaches; various levels of government in the United States also have tried different approaches. One approach – the provision of generous tax incentives for private gifts in support of the arts – is uniquely American. The dominant practice in some continental European countries is to support artistic production companies that are themselves government agencies. Most of the English-speaking countries prefer to offer government financial support to private (nonprofit) production organizations. In some cases, they make direct budgetary appropriations to specified organizations. But the dominant approach in this country, Canada, Britain, and Australia is to provide support to nonprofit organizations and individual artists through a government foundation that receives a lump-sum appropriation and makes its own decisions as to who shall be assisted. *[handwritten margin note: arts admin + councils.]*

It is usually very difficult to identify the effects of a given dollar

amount of subsidy, but the attempt needs to be made if past successes and failures are to be guides for future policy. Popular discus-
sions of public subsidy of the arts often suggest that the sole purpose of government support is to rescue artistic organizations from
imminent financial disaster. In fact, more often than not, both the
grantors and the recipients of public funds expect that those funds
will not only resolve the financial crisis, if one is present, but enable
arts organizations to change what they do: for example, to mount
more productions or exhibitions, to reach new audiences, to further
the careers of individual artists, to revive a disappearing art form, or
to facilitate the birth of a new one.

The purpose of this book is to evaluate the effects of public
support in light of these expectations. (The criteria for that evaluation include both the rationales for public subsidy that economic
theory provides and the grant-making organizations' own statements of their objectives.) On the basis of these findings I will make
specific recommendations for public policy.

2

The Case for Large-Scale Public Support of the Arts

"Everyone now agrees that the Government has an obligation to subsidize the arts in this country," wrote Hilton Kramer during the 1976 presidential campaign, and he was very nearly right.[1] Almost everyone considers the arts something different from the goods and services that we leave to the mercies of the marketplace. There are at least a half-dozen separate reasons for public support of the arts, and in the past decade the government arts funding agencies have referred to most or all of these reasons in providing money for hundreds of separate organizations and individuals. Public agencies necessarily base their priorities on an implicit or explicit recognition of the different reasons for grant making that are appropriate in different situations. But efforts to improve policies and means of public support also must be based on the grounds for public action that are pertinent to specific art forms and institutions.

Let us consider first the viewpoint of the rare person who opposes direct public support of the arts. Such a skeptic might be concerned, as many were a decade and longer ago, that government intervention conflicts with the individuality and independence of creators and consumers in the arts. The skeptic will surely observe that the arts in the United States are very market-oriented, with most performances subject to admissions charges and most books and works of visual arts usable only after someone has paid to acquire them from the artists who produced them. Thus, the skeptic might conclude, as one writer has, that the well-known financial difficulties of the arts, particularly the performing arts, are of their own making:

> Many performing groups could balance their books simply by increasing their prices or reducing the quality (and so the cost) of their output . . . . [T]hey reject the willingness-to-pay criterion of the economic market, at least to the extent that they are able to obtain charitable or public support. Their "plight," then, is to a considerable extent the result of deliberate choice.

15

They do not see themselves as engaged primarily in serving a market, but in propagating a cultural tradition. To this end, they wish to maintain as low a price for the service as possible and to avoid any dilution of quality which would impair the tradition. It does not follow that in so defining their mission they are motivated by concerns other than self-interest. The total resources, from both customers and donors, that they obtain by such a policy may be larger than if they pursued a narrower commercial purpose, which might dry up their sources of charitable and public support.[2]

Such reasoning assumes that our society is indifferent to the quality and quantity of artistic production and to changes in the size and composition of audiences. Clearly, most of us are *not* indifferent to these matters; most agree that the public interest is served by deliberate government action designed to make the arts more widely available, to preserve our cultural heritage for present and future generations, to strengthen cultural organizations, and to encourage the creative development of individuals with artistic talents (the stated objectives of the National Endowment for the Arts).[3]

In short, we as a nation agree not only that the arts are good for us but also that government intervention is necessary to assure more and better artistic production and consumption than would result from unaided pursuit of "narrower commercial purposes" by artists and artistic organizations.

Moreover, even if the artistic marketplace worked very smoothly, many people still would subscribe to the need for public support, much as voters and legislators subscribed to the need for massive and increasing subsidies in higher education during the 1950s and 1960s, when market-originated economic incentives alone were more than sufficient to induce individuals to attend colleges and universities.[4] To use an economic term, the arts are generally viewed as "merit goods," whose production and consumption should be encouraged by public subsidy simply because they are meritorious rather than because the market alone would not supply enough of them or because income barriers deprive some people of access to them.

The meritorious nature of the arts is the most general and perhaps the most widely espoused argument for public subsidy. It is a valid point of view but an inadequate guide for public policy; it tells us nothing except that more of what is good is better. It does not, for example, help fund-granting agencies to decide which activities and organizations are most deserving of additional subsidy.

Even if more artistic production is a good thing, more public subsidy may not be a requisite for increased production. Public agencies do not have limitless money to disburse; hence, they must consider intrinsic merit as only one measure of financial need and artistic promise. Other grounds for public subsidy of the arts provide rather more specific criteria for decision making. And in practice, the grant agencies have relied on these other grounds.

Over the years, economists have classified the conceivable reasons for government subsidization of worthwhile activities, including activities like the arts that are, for the most part, produced and consumed under private auspices. This classification scheme is a useful aid to thinking about the policy of arts subsidy because subsidies are, after all, economic or financial in nature. Admittedly, the systematic way in which economists approach policy formulation in the arts cannot be said to predominate in decision making for the arts. Systematic thinking about important social issues is difficult (otherwise, the country would have been able long ago to resolve such issues as welfare reform and national health insurance), especially when vital data are lacking, as they are for the arts.

The difficulty is compounded in arts policy by two additional factors. First, those involved in policy making for the arts are, and should be, creative and idiosyncratic individuals, not inclined to rigorous policy analysis. Second, within government, the amount of money spent on the arts is still relatively small. Government responsibilities for the arts are not central to the concerns of the principal decision makers – presidents, governors, and legislative majority leaders; they have much more urgent and, in monetary terms, more weighty responsibilities and pressures involving large constituencies. The stakes in the arts are low for politicians and high for people in the arts. But if relatively few people in the arts think like policy analysts, even fewer have the means to make use of the services of policy analysts to the extent that politicians and interest groups do when dealing with public issues involving large amounts of money. As a consequence, arts policy to date has been highly idiosyncratic, shifting with the attitudes and personal preferences of individual presidents, governors, and legislators – attitudes and preferences that are shaped in turn by the advice and importuning of those arts and advocates of the arts who have access to the key decision makers.

Yet it is worth noting that the founders of the American government assumed that rational discourse, rather than personal idiosyncrasy, should be the basis for public decision making. Thus, the use of economics as a framework for thinking about arts policy conforms to that old assumption.

Economic Arguments for Public Support

To the extent that society functions without government intervention, the sum of vast numbers of individual private economic decisions (the market, in the shorthand of economists) determines both the mix of goods and services that are produced by the human and material resources at hand and the distribution of income among individuals and families that enables them to acquire those goods and services. If no market mechanisms exist to bring about the production of valued goods and services or if the existing market mechanisms produce a shortfall—for any number of different reasons—in the goods and services that consumers value highly, economists maintain that government should use subsidies to stimulate the production of these goods and services. Most economists also agree that market processes, if left to themselves, will result in a distribution of personal income that is unacceptably unequal in twentieth-century industrial societies; therefore governments should intervene to make the distribution of income less unequal.

The obvious way to make the distribution of income approach equality is to levy taxes on people with high incomes and to provide cash to people with low incomes. In 1975, nearly one-seventh of all personal income in the United States took the form of "transfer payments" from different levels of government, mostly designed to equalize the distribution of income. Federal, state, and local governments also spend large amounts to redistribute income in kind, that is, to provide specific types of goods and services to people whose low incomes are presumed to be barriers to access to those goods and services. The most notable examples are Medicaid and some types of housing subsidies; public schools also involve a large element of income redistribution in kind. The collective judgment in these cases is that, even after a lot of cash income redistribution has taken place, large numbers of people will be unable to afford the standards of health care, housing, and education that are considered essential in our society. The goal of such measures, in economic terminology, is "equity."

The first of the stated objectives of the National Endowment for the Arts (and the first in the NEA's spending priorities) is "to make the arts more widely available to millions of Americans." Low income is, of course, a major barrier to wider enjoyment of the arts. Without subsidy, very few of the arts can be offered in the market except at prices that are high relative to the incomes of most people, especially the young. (Young adults generally are low on the earnings ladder, and most children are members of relatively low-income families. In 1970, for example, about 80 percent of the nation's children under eighteen were in families with incomes below $15,000.) There is something intrinsically abhorrent about a policy of making the cultural and artistic heritage of our civilization available to only, say, the richest 20 or 30 percent of the population, the group to which enjoyment of the arts would be limited in the absence of all support outside the marketplace.

Low-income Americans are markedly underrepresented among consumers of the "high culture" arts. In 1966, in their pioneering study on the economics of the performing arts, William J. Baumol and William G. Bowen published the results of a large-scale survey of the audience for the live performing arts, covering 153 performances of five art forms in twenty-one cities conducted from September 1963 through March 1965. The median income of the respondents to the survey was more than double that of the urban population as a whole. At a time when one-third of the urban population had incomes below $5,000, only 9 percent of the respondents had incomes below $5,000. About 40 percent of the respondents had incomes over $15,000, at a time when only 5 percent of the urban population was in the above-$15,000 income class. Even among the occasional attenders, low-income people were rare.[5] This research, of course, predated the advent of large-scale public subsidy.

Since the mid-1960s, public subsidy programs have provided support for numerous free and reduced-admission-price arts performances. In 1970–71, for example, free performances accounted for well over 25 percent of the total attendance of nonprofit performing arts organizations in New York State.[6] In that same year, roughly 13 percent of all ticket attendance at the 166 major professional nonprofit performing arts companies in the country surveyed by the Ford Foundation was on reduced-rate student tickets.[7] These surveys in combination suggest that if the 1970–71 experience was typical, close to 40 percent of all attendance at arts performances may be free or at reduced rates.

Nevertheless, a nationwide survey of the population sixteen years old and over, carried out in January 1973, revealed that people with incomes of $15,000 and above attended specified live performing arts (ballet and modern dance, concerts and opera, live theater) three times as often as those with incomes of less than $5,000. In part, of course, this higher rate of attendance is due not solely to affluence or the lack of it but to differences in education, location, and other conditions. But it is significant that those with incomes over $15,000 attended 70 percent more often than those with incomes in the $10,000–$15,000 range, who, like the highest income group, were largely urban residents (and thus had access to performances) and were reasonably well educated.[8]

Subsidizing performances apparently has failed to increase the representation of low-income people in audiences appreciably. Perhaps cheap or free performances have become widely available too recently to affect attendance patterns; perhaps sustained subsidy programs will require a long time to succeed in reaching low-income people. Or perhaps other approaches – performances and showings in unconventional settings or various uses of the schools – would be more effective in making enjoyment of the arts more widespread. Or it may simply be, as some observers maintain, that the audience for high-culture arts will always be predominantly middle-aged, well-educated – and affluent – and that no amount or form of subsidy will generate much attendance by low-income people.

But if government subsidies cannot make the arts more widely available, then the National Endowment for the Arts must abandon its primary objective, at least in regard to theater, opera, dance, and concert music. Because these important art forms are the most costly to audiences, it is difficult to believe that price has nothing to do with the underrepresentation of the poor.[9] Perhaps the appropriate conclusion is that, although income barriers to access to the arts clearly warrant government intervention in the form of subsidy, these barriers are difficult to overcome. The best strategy may be long-term subsidies for audience development, such as support for more production of live arts performances on television, which provides initial exposure to the arts to large numbers of people.[10]

The Failure of the Market

Another general justification for government subsidies, in economic theory, is "efficiency." Subsidies may be used to yield a more efficient allocation of resources, one that more nearly reflects the sum total of individual and societal preferences, taking into account the relative resource costs of satisfying those preferences. Markets can fail to be efficient for a number of reasons, for example, because they contain monopolistic elements. But the arts market fails in part because the arts have some of the features of what economists call "public goods."

A pure public good has two characteristics: first, one person's use of it does not prevent others from making use of it; second, no one can be denied access to it, whether or not he pays for his use. No rational person can be expected to pay for something he can obtain without paying. When society desires such a public good, it does not rely on market mechanisms to produce it. The classic example of a public good is the lighthouse: one mariner's use of the light as a guide to navigation does not prevent another from using it, and any mariner can use the light, whether or not he pays. Consequently, lighthouses are not bought and sold in the marketplace; governments supply and maintain them and finance them from general tax revenues. National defense, the maintenance of public safety, and street lighting, are other pure public goods.

Few artistic goods and services meet the criteria that characterize pure public goods. Access to most artistic output is through market transactions – tickets of admission to the performing arts or purchase of literary and visual art works – or could be restricted to those who are willing and able to pay (even if now free). But, for example, the present organization of television broadcasting in the United States closely approximates a public good. As such, it provides an argument for subsidies to public television that features a substantial portion of high-culture programming.

At present, pay television is confined to a few experimental situations and the showing of films in hotel and motel rooms. For the most part, individual viewers and listeners in the United States do not pay for the specific programs they watch. Most television signals are delivered over the air, using the electromagnetic spectrum, rather than by cable. The radio spectrum is limited and can provide only a small number of video channels. Because commercial television broadcasting is supported entirely by advertising, those few channels will be devoted to programming that attracts large audiences and hence substantial advertising revenue. Sponsors will tend to slight the tastes of minorities – even rather substantial minorities. Only subsidy from government or private sources can accommodate anything less than a mass audience.

If more channels were available (for example, via cable transmission of signals), some of them might be able to cater to modest audiences.[11] Voluntary "subscription payments" by viewers and listeners do provide financial support for noncommercial stations. But voluntary payments are inherently unstable. Because individual viewers and listeners can enjoy the programming without contributing, noncommercial broadcasters who rely on voluntary audience support lead a rather precarious existence. Those stations work hard for their contributions, as anyone tuning into a large-city public television channel or the radio stations of the Pacifica group can attest. They find it virtually impossible to raise funds in this way to finance, in advance, major new undertakings, such as the production of a new dramatic series.

Large works of art, such as murals and monumental sculptures, have some of the characteristics of public goods. Such works often are located in public places to which access cannot be readily restricted via tickets. Such works are seldom sold by artists and dealers to collectors and museums; most are financed by commissions from government agencies, churches, or big corporations.

External Benefits

The large sculpture in the plaza of a new corporate headquarters provides what economists call "external benefits" – that is, benefits to people other than the parties directly involved in a transaction in the market – in this case, the sculptor is the seller and the corporation the purchaser; everyone else who passes through the plaza and sees the sculpture partakes of its "positive externalities," or external benefits. (Some transactions also involve external costs.) External benefits are basic characteristics of public goods.

Most public and quasi-public services yield significant external benefits. For example, recent history suggests that Western-style democratic governments require a reasonably well-educated voting population; public education may be assumed to benefit society by producing an adequately educated electorate, as well as benefiting the student and his parents. It is all too easy to exaggerate the extent and value of external benefits, and most proponents of public subsidy (for any purpose) do so. But to the extent that market transactions provide such benefits, subsidies to increase output may be essential to the efficient use of economic resources.

Four major types of external benefits are relevant to the case for subsidy to the arts. First, some art forms are interdependent. Virtually all the musical art forms – opera, dance, concert "serious" music, jazz, and the "popular" music forms – tend to support one another. They draw materials from each other and, more important, provide training and employment opportunities for professionals in the field. Thus, the consumer of one form of music is likely to derive some benefit from the flourishing of another form even if he does not patronize it and may actively dislike it. If that form cannot flourish on its own, it may have a legitimate claim to public subsidy financed by tax payments from consumers of the other forms.

Of course, subsidies are not equally effective in all situations in fostering related art forms. In order to encourage the creative development of talented individuals, the NEA may supply a subsidy that enables a symphony orchestra to employ a cadre of musicians on a permanent basis. This subsidy may, indirectly, enable the local opera company to mount higher-quality performances than it otherwise would. But this external benefit will materialize only if the orchestra's season has gaps during which orchestra musicians may take other engagements. Several of the country's most eminent orchestras no longer have such gaps.

A second type of positive externality is implicit in the Arts Endowment objective of preserving the cultural heritage. Future generations can benefit from contemporary activities in the arts – but these activities need financing now. Despite widespread environmental depredation, there is abundant evidence that most people in our society have concern for a posterity beyond their own children. That concern justifies some current public subsidy of the arts and culture, directed at preserving continuity and access in future years to the product of current artistic endeavor. Museums, archives, and scholarly activities relating to the arts are obviously meritorious claimants on behalf of future generations of arts consumers. Good collections also enhance the research and educational activities of museums; thus, subsidy may be warranted for acquisitions that also benefit today's museum visitors.

Museums are not the only meritorious claimants for subsidy on these grounds. Almost any artistic activity striving for a long-term impact – whether or not it achieves that impact – is also a candidate for support. The objective of benefiting future generations may justify a subsidy policy that distinguishes between high art culture and popular art culture. Much popular culture is deliberately evanescent and not meant to endure even a few years, much less for future generations; such culture can be reasonably asked to pay its own way through charges to the immediate consumers.

Artistic undertakings are essentially experimental. Because artists take chances, inevitably many will fail. Sometimes, the artist or artistic organization profits from the failure; it contributes to later success. Often, however, failure costs the individual artist or organization dearly. Failure may cause a theater company to go out of business or a writer to stop writing, but other artists and society at large may learn a lot from the failed experiment and thus profit from it. Those external benefits constitute still another justification for subsidy to the arts.[12] Under this rubric, government should provide subsidies to support risk-taking artistic institutions and individual artists and should directly commission new works that may not be lasting in their effects. This argument for subsidy may serve as a corrective, to prevent subsidy policies that are intended to benefit posterity from supporting only the conventional. It is impossible to predict what will last and what will not, and in any case, the failed experiments may be useful, too.[13]

Of course, not all experiments are failures; but the high costs of possible failure inhibit artists and organizations that may wish to undertake experiments on their own. Subsidy removes this inhibition. Government may also use subsidies to publicize successful experiments. Successful experimenters in the arts generally are preoccupied with the ends to which a given experiment may have been merely a means. They seldom have any personal incentive to incur the costs of publicizing their successes for the benefit of other people in similar situations. For example, in recent years, local arts groups have been converting unlikely structures – a water-storage tank in North Carolina; a bowling alley in Burbank, California; an explosives plant in Hartford, Connecticut – to artistic uses. The National Endowment for the Arts has therefore provided funds for the Educational Facilities Laboratory to prepare a booklet reporting on such experiences and providing advice – external benefits – for others.[14]

Finally, the arts and culture may be an important element of economic life in some large cities, attracting visitors, keeping the affluent attached to the city, and generating income for those in ancillary services – restaurants, hotels, and the like.[15] Accordingly, public support of the kind that New York City now extends may be justified on grounds of ordinary economic self-interest: external benefits to the local economy and state and local government treasuries. Clearly, this argument is most forceful for cities, such as New York, where the arts are a significant industry or for areas whose attractiveness to visitors can be appreciably improved by expanded artistic activity. Tourism is important to the economies of relatively few American cities. Other cities may well choose to subsidize museums or symphony orchestras, but they should not justify this choice by claiming that it promotes economic development more effectively than would the expenditure of the same amount of money on, say, raising the salaries of municipal employees.

Production Costs in the Arts

Private markets work efficiently, in economic terms, only if the costs of production meet certain criteria. One such criterion is the absence of economies of scale in production, that is, reductions in cost per unit of output as total output increases. (In the arts, the unit of output may be a consumer visit to a museum or an individual's attendance at a performance.) The economically efficient price to charge is the cost of providing an additional unit of output, but in situations of declining unit costs, a price set at that level will be below the average cost of all units of output and will result in a deficit.

Museums typically operate under these conditions. The costs of maintaining a museum in good condition are quite high. If museums had to rely on admission prices to cover these costs, those prices in most cases would be so high as to discourage attendance. But beyond the basic maintenance costs and unless attendance is so heavy as to create new costs (increasing the number of exit guards or elevator attendants, for example), the cost of accommodating each new visitor is little or nothing. Hence, the economically right price for admission in such cases is also little or nothing. Concern for economic efficiency is an argument for a subsidy to make museum admission free or nearly so, even if museum visitors are not necessarily poor. Efficiency in this case also coincides with the objective of making the arts more widely accessible (because they are intrinsically worthwhile).

Another cost problem in the arts has to do with what can be described loosely as lack of information on the part of either potential consumers or potential producers. Because enjoyment of the arts tends to be an acquired taste, efforts to expand both the potential market of paying consumers and the pool of future performers or other participants in the production process involve giving a great many people an opportunity to sample the arts.

Of course, many ordinary commercial activities also deal with this problem, usually through advertising or other promotional activities. Promotional costs also are characterized by economies of scale. Mass-media advertising campaigns are very expensive, but their audiences are so vast that the costs of reaching the individual consumer are very low. Such economies of scale are available in the arts only to commercial film and television productions. The markets for most art forms are segmented, specialized, and too modest in size to make mass advertising campaigns profitable. A few communications media lend themselves to advertising or promotional efforts aimed at the specific modest markets that characterize particular artistic enterprises. Some arts organizations publicize their activities through public announcements or low-cost advertising on the "serious" FM radio stations in some large cities.

In general, though, advertising is not useful in overcoming actual ignorance of the arts. Perhaps the only way of dealing with this problem is to subsidize more widespread production of the arts specifically designed to give large numbers of potential consumers and producers firsthand experience of them. The objective of economic efficiency thus justifies the public education, awareness, and so-called outreach activities that government arts-funding agencies subsidize in pursuit of the stated objective of making the arts widely accessible.

Information costs can be an especially severe handicap to the development of wholly new types of artistic activities as well as to the development of more conventional activities in regions where they are unfamiliar. Most economists favor nurturing and protecting "infant industries" until it is determined that they are ready to make it on their own in the marketplace. To some extent, promotion of the arts by federal and state agencies in underserved areas can be justified on this basis.

Merit Goods

In addition, several quite specific merit-goods arguments have been used to justify subsidies. For example, private demand for some art forms is quite thin; these art forms would be produced in very small quantity if the market were left to its own devices. Poetry, in general, falls into this category. Books of poetry have such small sales that even relatively well-known poets are generally unable to earn their livings from sales of their work, even if they devote themselves full time and exclusively to poetry. Few American poets, including the most eminent, have subsisted entirely on the proceeds from sales of poetry without patronage, independent means, an academic post, or earnings from other literary or nonliterary endeavors. These sources of funds may be said to subsidize the production of poetry. Without subsidy from *some* source, little poetry would be produced, and the creative development of some talented poets would be frustrated.

In the absence of subsidies, the performing arts and museums tend to be strongly centralized. Centralization results in part from artists' inclinations to seek the company of other artists and to congregate in major cities. But strong market forces also are at work. For example, there are significant economies of scale in the development of high quality museum collections. Moreover, in many areas, market demand is not sufficient to support the minimum conditions of professional quality art production. The market in a given region may, for example, be adequate to support a two-week season for opera, ballet, or repertory theater. But performers, supporting artists, and craftsmen who function as such only two weeks a year cannot produce performances of professional quality. Some amateurs may devote their lives to the local opera, ballet, or repertory company, but there is a world of difference between amateur and professional performance. Resident performing companies outside the largest cities may therefore require subsidies. Subsidies also may be essential to defray the extra costs for touring or traveling exhibitions that bring the arts to consumers living in smaller communities.

A government arts-granting agency may decide, as the Arts Endowment has, that it is important to make modern dance more widely available throughout the nation. Underlying that decision is the general merit-goods assumption that more exposure to modern dance is a good thing. But this assumption does not determine either the form or even the amount of subsidy. Agency officials may decide to subsidize a touring company, for example, in order to reach the potential audience for modern dance outside the few big cities where the market for modern dance is relatively strong, or to enable the modern dance company to test new works on less sophisticated audiences for the sake of furthering its creative development, or as an experiment, or to nurture an infant industry. The grantors' objectives and the way in which they formulate the problem will have some bearing on their decisions as to the dance companies that will receive the touring subsidy, where they tour, the ticket-pricing policy that is encouraged, the relative emphasis on touring versus big-city seasons, and the division of subsidies between live and television performances.

The Baumol-Bowen Thesis

Most arguments for subsidy hold that government intervention is warranted to *expand* artistic output, for one reason or another. But in 1966, in *Performing Arts: The Economic Dilemma,* economists William J. Baumol and William G. Bowen suggested that pervasive, long-term economic trends might make government subsidy essential to *maintain* artistic output.[16]

Baumol and Bowen pointed out that the performing arts are inherently labor-intensive services with limited means of substituting machinery and other forms of capital for labor or for reorganizing the use of labor. Services with these characteristics—which also are ascribed to education, police protection, and some types of health service—have little capacity to increase in productivity over time. When productivity in the rest of the economy is rising, then wage rates in all sectors of the economy must rise, including those in labor-intensive sectors unable to register productivity gains. Rising wages rates, in the absence of productivity increases, raise the costs of production, and the prices at which services are sold. Hence, Baumol and Bowen argued, without subsidy, admission prices for the performing arts will rise substantially over time. And unless demand on the part of paying customers is completely insensitive to these rising prices, the result will be a decline in production of the performing arts.

The scarcity of good data makes it difficult to evaluate the way in which consumers of the performing arts have responded to rising prices in the decade since Baumol and Bowen first presented this argument. But demand appears to be at least somewhat sensitive to price. The Ford Foundation study of the major performing arts organizations indicates that from 1965–66 to 1973–74, average ticket income per attendee increased by 45 percent, about 10 percent more than the overall rise in the consumer price index. Average attendance per performance declined slightly over this period. Two different methods of calculating the price elasticity of demand suggest that each 10 percent rise in average ticket prices caused attendance to drop roughly 2.5 percent below attendance projections based on ticket prices that rose no more than the consumer price index.[17]

Conceivably, the negative effects of rising prices on the demand for the performing arts over time could be offset if demand increases steeply as incomes rise or if we could be certain that the rise in education levels and other social changes would increase appetites for the arts. But the available evidence indicates that consumer demand for the live performing arts does not rise over time appreciably more rapidly than incomes. Data for the 1929–63 period published in the Baumol-Bowen study show that consumer expenditures for the live performing arts varied very little as a percentage of disposable personal income, save in the worst part of the Great Depression.[18] Since their study appeared, the basic data series on which they relied has been substantially revised by the U.S. Department of Commerce for the years from 1947 to 1963.[19] For this study, the relationship between consumer spending and income in the 1960–75 period was recalculated, using the revised data. Covering a period in which the number of performances and performing companies increased substantially, these data show that for each 1 percent increase in disposable personal income, consumer expenditures for the live performing arts rose by only 0.81 percent, that is, less rapidly than income. If this figure is adjusted (on the basis of the crude data at hand) to reflect the rising relative price of the live performing arts, it is still less than 0.9 percent.[20]

Thus, the data indicate that demand *is* somewhat sensitive to price and does *not* rise so sharply with rising incomes as to compensate for rising prices. But the actual dimensions of the productivity problem and the complex nature of the real economic world seem to differ somewhat from the simple economic model Baumol and Bowen developed, and public policy must respond to the real-world consequences of slow productivity increases in the performing arts.

The proposition that slow improvements in productivity will lead inexorably to rising relative prices is valid only when all sectors are operating as efficiently as they possibly can. Like all other industries, the performing arts generally fall short of maximum efficiency. Hence, they have significant unexploited opportunities to increase technical efficiency. Subsidies are difficult to justify for arts organizations that have not made the most of such opportunities. And in fact there is abundant evidence that productivity in the arts is not completely stagnant, in part because of new technology, in part because of more efficient use of existing technology.

For example, none of the older Broadway theaters have permanent lighting systems; instead, they rely upon temporary lighting arrangements put up for a particular production or for a season. The permanent lighting systems that all new Broadway theaters have should – union rules permitting – be significantly cheaper to operate. Similarly, because the old Metropolitan Opera House had virtually no storage space for sets or costumes, the company used moving vans each morning to take the sets and costumes from the previous night's performance to the warehouse. The new Metropolitan Opera House at Lincoln Center has the storage space necessary to eliminate this cost.

New sound-amplification technology permits the use of halls and theaters that were previously considered unsuitable for performances. By using video tape, the Eastern Opera Theater of Maryland brings high-quality performances to small communities. Income realized from orchestral recordings and televised production of plays originally produced live also may be considered the result of productivity improvements that partly offset the rising costs of live performance.[21]

Of course, there are limits to improvements in productivity. It takes four musicians to play quartets and at least one actor to put on a play. No one would want cost pressures to speed up the performance of a Schubert quartet or Richard II's discourse on "sad stories of the death of kings."[22] However, even the most traditional aspects of the performing arts may change somewhat in response to crass economic pressures without justifying public intervention. Eighteenth-century chamber music was written to be performed in stately houses, not at Carnegie Hall. A Mozart quartet commissioned by the Prince-Archbishop of Salzburg sounds very fine when played in the great hall of the Schloss Leopoldskron,[23] but without a noble patron of great wealth, the Schloss could not remain the standard venue for Mozart quartets.[24] Public intervention to prevent economic pressures from causing *any* change whatever in the arts is a reductio ad absurdum of the Baumol-Bowen thesis. Moreover, if public intervention offset all cost pressures fully, productivity would almost certainly remain stagnant, and arts organizations would be vulnerable to union featherbedding and other practices that do not enhance the quality of performances.

The Baumol-Bowen thesis should not be assumed, as it usually is, to prove the case for open-ended public subsidy to all art forms. Productivity improvements seem harder to achieve in concert music than in the theater; the demand for symphony orchestra performances seems rather less sensitive to increases in ticket prices than the demand for some other art forms; and the demand for a specific art form, like ballet over the past generation, may rise steeply with rising incomes, although the demand for all of the arts combined does not.

Moreover, the available evidence indicates that consumer demand is only moderately sensitive to rising ticket prices. Quite apart from the direct evidence, the elasticity of demand for the performing arts with respect to price may well be low because most alternatives to the performing arts as objects of consumer spending also are labor-intensive "luxuries." The prices of other arts, recreational activities, and restaurant meals also are likely to rise relatively rapidly because of slow productivity gains. If the price elasticity of demand is small, then rising labor costs in the performing arts can be offset by higher ticket prices with relatively minor reductions in attendance, probably resulting in marginally smaller attendance at each performance, rather than a reduction in the number of performances and thus in the output of the arts.

For example, over a ten-year period, productivity in the performing arts might increase annually by 1.4 percentage points less than productivity in the economy as a whole. (This figure is based on long-term historical data on productivity trends in the services generally.) If wage rates increased uniformly for the arts and all other economic sectors, then over the decade labor costs per unit of output in the arts would rise by 15 percent relative to the rest of the economy. If the price elasticity estimates cited earlier are valid, a typical performing arts organization could maintain its financial position over the period (holding all sorts of other things constant) by increasing its ticket prices by 21.5 percent more than prices in the general economy; it would then suffer a decline of 5.4 percent in attendance.[25] Neither this estimated rise in relative ticket prices nor the decline in attendance seems large enough, in the absence of other considerations, to constitute an ironclad case for public intervention.[26]

Finally, it is not clear that wage rates in the arts must rise more rapidly than productivity or in sympathy with rising wage rates elsewhere in the economy. Performing-arts organizations may not have to match wage rates paid elsewhere in the economy in order to attract an adequate supply of labor (nor may other slow-productivity-growth sectors). In practice, changes in relative wage rates over time are affected by barriers to movement of labor among the sectors, other imperfections in labor markets, and the specific characteristics of the demand for and supply of labor in different parts of the economy (the slope of the relevant schedules, in the language of economists). In the absence of large-scale subsidy to the arts, the main result of lagging improvement in productivity may be not cost pressures on arts organizations but a decline in wages in the arts relative to those in other sectors. In earlier periods, before so much public support was forthcoming, wages in the arts apparently did decline in this way.

Such relative deterioration in the money rewards of people in the performing arts may be a cause for concern. To prevent the prospect of relatively low money earnings from discouraging talented people from pursuing artistic careers, government may provide selective assistance to individual performers and artists. But an institutional subsidy to finance wage increases seems a clumsy way of attracting able people. Subsidies for this purpose should take the form of fellowships or other awards to promising individual artists, support of training institutions, and grants that increase the total number of performances and performing companies (thus increasing employment opportunities for artists) because the prospect of protracted periods of unemployment is probably more discouraging than relatively low earnings for relatively steady employment.[27]

The Baumol-Bowen thesis has been used to justify across-the-board support, especially of the performing arts, on the ground that their long-term financial prospects are poor as a result of basic economic conditions that only subsidy can counteract. But not all performing-arts organizations uniformly and inevitably confront dismal economic prospects over the long run. To assist those organizations that are functioning at maximum efficiency but nonetheless are forced to raise their ticket prices relatively over time, government may use subsidies to reduce ticket prices selectively and thus overcome the income barriers that rising ticket prices will create. Such subsidies might conceivably be large ones.

Hazards of Subsidy Programs

Like other forms of government intervention, subsidy of the arts may fail to achieve its objectives or have harmful side effects. A harder question is whether a given subsidy is necessary to achieve its objectives. Could the same result, as far as society in general is concerned, be achieved without subsidy? For example, most economists argue that the conventional form of subsidy to public universities, low tuition for all students regardless of their economic status, is inefficient and unwise. The objective of the subsidy is to encourage people who could not otherwise afford to go to college. Many students at public universities come from affluent families and would go to college even without the subsidy. Other forms of subsidy might more effectively or less expensively reach those who could not otherwise attend.

On the other hand, most subsidy for "pure" research and scholarship is efficient in the sense that without subsidy some pure re-searchers would instead do applied research that could be sold in the marketplace. The situation with regard to the arts is more equivocal because the arts are so largely market-oriented. Subsidizing any product or service that is highly market-oriented, whether food and housing or legitimate theater, may increase the incomes of those involved in its production or lower prices to current consumers without greatly changing the quantity and quality of the product or service produced.

Musicians, actors, and museum staffs can be expected to take into account the existence or possibility of public financial support in staking their wage claims. Increased public subsidy has contributed to the recent rise in militancy among some groups of professionals in the arts.[28] To some extent at least, increased subsidy is absorbed by higher pay for producers of art, including star solo performers and rich painters and sculptors as well as starving actors, dancers, and assistant curators.[29] But these individuals are not the intended ben-eficiaries of public subsidy for the arts, any more than workers in the building trades are the intended beneficiaries of housing subsidies.

Even in a situation to which the Baumol-Bowen thesis applies, a public subsidy to lower admissions prices may be inefficient. For example, for many years the New York City Center has kept its maximum ticket prices low. This low maximum price benefits the richer members of the audience. Raising the price would not reduce access, for low-income people or anyone else, to the City Center's productions, nor would such prices reduce the number of produc-tions that were mounted.[30]

Other Forms of Inefficiency

Subsidy policy also may have unequal impacts on art forms that involve many of the same professionals and compete for similar audiences: for example, opera versus concert music, television ver-sus sound radio, or sculpture versus painting. When the arts depend entirely on sales in the market, those forms with inherently high costs of production tend to suffer, in quality if not in quantity; opera, television, and sculpture are costly relative to their immedi-ate competitors. But the availability of subsidy policies may differ-entially encourage the most expensive forms, which are produced by well-established institutions that often incur large deficits and can persuade public agencies that they are in danger of extinction.

The less well-established organizations that often are active in the less expensive art forms are at a disadvantage in soliciting public support even when they have serious financial problems.

Subsidies for the arts, like other subsidies, may eliminate market pressures for economies in producing the goods or services; the effects of subsidies may appear to confirm the Baumol-Bowen argument that productivity in the arts is inherently stagnant. But subsidies need not have these effects; granting agencies can find ways of rewarding organizations or individuals for ingenuity in dealing with production costs.

Subsidy policy all too often encourages construction rather than art activities. Construction financing is attractive in part because new buildings are tangible and reassuringly permanent. Moreover, state and local governments often find it easier to borrow funds in the bond market for capital purposes than to draw on general revenues for recurring operating and maintenance costs. The spread of new performing-arts centers testifies to the popularity of the bricks-and-mortar approach. Unfortunately, the high operating and maintenance costs of these centers can impoverish the arts groups occupying them (a real problem for, among others, the Metropolitan Opera). Most of the theoretical justifications for public subsidy apply to support of artistic production rather than for buildings to house the arts.

The Accountability Problem

In recent years, the alleged lack of accountability on the part of all sorts of public and private institutions, especially for the use of money and real resources, has provoked considerable public debate. In part, this problem arises because it is difficult to keep track of things in a large and complex society. In part, it stems from the growth of institutions and activities that reflect a mixture of public and private interests and resources. In a simpler era – say, early in this century – decisions about resource allocation were made either in the marketplace or through explicit political processes that were relatively easy to scrutinize. The users of resources were accountable for their actions to consumers voting with dollars or to citizens voting in elections. For all the many imperfections of those systems of accountability, the lines were clear-cut.

Government support of the arts in the United States involves a blend of public and private interests, with considerable potential for personal conflicts of interest. Equally important, much government support is provided through government arts foundations – agencies that receive large blocks of public money and redistribute it to a host of organizations and individuals. The staffs and boards of these government arts foundations make decisions about critical resource allocations, and in doing so they are substantially insulated from both politics and the marketplace.

This insulation, which is itself the result of a deliberate policy decision has important advantages. Most direct public support takes the form of small grants. The use of intermediaries for decision making frees the political processes from what would be an intolerable overload; Congress cannot vote in any sensible way on annual lists of several thousand proposed grants. Moreover, when elected officials make explicit decisions about lists of specific claimants for subsidy to the arts, the dangers of favoritism and political retaliation are very great. In addition, the task of evaluating proposals for individual grants calls for a degree of expertise; it does not lend itself readily to explicit political decision making.

But the decision makers must be accountable to the public if only because hundreds of millions of dollars in public funds are involved. The undoubted merits of the arts do not vitiate the need for precautions to minimize personal conflicts of interest; for complete, intelligible, and informative reporting on the grant-making activities of the funding agencies; and for continuous evaluation of the results of public subsidies. To date, the arts-funding agencies have been rather casual in dealing with these problems, largely because the amount of public money at their disposal has been, until recently, so small. Today, failure to address these problems may undermine widespread acquiescence in the provision of large-scale public subsidy to the arts.

Public Subsidy and Government Interference

The accountability problem could be resolved easily by close bureaucratic scrutiny of all the decisions of the arts agencies; they could function as conventional government departments, and the appropriations legislation or some other control document could make specific mention of all grantees. There are substantial costs to such official scrutiny, including dollars. University presidents have complained bitterly about the dollar and other costs of complying with the regulations that are conditions of federal grants. In June

1976 at the annual meeting of the American Association of Museums, S. Dillon Ripley, secretary of the Smithsonian Institution, sounded a warning along these lines:

> As museums come closer to success in establishing a precedent for government funding for services and for services rendered, akin to the massive support for colleges and schools, it would be wise to look ahead and consider that with federal funding come certain reciprocals: oversight, control, bureaucratic management, accountability and increased administrative and overhead responsibilities . . . . Money begets power, but the ultimate power rests with the dispenser of the money. Vast money produces regimentation and pedantry.
>
> At the Smithsonian, we have our own direct relationship with our appropriations' committee. We have a tried and true group of people who are familiar with our problems, which is a far cry from the experience of any institution that first goes to the government for funding and then discovers the headaches of bureaucratic processes: not only the usual accounting for every pencil bought, but detailed analyses of hiring practices and other modes of accountability that most organizations are not capable of.[31]

Such scrutiny would lead to a substantial degree of governmental intervention in and control over the actual production of the arts. The accountability problem may have had too little attention, but the danger of governmental interference is well understood. Public subsidy policy must navigate between the two hazards, and the arts are unlikely to remain unaffected by either.

Few people connected with the arts have ever seen large-scale public subsidy as an unmixed blessing. In fact, prior to the 1960s, many of those most concerned feared that direct subsidy of any real dollar importance would come at the price of heavy political intervention in artistic decision making, a cost that would exceed the benefits. There was apprehension about philistine legislators and elected officials straight out of H. L. Mencken's gallery, who would seek to censor avant-garde program choices, witch-hunt for obscenity and subversion, and generally favor the bland and mediocre over the exciting and distinguished.

Despite these widespread fears, during the past decade, this sort of intervention has been a rarity. The single open intervention by a governor (of New Hampshire), to stop a grant to publish poetry he found objectionable, was so unusual that it received nationwide attention – and the event was treated, in the press and broadcast media, as a throwback to the 1920s, not as accepted political behavior. The only truly serious and continuing form of political intervention was both expected and accepted: legislative bodies insisted that public largesse be dispersed geographically rather than spent in only a few places.

The National Endowment for the Humanities has been somewhat less fortunate in this respect. In October 1976, the U.S. Senate adjourned without acting on the presidential nomination of Ronald S. Berman for reappointment to another four-year term as chairman of the Humanities Endowment. The Senate's failure to act was largely due to the opposition of Senator Claiborne Pell, a principal sponsor of the 1965 legislation creating both the Arts and Humanities Endowments. Pell charged that the endowment had too little visibility, that it was too academically oriented and too little concerned with "average citizens who have had no advanced formal education," that it dominated intellectual life in the nation, and that Berman had had the temerity to disagree publicly with the senator.[32] Pell apparently believes that the two endowments are to a large extent in his charge and are obligated to act in accord with his predilections. Unless he is disabused, the Arts Endowment may someday have similar problems.

Even if no inappropriate political pressures distort the decision-making process one way or another, governments must choose among the claimants for funds, for total appropriations will never be sufficient for all. And the mere existence of a public subsidy – for some arts organizations – may make private fund raising more difficult for all. Disappointed organizations may even discover that their failure to secure public support marks them as unworthy to some private donors. Successful claimants may be chagrined to find that governments do not give money away without imposing conditions on the recipients. The conditions may be relatively mild, such as requirements for financial reporting, or onerous, such as difficult fund-matching requirements or an insistence that wholly new and perhaps unwelcome programs be undertaken. Government cannot be expected either to turn over unconditionally large sums of money to high-minded mandarins of the arts who "know best" how to spend this money or to ask fewer questions of artistic recipients of public money than it asks of the rest of us.

Of course, the private foundations, corporations, and individuals who make choices in their support of the arts and impose conditions on the recipients may not be any more "qualified" than public officials. Some leading and thoughtful people in the world of the arts, including Robert Brustein, dean of the Yale Drama School, and Zelda Fichandler, founder and director of the Arena Stage in Washington, D.C., have complained that foundations or local private sources interfere more and are more philistine in their views than the National Endowment for the Arts.[33] People in the arts have complained for decades that reliance on earned income from admissions and sales leads to emphasis on the tried-and-true and avoidance of the new and different. For example, Professor William Hutchinson of UCLA argues that symphony orchestras perform so limited a portion of the total orchestra repertoire that American universities, not the musical performing arts organizations, must be considered the true carriers of "the art of music."[34]

What compensates for the pressure of private donors and audiences as sources of funds is that they are many and divided. In contrast, there is only one federal government, only one state government, and only one city government for a symphony orchestra or resident theater to deal with. Large-scale government support inevitably must produce artistic results that differ from what would take place if money simply rained from the heavens on artists and artistic organizations.

The advantages and disadvantages of public support for the arts may appear academic to many people who are convinced that the arts are in crisis and that a massive application of government funds is all that can remedy the situation. They can cite numerous and frequent surveys by organizations representing specific art forms, such as opera, symphony orchestras, and nonprofit theater groups, as well as organizations concerned with a variety of different forms and activities. Often, the survey questionnaires invite respondents to report on activities that were cancelled, postponed, or not initiated for lack of funds. The many woeful tales elicited by such questionnaires are doubtless true, but they are also misleading. An imaginative and ambitious manager always should have at hand a long list of activities and projects his organization would gladly undertake if only the funds were available. If public support of the arts were to increase tenfold in the next five years, it is to be hoped that, at the end of that time, responding organizations would produce even longer lists of unfunded projects.

The Ford Foundation's analysis of the financial needs of the arts is far more persuasive. This study covers the finances of 166 major nonprofit performing arts organizations in theater, opera, symphonic music, and dance, which account for roughly 90 percent of the roughly $175 million spent by all such organizations (in these fields) in the United States in 1970–71. Data for the six seasons, 1965–66 through 1970–71, were assembled in the study on a fully consistent and carefully defined basis. The study staff calculated the trends that had emerged during the six-year period and, on this basis, projected the finances of 165 of these organizations to the 1980–81 season.[35]

In 1970–71, these organizations:

- had operating expenditures of $138 million;
- earned, largely from performances, $76 million;
- filled the resulting "earnings gap" of $62 million with $52 million in gifts and grants from public and private sources, $8 million from earnings on endowment funds, and nearly $3 million of the principal of endowment funds for operating purposes. (Of the surveyed institutions, only symphony orchestras and a handful of other organizations have endowment funds.)

The Ford Foundation projections for 1980–81 are shown in the top part of Table 2-1. The table shows both the projections of the earlier trends, assuming away cost inflation, and the projections assuming inflation at the rate of 4.5 percent annually over the decade.[36] Without inflation, expenditures are expected to. double and earned income to go up far less rapidly to yield an earnings gap of $180 million, three times the 1970–71 level. Even if, as the table assumes, local private contributions more than double, a gap of $100 million – nearly four times the 1970–71 level – will remain to be covered largely by grants from public agencies and national foundations.[37] The study assumes that national foundations will not increase their support of the arts; it implies that total public support for these organizations will increase from less than $8 million in 1970–71 to as much as $80 million in 1980–81.

These projections are, of course, straight-line extrapolations of earlier trends. The study indicates that a plausible range for the earnings gap is from $95 million to $335 million, without inflation, with a corresponding range of from $45 million to $200 million to be filled by public support. Then there is the problem of inflation. Using the trend extrapolation and a 4.5 percent annual inflation rate, the study projects a huge earnings gap of $285 million, four and one-half times the 1970–71 level.

The lower part of Table 2-1 presents data through the 1973–74

Table 2-1. *Finances of Large Performing Arts Organizations, Actual and Projected, 1970–74, and 1980–81 (in Millions of Dollars)*

Organizations and date	Total expenditures	Earned income	Earnings gap	Local nongovernment contributions	Remaining gap
165 Organizations					
1970–71 actual	138	76	62	36	26
1980–81 trend value, constant dollars	275	95	180	80	100
1980–81, 4.5% annual inflation	435	150	285	125	160
152 Organizations[a]					
1970–71 actual	127	71	56	32	24
1980–81 trend value, constant dollars	253	90	163	71	92
1980–81, 4.5% annual inflation	400	140	260	111	149
1973–74 trend value, interpolated	156	76	77	41	36
1973–74, 4.5% annual inflation, interpolated	179	87	89	46	43
1973–74 actual	173	94	79	44	35
1973–74 actual in 1970–71 dollars[b]	149	81	68	38	30

[a] Actuals from unpublished data provided by the Ford Foundation for the 153 organizations covered in the 1970–71 through 1973–74 surveys, with the Metropolitan Opera excluded on the basis of data for 1973–74 provided by Opera America. Projections for 1980–81 assume that the percent changes projected for the 165 organizations also apply to the 152 organizations. Interpolations are based on three years of increase at the averge annual rate for the decade. [b] The 1973–74 actuals divided by 1.16, reflecting the increase in consumer prices from the 1970–71 season to the 1973–74 season.
Source: From the Ford Foundation, *The Finances of the Performing Arts*, vol. I, 1974, pp. 104–105.

season, provided by the Ford Foundation and covering a slightly smaller sample of organizations. During the first three years of the decade, total expenditures rose roughly in accord with the projections if inflation is taken into account – a bit more slowly, but not wholly out of line. However, earned income rose significantly more rapidly than would be suggested by the projections, no doubt because average ticket prices rose considerably (without producing devastating effects on attendance). The earnings gap was smaller than projected; because local nongovernment contributions came close to the projections, the "remaining gap" proved to be below the projections.[38]

But these developments hardly mean that all is well. The trends of the first three years of the 1970s extrapolated to 1980–81 (that is assuming that both prices and the real levels of spending and income will increase at the rates of the first three years for the entire ten-year period) produce these results for the 152 organizations (in millions of dollars):

	1973–74	1980–81
Total expenditures	173	356
Earned income	94	181
Earnings gap	79	175
Local nongovernment contributions	44	93
Remaining gap	35	82

If grants from national foundations and endowment income remain at 1973–74 levels (roughly $20 million), then public support would have to increase from about $13 million in 1973–74 to over $60 million in 1980–81, holding everything else at the projected levels. And if the share of total public support going to these organizations remains constant, total public support of the arts would have to increase from less than $300 million in 1975 to more than $1.1 billion in 1980–81.

This analysis suggests that even under the most favorable circumstances, such as a moderate rate of inflation and fairly aggressive increases in earned income, the financial needs of the arts will present serious public policy problems in the next few years. Given the fiscal pressures on governments at the local, state, and federal level, public support is unlikely to triple or quadruple within the next few years. Moreover, other sectors – such as higher education – have similar financial prospects and can also mount strong claims for public support.

Citizens and decision makers confront tales of financial woe constantly. All agree as to the general needs and merits of the arts, but artists and arts organizations will be demanding many more public dollars than are likely to be available. Both social philosophy and ingenuity must be employed to establish priorities among the arts claimants and to modify the economics of the arts to cope with the realities of fiscal stringency.

3

Patterns of Public Support

The pattern of public support for the arts in the United States is a distinctive one, shaped by our peculiar political and social development. Yet it contains elements in common with the various patterns of those other countries where life is dominated by private decision making but governments provide support, in one form or another, for the arts. Even among such countries, though, government support for the arts takes a variety of forms.

Indirect Support

Exempting the activities and assets of nonprofit organizations and institutions themselves from taxation is administratively feasible and of quantitative importance only in such countries as the United States, Britain, most other English-speaking countries, and Scandinavia, which derive a substantial amount of their revenues from direct taxes on income and property. Countries that collect most of their revenues from excise taxes and import duties on widely used consumer goods, as do most developing countries and several countries of continental Europe, cannot provide much tax-exemption assistance to nonprofit organizations. Symphony orchestras and opera companies have little to gain from tax relief on purchases of tobacco, liquor, gasoline, cooking oil, or machine tools, although they can benefit if tickets and certain other items are exempted from value-added taxes.

In the United States, taxes on property (prior to 1913) and on income and property combined (since 1913) have dominated the tax system. And from the earliest days of the Republic, state and local governments have exempted nonprofit artistic and cultural organizations – along with a long list of religious, educational, and eleemosynary organizations – from property taxes in order to promote artistic and cultural activities.[1] In 1913, when the federal income tax was instituted, most of the nonprofit organizations exempt from property taxes also were exempted from income taxes.

Support by tax exemption has certain obvious advantages: it relieves government agencies of the burden of making invidious distinctions among worthy activities (the amount of the subsidy that a given tax-exempt organization receives depends on the organization's success in eliciting funds from *private* sources); it also relieves governments of the burden of openly drawing on general tax revenues to make direct cash payments to beneficiaries, and it conceals the costs of the subsidy in terms of resources that might otherwise be available for other public purposes. Tax exemption has its disadvantages, too. It is of no value to organizations that rarely have positive net income. And because *property* tax exemption benefits only those nonprofit organizations that own expensive buildings situated on high-value land, it encourages them to use their financial resources for land and buildings rather than for the program operations that make the organizations socially valuable.

At most, property-tax exemption provides a subsidy worth $150 million annually for the arts in the United States.[2] A far more valuable source of support is the exemption from taxes – federal, state, and local, income, death, and gift – of contributions, gifts, and bequests to nonprofit arts organizations. Ever since it began taxing income and estates early in this century, the United States has provided far more comprehensive and generous tax deductibility of charitable gifts and bequests than does any other country. In other countries, such gifts and bequests are either not deductible at all or deductible only in limited amounts and under special circumstances. No other country has specific tax-law provisions that make it possible for a donor to register actual cash gains from giving by deducting from tax liability the current market value of donated assets (such as paintings) that he originally purchased at much lower prices.

Although I have estimated that this form of subsidy for the arts costs government roughly $400 million annually at present, some evidence indicates that the total may in fact be substantially larger.[3] Not only is this form of public support far more important in dollars than property-tax exemption; it is also more pertinent to current financial planning in the arts. An arts organization has to invest more in land and buildings to increase (hypothetically) the value of its property-tax exemption; the property-tax exemption does not enable it to become better off financially than it is at the moment. But the tax deductibility of gifts and bequests generates cash and valuable assets for the recipients. By lowering the cost of gifts to the donors, tax deductibility makes it easier for arts organizations to raise money. Some social critics deplore tax exemption on the general grounds that all subsidies, no matter how worthy the recipient, should be open, measurable, and subject to periodic review, rather than hidden, unquantified, and virtually permanent, as is tax-exemption assistance.[4]

A third, minor but real, form of indirect support for the arts is only occasionally noted: because so much employment in the arts, especially the performing arts, is seasonal or irregular, large numbers of arts professionals live on a combination of irregular earnings from the arts and unemployment insurance. A number of performing-arts organizations plan their seasons and design their policies to qualify their employees for the fullest possible unemployment insurance benefits. Union contracts are sometimes written with explicit provision for unemployment insurance. Of course, unemployment provisions differ from state to state, but two states with heavy concentrations of the performing arts – New York and California – have relatively liberal provisions. Few sectors of the economy other than the performing arts seem able to rely so heavily on unemployment insurance as an economic prop. The use of unemployment insurance as a form of indirect support for the arts may be unique to the United States.

Direct Support

In the United States, Britain, and most other English-speaking countries, arts organizations, for the most part, are either commercial enterprises or nonprofit organizations. Therefore, direct public support of the arts primarily takes the form of grants to nongovernmental organizations and individuals. In making such grants, governments are not themselves organizers and promoters of the arts; rather, they respond with subsidy to nongovernmental initiatives.[5]

In addition, even in the English-speaking countries, governments themselves operate some artistic and cultural organizations and institutions as government departments. For example, national governments, and some local and state governments as well, are proprietors of museums. In the infancy of broadcasting in the 1920s, the state of Wisconsin and the city of New York became proprietors of radio stations, setting a precedent for government ownership and operation of noncommercial broadcasting stations and networks that place a fair amount of emphasis on the performing arts. In Britain, the British Broadcasting Corporation (BBC) – a government corporation financed from the receipts of the license fee collected from individual owners of radio and television sets – may well be the largest single source of public funds expended for the arts.[6] In continental Europe, direct government ownership and operation of artistic organizations – including most of the great European orchestras and opera, dance, and theater companies – is the rule rather than the exception, and many of the professional artists in such organizations are civil servants.

Government proprietorship has obvious monetary advantages. Governments do not ordinarily permit the complete financial collapse of their departments, nor do they readily fire civil servants. The empire-building proclivities of bureaucrats work to expand budgets, as do "fair-share" rules, under which all government departments annually receive more or less equal proportional increases in appropriations. Elected officials are likely to bask in more reflected glory from their governments' artistic enterprises than from subsidized nongovernmental ones. At the same time, government proprietorship considerably increases the temptation and opportunity for political and bureaucratic participation in artistic decisions, as French experience over many years testifies.

Even when artistic organizations are not government departments, government as patron and sponsor may play a fairly direct role in their operations. It is not uncommon for governments to build and/or operate physical facilities to house nongovernmental artistic organizations. The city of New York began doing this in the last century, and it continues to spend the great bulk of its $50 million annual expenditure in support of the arts on maintaining and operating buildings housing the arts. State universities subsidize the performing arts by providing facilities at less than full cost for performances by touring organizations. And government appropriations covering part or all of the capital costs of new physical facilities are widespread. Notable examples include the Kennedy Center in Washington and the New York State Theater at Lincoln Center in New York.[7]

Governments also commission and purchase artistic services and products. In recent years, local government sponsorship of free performances (typically outdoors in parks) has increased, and the great wave of public office-building construction that began in the United States around 1960 has been accompanied by purchases of works of visual art for display in the new buildings or in the plazas

associated with them. Most of the public financial support for literature consists of public-library purchases of books and periodicals. In
those Western European countries in which public-library use is
especially frequent, writers' organizations have campaigned for payments of royalties to authors for books circulated by public libraries. In the 1950s, both West Germany and Sweden instituted
versions of such payment to authors. In Sweden in 1969–70,
$620,000 was distributed in "library compensation"; $160,000 in
direct payments to authors and the rest in scholarships, awards,
and pensions to authors, illustrators, and translators and their depen-
dents.[8] The British government in March 1976 introduced legislation to establish this sort of payment for what is called, in Britain,
"public lending right."

As a form of government support, the purchase of artistic goods
and services has the virtue of channeling public funds directly to
individual artists, such as writers and visual artists, who, unlike
performing artists, operate on their own, not as members of companies, orchestras, or other organizations. Such direct patronage
also enables governments to specify the characteristics of the artistic
services and products being purchased. In this respect, it is a mixed
blessing for the arts, because public officials, aware that purchase of
the unconventional may expose them to criticism or, worse, ridi-
cule, have an incentive to purchase very conventional expressions of
the arts.

Government also may channel public funds directly to individual
artists through outright grants. This approach has rich historical
precedents, including the royal patronage of individual artists,
which flourished in the Renaissance and the Enlightenment, and the
appointment of favored artists to public sinecures, a practice that
was common before the development of the "merit system" of
recruitment for civil service in the middle and late nineteenth century in North America and Europe. By far the largest effort in
history – ancient or recent – to aid individual artists directly was the
(Franklin D. Roosevelt administration) Works Progress Administration (WPA) Arts Project in the 1930s. Currently, a portion of the
funds appropriated under the Comprehensive Employment and
Training Act (CETA) is being used in a number of cities to employ
artists qua artists on government arts projects.

Several European countries, including Denmark (which began
such a program early in this century), Sweden, and Britain, have
formal programs of grants, awards, prizes, and fellowships to individual artists. In Sweden, such payments to individual artists consti-

tute an unusually large element of direct public support of the arts –
about 9 percent of total central government support and 5 percent
of combined central and local government support in 1970–71.[9] In
Britain in 1973–74 awards of various kinds to individual artists
totalled only a little over 1 percent of the Arts Council's expenditure.[10] In the United States, since 1965–66 the National Endowment for the Arts (NEA) has been making direct awards to individual artists, and ten of the state arts councils also make such grants.
In fiscal 1974, when NEA's total obligated funds amounted to $67.6
million, it awarded $2.5 million directly to artists in its various
fellowship programs.[11] State arts councils awarded an additional
$800,000 or so.[12]

In its first year of operation, NEA initiated the policy of making
direct grants to individual artists – something that pre-existing organizations, such as the British Arts Council and the New York
State Council on the Arts, had not done – in part, apparently, because of "sheer lack of money to do anything else." The first NEA
appropriation was so small that the endowment could make only
small grants to individuals, not large grants to institutions.[13] Since
then, as its appropriations have increased, NEA has increased and
diversified its awards to individuals, despite the difficulties of administering and making sensible choices in a fellowship program
that generates 5,000 applications a year.[14]

Still another form of direct government action that does not
involve the use of nonprofit intermediaries is government operation
of schools or training institutions for the arts. This type of support
is very widespread abroad, where most education and training institutions are government-operated. In the United States, most of the
schools that train artists are in the private sector and many are
proprietary; hence, in subsidizing the training of artists, government supplies funds to both state-university conservatories and performing-arts schools and nonprofit intermediaries.

Grants of government funds to nonprofit arts organizations to
support program operations are not new in the United States, although such large-scale grants are. For years, a few state and local
governments have made such grants, in the form of line-item budget
appropriations, to specified organizations, notably museums. (Line-
item appropriations are designated for particular recipients as opposed to categories of recipients or grant-making intermediaries.) A
nonprofit arts organization that has a line-item appropriation is almost as secure financially as a government-operated institution but
presumably has more artistic freedom. However, in order to obtain

such appropriations, individual arts organizations must assert their claims to public support against the competing claims not only of other arts organizations but of all the other purposes among which legislative bodies allocate public funds. Few arts organizations feel confident of success in such a competition. Hence, most American groups and institutions lobbying for public support of the arts heatedly oppose line-item appropriations for particular organizations.

Instead, these groups favor an approach that now is the dominant form of public support for the arts in Canada, Britain, and the United States: the government arts foundation. This institution (examples include the Corporation for Public Broadcasting, the California Cultural Commission, and the Canadian Film Development Corporation) receives a relatively large line-item appropriation of public funds. It disburses these funds to a sizable number of nonprofit organizations and individuals who are themselves the producers of the arts. The government arts foundation allocates its funds usually on the basis of very general statutory guidelines, with specific decisions influenced largely by the recommendations of expert advisory panels. The degree of discretion in policy making that government arts foundations enjoy is unusual in American government, and the foundations' reliance on the advice of people from outside the civil service is also unusual.[15]

The British were the first to use this approach. The British Arts Council was chartered in 1946.[16] (A predecessor council had been founded early in World War II.) However, until the late 1960s, the funds available to the Council were very modest. In 1965, a government white paper was published, recommending generous public support of the arts. The public obliged. In 1957, the Canada Council was established and given a $50 million endowment fund; in recent years, the income from this fund has been supplemented by sizable annual parliamentary appropriations. The first government arts foundation in the United States was the New York State Council on the Arts. It was established in 1961 but, like the British Arts Council and the Canada Council, had relatively little money to disburse in its early years. The NEA was founded in 1965, again with very small appropriations at the outset but large increases in the early 1970s.

Today, the British Arts Council accounts for about one-fourth of total public spending in support of the arts in Britain. The rest goes to the BBC, central and local government operation of museums, central and local government grants for the construction of artistic buildings, and local government line-item subventions to specific nonprofit artistic organizations.[17] In contrast, in the United States, arts foundations, including the NEA, the National Endowment for the Humanities, the Corporation for Public Broadcasting, and the state arts councils, all of which operate in similar ways, account for at least two-thirds of direct public spending for the arts. Similarly, in Canada in the early 1970s, the Canada Council, its provincial government counterparts (notably in Ontario and Quebec), and the Canadian Film Development Corporation, which is a type of government arts foundation, appear to have provided roughly 60 percent of total public support of the arts.[18]

Both the absence of requisite data and conceptual difficulties preclude the valid comparison of aggregate government funding of the arts in different countries. Apparently, there are no countries in which comprehensive data on public subsidy covering all levels of government are collected in a form that permits international comparisons on a recurring basis, and only in a few countries have efforts been made to assemble such data for a given year. (The United States is *not* an exception to this generalization, despite the celebrated American predilection for collecting statistics on every conceivable subject.)[19]

Proper international comparisons also should take into account indirect assistance through preferential tax treatment and place government financial assistance in perspective by comparing it to the aggregate size of the arts sector and to the income that artistic activities generate. For example, in 1971–72 per capita direct public support for the arts in Canada reached a level that the United States did not reach until 1975, but in Canada, corporate and private foundation support for the arts is negligible and individual giving very small, reflecting the differences in the tax systems. In 1975, in Australia, central government support of the arts through the Australia Council on a per capita basis was about 50 percent above the public support provided by all levels of American government combined.[20] (Per capita income levels in Australia are only about 70 percent of the U.S. level.) But Australia's tax laws do not foster large private giving, whether by individuals, corporations, or private foundations.

Anecdotal evidence – regarding such matters as the heavy public subsidy of opera companies in German, Austrian, and Italian cities and the French national government's direct operation of so many artistic organizations and institutions – suggests that the role of public financial support is much larger in continental Europe than in English-speaking countries. In Germany in 1971, expenditures for "cultural services" – almost all of them provided by the provincial and municipal governments – were the equivalent of more than $700 million, or $12 per capita, although that category includes libraries, adult education, other educational activities, and nonart museums, as well as the arts. In 1972, public expenditures for the performing arts (mostly provided by municipal governments), amounted to the equivalent of more than $5 per capita, compared to less than $1 per capita in the United States in 1975.[21]

Sweden may well hold the record for per capita government support of the arts. In 1970–71, Sweden's total public support of the arts was the equivalent of just under $60 million, or about $7.30 per capita. Local governments provided 44 percent of this amount. Grants to performing arts organizations, including film, accounted for 82 percent of the total, grants for arts museums and other support of the visual arts for 13 percent, and payments to individual artists for the remaining 5 percent.[22]

In France in 1975, central government expenditure for the arts appears to have been the equivalent of roughly $100 million and, although the data are somewhat contradictory, local governments seem to be spending another $50 million, altogether the equivalent of roughly $3 per capita.[23] The literature on subsidies to the arts in France includes one spectacular figure: the government subvention to the Paris Opera is equivalent to about $46 per seat at each performance.

The French also provide a variety of quasi-governmental aids of lesser magnitude, such as a redistributive fund for the Paris theaters, which receives the proceeds of an admissions tax (plus some other public funds) and assists theaters with deficits at the expense of those with surpluses. But like most countries outside the United States, neither Germany nor Sweden nor France has an income-tax system that encourages large-scale private giving to the arts: in Germany, individuals may deduct up to 5 percent of their incomes for contributions; in France, a relatively recent law permits corporations to deduct up to 1 percent and individuals up to one-half of 1 percent for contributions.[24]

In Britain in 1975–76, direct public support of the arts totaled, in dollars, about 70 percent of the American aggregate for calendar 1975 (see Table 1-1). In Britain in that year, direct public support amounted to nearly $4 per capita, about three times the per capita public support in the United States. As a percentage of gross national product, public support for the arts in Britain was nearly six times as high as in the United States. But in all probability, the amounts that British nonprofit arts organizations (and public bodies as well) pay in local property taxes and value-added tax[25] equal or exceed the very modest tax preferences they receive as individual and business contributions, gifts, and bequests to the arts.[26]

If American tax preferences for the arts are worth at least $400 million annually and conceivably as much as $800 million, the United States probably provides as much public financial support for the arts as Britain on a per capita basis and about half what Britain provides as a percentage of gross national product. Moreover, it is reasonable that public support in the United States should represent a smaller fraction of the receipts of some important types of artistic organizations than it is in Britain because American consumers enjoy much higher levels of per capita real income than British consumers and should be able to provide artistic organizations with substantially greater earned income derived from sale of their services. Major "international-class" arts organizations – the premier opera and ballet companies and art museums, for example – should be able to mount comparable performances and exhibitions with less subsidy in the United States than in Britain simply because Americans, being richer, are able to pay substantially higher prices for admissions.[27] However inadequate the level of public support is in this country on other grounds, I do not consider it strikingly low compared to that in Britain, which is one country for which reasonably reliable up-to-date comparisons can be made and which is generally acknowledged to provide strong government support for the arts.

4

Direct Subsidy Programs in the United States

The pronouncements of several highly visible and activist Presidents in recent years have led many Americans to believe that, in our governmental system, the federal government introduces most or all innovative measures and then coaxes recalcitrant and unenlightened state and local governments into following its example. In fact, more often than not, one or another state serves as a laboratory for new initiatives that are later adopted by Congress. Most federal legislation on income maintenance, social services, health services, and housing is patterned after measures first adopted at the state or local level. So it is with public support for the arts. The city of New York was providing large-scale support to a number of local arts organizations years before any state government did so, and the state of New York was on the scene before the federal government.

Federal Programs in the Arts

In fact, before the 1930s, the federal government showed little concern for the arts. Although in 1846 Congress created the Smithsonian Institution and in 1859 President James Buchanan appointed a National Art Commission (which was disbanded two years later), it was not until 1910 that Congress passed a bill establishing the National Commission on Fine Arts[1] (whose sole function was to suggest designs and decorations for federal buildings).

The state of government support for the arts during this period reflects two aspects of life in the United States. First, the arts were considered elitist and as such undeserving of direct public support. Second, the great industrial and financial barons who prospered in the late nineteenth century were establishing and subsidizing their own museums, symphony orchestras, and opera companies in the major cities, although they did persuade some city governments to provide support early on.

In the 1930s, the federal government undertook its first large-scale intervention in the world of the arts in the form of the celebrated Arts Project of the New Deal's Works Progress Administration (WPA). The impetus for this effort was not special concern for artistic activity and still less a commitment to a permanent federal role in support of the arts. The purpose of the program was simply to reduce the unemployment caused by the Depression. (The arts did prove useful in the pursuit of one important long-term New Deal objective, the provision of urban amenities to rural and small-town America.) The New Deal's support of the arts is now celebrated as a happy marriage of big government and the arts, but at the time the programs had as many critics as friends. The programs were attacked by political conservatives and by a fair number of people in the art world on the ground that the restrictions inherent in work-relief programs necessarily conflicted with artistic merit and talent.[2]

A modest program of support for the arts began early in the New Deal era – in November 1933 – with the creation of the Civil Works Administration (CWA) as part of the Federal Emergency Relief Administration (FERA). The Public Works of Art Project, a CWA program, was organized as a selective white-collar employment program for artists. This program lasted four months and cost $1.3 million.[3]

In early 1934, the FERA established a temporary Emergency Work Program, which was administered by the states and employed about 1,000 individuals on arts-related projects.[4]

In January 1935, Congress approved President Roosevelt's proposal for a large-scale national employment program and established the WPA, with an initial $5 million appropriation. Cultural activities were administered within the professional and service section of WPA and were designated as Federal Project Number One.

Federal One consisted of five programs – the Federal Art, Music, Theatre, Writers, and Historical Records Projects. Each program was directed by a leading professional in its field. Unlike the administrators of the New Deal's earlier programs, those running Federal One were concerned with maintaining professional standards of production rather than with altering the art form in order to provide educational or recreational secondary benefits to the public.

The purpose of WPA itself was to alleviate the unemployment problems resulting from the Depression, to take people off the relief rolls and put them to work. The administrators of Federal One found it particularly difficult to meet the requirement that between

75 and 90 percent of WPA fund recipients be chosen from relief rolls. Most artists were ineligible either because they had been self-employed or without full-time employment before the Depression or because they were not financially impoverished even during the Depression. For reasons inapplicable to conditions in the arts, WPA regulations also restricted relocation of program beneficiaries. As a result:

> Federal Theatre Project (FTP) plans for regional theatre were thwarted largely by relief regulations, which stated that individuals could not be transferred from the location where they originally signed on. FTP administrators had hopes to move some of their actors from metropolitan areas, especially New York City, to parts where their talents were needed. But Washington answered with a resounding no. Thus New York City became a major center of activity while many other parts of the country were virtually untouched by the FTP.[5]

The FTP was far from the only Federal One program with a heavy concentration of personnel and funds in major population centers. The desire of administrators to maintain high artistic quality led them to operate where the best artists were already located. When Federal One came under congressional criticism, beginning in 1938, the program's heavy concentration in a few large cities, particularly in New York, rather than in rural America, contributed to its demise.

The scale of the WPA program was immense. Federal One employed 45,000 in June 1936; 37,250 in May 1937; 28,000 in June 1938; and 39,000 in February 1939. Its production was even more impressive. By September 1938, the Art Project had produced 355,126 photographs, 17,000 pieces of sculpture, 108,000 easel paintings, 2,500 murals, 95,000 prints, 1.6 million posters, and a 20,000 piece Index of American Design, and had operated over 100 community art centers. As of September 1939, the Music Project Concerts Division had employed over 8,000 musicians in the following organizations:

> 28 symphony orchestras employing 1,907
> 90 small orchestras employing 2,075
> 68 bands employing 2,114
> 55 dance bands and orchestras employing 663
> 15 chamber music ensembles employing 114
> 33 opera and choral units employing 1,100
> 1 soloists' unit employing 10

The core of the Writers Project was the *American Guide* book series. Guidebooks were produced for each of the states, as well as for a number of cities (and towns). The Federal Theatre Project at its height employed 13,000 people, covered 31 states, reached an audience of 25 million people, produced 830 plays, and returned $2 million in admission fees to the Treasury Department.[6]

In addition to sponsoring Federal One, in July 1935 the WPA gave a $500,000 grant to the Treasury Department so that it could hire visual artists and sculptors to decorate the nearly 2,000 buildings across the country under the department's jurisdiction. This program, known as the Treasury Relief Art Project (TRAP), lasted a year and was to provide work to 450 artists then on relief rolls.[7] The administrators of TRAP were even more insistent on professional standards than their Federal Art Project (FAP) colleagues. As a result of this concern for quality above all, TRAP hired only 300 artists and was labeled "elitist." Under pressure to expand employment, TRAP "borrowed" a few more artists from FAP rolls, bringing its employment list up to 356 by the time it was phased out in 1936.[8]

Throughout its existence, Federal One had come under various attacks, but in August 1938 it met with a new and powerful source of opposition. The House Committee on Un-American Activities, under the chairmanship of Martin Dies, began an investigation of Federal One, concentrating on its theater and writing projects. The programs were criticized for inefficiency and lack of conformity with WPA regulations; certain writers, actors, and artists also were labeled as subversive and indecent. The Dies Committee exploited the presence on Federal One's employment rolls of a number of known Communists. In a few instances between 1935 and 1938 the theater, writing, and arts projects had experienced censorship restrictions, but the Dies Committee found the censorship insufficient.

Under pressure from the committee, the Emergency Relief Act of 1939 abolished the Federal Theatre Project and transferred the remaining Federal One programs to state control, which the committee apparently considered less "liberal." The destruction of Federal One's most controversial project was a victory for anti-New Deal forces, but in the four years of its existence, FTP had supported a number of experiments and encouraged the development of black theater, children's theater, and, indirectly, National Public Radio, which had its origins in the nearly 6,000 FTP radio productions aired on free time donated by the CBS and NBC radio stations.[9]

The decline and fall of Federal One cannot be attributed entirely to the House Committee on Un-American Activities. In early 1938, two members of Congress, John M. Coffee of Washington and Claude Pepper of Florida, recommended that a permanent and independent Bureau of Fine Arts be established "to assume all functions, powers and duties exercised by the WPA in the arts."[10] This proposal generated extensive debate among artists, politicians, and the press and provided new fuel for the Dies Committee. Because the bill provided for a controlling role by labor unions involved in the arts, many leaders in the arts voiced concern about the quality of the artistic endeavors to be funded under such a permanent agency.

With the United States involved in World War II, unemployment dropped sharply. The WPA was gradually phased out and with it Federal One. In 1943, President Roosevelt halted *all* WPA activities. Despite its extensive activities, Federal One did not set a precedent for a permanent role for the federal government as a supporter of the arts; it may have had a negative effect on public opinion. As a historian of the period has observed:

> The arts units needed to prove that they were in every way exemplary and uplifting. In that, they failed. They could not escape the stigma of make-work relief or the taint of Rooseveltian politics.[11]

During the 1950s, the executive and legislative branches showed only limited interest in the arts. In 1951, President Truman requested that a report on the state of the arts be submitted to his office. That report, completed in 1953 during the Eisenhower administration, recommended increased support for the Smithsonian. In 1954, President Eisenhower initiated a Program for Cultural Presentations Abroad, which sponsored tours of performing and creative artists. From 1955 to 1961, Congress appropriated $16.2 million in funds for this program (which also supported touring of sports organizations).

In 1955, President Eisenhower proposed the establishment of a Federal Advisory Commission on the Arts (without fund-granting authority), within the Department of Health, Education, and Welfare. Congress did not act on this suggestion. But in 1958, Congress approved legislation calling for the construction of a National Cultural Center in Washington, D.C. Although the legislation provided land for the center, it stipulated that construction funds be raised by private sources. In 1964, however, Congress authorized an initial $15 million for construction funds.

In 1961, the Kennedy administration also proposed the creation of a Federal Advisory Council on the Arts. It was defeated on a roll-call vote.[12] A year later, President Kennedy appointed August Heckscher, director of the Twentieth Century Fund, as his special consultant on the arts with the primary task of reporting on the status of the arts and the federal government. Heckscher's report recommended the creation of an Advisory Arts Council to review federal policies and to make program recommendations for involving the artistic community in government activities. Heckscher's most controversial recommendation was the establishment of a National Arts Foundation to offer grants-in-aid to organizations and state arts councils. In response to the report, President Kennedy commented: "Government can never take over the role of patronage and support filled by private individuals and groups in our society. But government surely has a significant part to play in helping establish the conditions under which art can flourish – in encouraging the arts as it encourages science and learning."[13]

The Heckscher report also recommended that the federal government substantially expand its acquisition of works of art; raise its design standards; assume more responsibility for preserving cultural assets and the cultural environment; give motion pictures an important role in the National Cultural Center; consider the provision of arts facilities in all federal building and urban renewal plans; offer support for international fairs and conferences; give the arts a higher priority in federal education, training, and research programs; and provide official recognition of the achievements of creative and performing artists (perhaps in the form of a medal).

In addition, the report recommended changes in the tax laws: a fair income-averaging provision for artists, greater tax incentives for private contributions to the arts, and repeal of the then-existing 10 percent federal tax on theater admissions. It also advocated low postal rates for cultural materials, revision of copyright laws, use of government surplus property by cultural institutions, and better use of federal media programming in the arts.

In June 1963, President Kennedy issued an executive order establishing an Advisory Council on the Arts, but this council never went into operation. Following the assassination, the Senate approved a bill establishing a National Arts Foundation, authorizing it to award matching grants to states and nonprofit professional arts organizations and appropriating $5 million for its first year and $10 million for each succeeding year. This bill, whose main backers were Senators Claiborne Pell and Jacob Javits, did not reach the floor of the House. The opponents of the bill feared that federal support would lead to government control of the arts. But six months later, in mid-1964, the same Congress enacted a new version of the bill, establishing a National Council on the Arts as an arts advisory body in the Executive Office. (This organization, composed of a chairman and twenty-four private citizens appointed by the President, did not have funds to offer grants-in-aid.)

The Arts Endowment

In 1965, the Johnson administration introduced a new bill offering federal grant support to cultural institutions in both the arts and the humanities. The supporters of the bill emphasized that it was part and parcel of all the other Great Society and foreign policy programs. But the bill was strongly opposed by conservative Republicans and southern Democrats. The Republican Policy Committee, a major opponent, stated: "The arts and humanities are thriving today and will continue to thrive so long as the deadening hand of the Federal bureaucracy is kept from the palate, the chisel and the pen."[14] Opponents also feared that federal support would reduce the incentives for private support and that government intervention would produce mediocrity.

Opposition to the bill arose not only in congressional circles but also in the arts. Artist Larry Rivers commented: "The government taking a role in art is like a gorilla threading a needle. It is at first cute, then clumsy, and most of all impossible."[15] So persuasive was the fear of government control that symphony orchestras did not apply for federal assistance until 1970.

But Congress finally passed – and on September 29, 1965, President Johnson signed – a bill establishing the National Foundation on the Arts and Humanities. The bill stated that "a high civilization must not limit its efforts to science and technology alone but must give full value and support to the other great branches of man's scholarly and cultural activity." It defined the humanities as including, but not being limited to, the study of language (both modern and classical), linguistics, literature, history, jurisprudence, philosophy, and archeology. (In 1970, at President Nixon's recommendation, comparative religion and ethics were added to this list.) It defined the arts as including, but not being limited to, music, dance, drama, folk art, creative writing, architecture and allied fields, painting, sculpture, photography, graphic and craft arts, industrial design, costume and fashion design, motion pictures, television, radio, and tape and sound recording.

To preclude government censorship or interference in the arts, the bill stated that "no department, agency, officer, or employee of the United States shall exercise any direction, supervision, or control over the policy determination, personnel, or curriculum or the administration or operation of any school or other non-Federal agency, institution, organization, or association."

To encourage private contributions, the legislation specified that all grants to nonprofit institutions must be in the form of matching grants[16] and established the Treasury Fund. (When a donation is received, it frees an equal amount from the Treasury Fund, and the doubled amount is then made available to the grantee to match. Thus, for every dollar given by private sources under this program, another dollar is released from the Treasury. The grantee then matches the two dollars with two more dollars because almost all endowment grants are for only half the total budget of an approved project.) The act also makes assistance available to the states for arts projects and provides for grants-in-aid to individual artists. The act authorized appropriations of $10 million a year for 1966, 1967, and 1968 for each of the two endowments.

The National Foundation on the Arts and Humanities is composed of three institutions: the National Endowment for the Arts, the National Endowment for the Humanities, and the Federal Council on the Arts and Humanities. (Each endowment has a National Council, a policy board consisting of a chairman and twenty-six private citizens appointed by the President.) The Federal Council on the Arts and Humanities, composed of twelve federal agency administrators including the NEA and NEH chairmen, promotes coordination of the foundation's activities with other federal programs. The first chairman of the Arts Endowment was Roger L. Stevens; the first Humanities chairman was Henry Allen Moe, who served only a short time; he was succeeded by Barnaby Keeney. In 1969, President Nixon appointed Nancy Hanks to the Arts chairmanship and, in 1971, Ronald Berman to the Humanities chairmanship. Wallace Edgerton served as NEH's acting chairman during 1970.

Both endowments had three-year authorizations; hence, by 1968 legislation was needed to continue them. The 1968 re-authorization act modestly increased the ceilings on endowment spending. In 1970, President Nixon interrupted the cycle by requesting a new authorization statute, with increased ceilings, for fiscal 1971–73. The 1973 re-authorization, for the subsequent fiscal years, provided further large increases. Like other legislative authorizations, these

Table 4-1. *Appropriations for the National Endowment for the Arts, Fiscal Years 1966–76 (in Thousands of Dollars)*

Fiscal year	Program funds	Bloc grants to state agencies	Funds to match private donations	Total[a]
1966[b]	2,500	–	34	2,534
1967	4,000	2,000	1,966	7,966
1968	4,500	2,000	674	7,174
1969[b]	3,700	1,700	2,357	7,757
1970	4,250	2,000	2,000	8,250
1971[b]	8,465	4,125	2,500	15,090
1972	20,750	5,500	3,500	29,750
1973	27.825	6,875	3,500	38,200
1974[b]	46,025	8,250	6,500	60,775
1975	67,250[c]	–	7,500	74,750
1976	74,500[d]	–	7,500	82,000

[a]These amounts are all available for grants. NEA's administrative expenses, like those of the Humanities Endowment, are provided from a separate appropriation for that purpose, to the National Foundation on the Arts and Humanities. [b]New authorization act effective beginning in this fiscal year. [c]At least 20 percent must be allocated to state arts agencies and regional groups. [d]The appropriation request proposed that over $15 million be allocated to state arts agencies.
Source: National Foundation on the Arts and Humanities releases.

are well above the amounts actually appropriated by the Congress or requested by the President in his budget. Table 4-1 shows the growth in the amounts actually appropriated to NEA.[17] That growth has been spectacular, from an average of about $8 million a year through 1970 to more than $80 million in fiscal 1976.[18]

The political history of the Arts Endowment follows the pattern of other new federal government activities. It had a long gestation period, during which repeated efforts to enact legislation failed. Rather suddenly, the political requisites for passage of a bill appeared: a friendly, if not aggressively promoting, White House; a number of very strong supporters in the Congress (in this case, Senators Pell and Javits and Congressman Brademas); and opponents who viewed the bill more as a poor idea than as a threat to their vital interests. The White House viewed the bill as a minor part of a major effort, involving vast federal spending, to reconstruct the United States as a Great Society. President Johnson also sought to prove himself an appropriately cultivated successor to President Kennedy and at least as much of a public patron of the arts as Nelson Rockefeller, who in 1960 had launched the New York State Council on the Arts.

With very few exceptions (most of which, like Medicaid, have unhappy histories), new federal government activities in the United States start off, as did NEA, with very modest appropriations, which grow rapidly as the new venture confirms the expectations of its advocates, allays the fears of its original opponents, and builds a new constituency among the program's beneficiaries. In all these respects, NEA has been very successful: the White House has remained strongly positive through successive administrations; NEA's original congressional friends have remained close and sympathetic; some opponents, such as the boards of museums and symphony orchestras, have undergone conversion; and large numbers of organizations and individuals, as grant recipients, stand to benefit from NEA's continuation and expansion.

The success of the endowment is due both to its merit and to the changing climate of American opinion. By the mid-1960s, most Americans no longer looked upon the arts with suspicion. The spread of mass middle-brow cultural standards had rendered obsolete P.T. Barnum's dictum: "no one ever went broke underestimating the taste of the American people." Today, NEA's potential critics in Congress and elsewhere hesitate to appear hostile to culture and the arts and fear being labeled by the media as barbaric yahoos. In the 1930s, it took courage for a politician to speak out in defense of Federal One; in the 1970s, it takes no courage at all for a politician to praise NEA.

NEA's Programs

The stated objectives of NEA are to make the arts more widely available to millions of Americans; to preserve our cultural heritage for present and future generations; to strengthen cultural organizations; and to encourage the creative development of talented individuals. The endowment seeks to achieve these objectives through grants to official arts agencies of the states (and overseas U.S. territories), to nonprofit tax-exempt organizations, and to individuals "of exceptional talent." It does not provide supplementary funding (at least not directly) to arts organizations operated on a for-profit basis, as the British Arts Council has done occasionally and the French government does regularly. Nor does NEA make grants to nonprofit organizations to cover deficits, to provide "general support" of the organization, or to pay for capital improvements and construction, purchase of permanent equipment, or real property, except where such expenditures are essential to a specific program being supported (for example, assisting museums in the conservation of collections often involves some capital improvements). The endowment's funds go to finance specific programs, projects, or activities. In general, NEA grants to organizations pay no more than one-half the total cost of a project. And NEA does not provide tuition assistance grants to individuals for college-level study.[19]

The endowment operates twelve major programs: Architecture, Dance, Education, Expansion Arts, Literature, Museums, Music, Public Media, Special Projects, Theater, Visual Arts, and Federal/State Partnership. These programs make grants to individuals and arts organizations, sponsor art education programs and touring, and provide financial and technical assistance to state, local, and community groups.

The endowment does not have to beat the bushes to flush out worthy candidates for grants for its various programs; artists and art organizations generally take the initiative in applying to the endowment. Each NEA program has a staff and an advisory panel of artistic professionals who screen the applications. The National Council on the Arts then reviews the recommendations of NEA's staff and the panel. Smaller grants are processed by the chairman of the council, with subsequent council review. Most programs that award grants to individual artists must choose among several applicants for each award. But a high proportion of the arts organizations that meet formal eligibility requirements receive grants. The reason for this difference is that the organization grant programs are designed to provide assistance to virtually all truly professional opera companies, symphony orchestras, dance companies, and resident theaters, and the allocation of funds among the programs presumably reflects this intention.

Earlier in the grant-making process, the advisory panels also advise on program design, eligibility requirements, and the allocation of funds by subprograms within the major program entity. The National Council on the Arts reviews this advice before making its decisions on these subjects and on the allocation of funds among the major programs.

Table 4-2. *NEA Grants by Program, Fiscal Years 1971–74 (in Thousands of Dollars)*

Program[a]	Fiscal year				4-year totals
	1971	1972	1973	1974	
Architecture	179	785	1,564	4,202	6,730
Dance	1,251	2,268	2,759	3,942	10,220
Education	154	334	319	494	1,301
Artists-in-Schools	697	1,536	2,211	3,082	7,526
Expansion Arts	308	1,137	2,525	4,099	8,068
Literature	201	517	775	1,394	2,886
Museum	927	4,149	4,615	9,051	18,742
Music	5,188	9,746	10,382	16,116	41,433
Public Media	1,264	1,980	2,767	4,682	10,693
Special Projects	530	656	1,014	894	3,094
Theater	2,021	2,696	3,335	4,957	13,010
Visual Arts	552	941	1,981	2,336	5,809
Federal/State Partnership	4,125	5,500	6,871	10,558	27,055
Total	17,397	32,244	41,117	65,808	156,566

Note: Because of rounding, detail may not add to totals.
[a]Some activities were shifted among programs during this period; here they are treated as if they had been consistently classified according to the fiscal 1974 program location.
Source: Compiled from NEA *Annual Reports.*

NEA's Spending

Tables 4-2, 4-3, and 4-4 present data on grants by program, compiled from NEA *Annual Reports* for the first nine years of NEA's existence. The record of the 1971–74 period (shown in Table 4-2) is particularly significant because it reflects relatively recent decisions involving relatively large amounts of money. Earlier, NEA had much less money to spend and defined its scope and objectives in somewhat tentative terms. In both periods, grant totals for individual programs varied so much from year to year that trends are difficult to identify from annual data.[20]

In fiscal 1966, NEA's very first year, dance and theater companies received 60 percent of all NEA grant funds and, in NEA's first five years, accounted for 27 percent of all allocated funds. Since then, organizations in other art forms have become more active and

Table 4-3. *NEA Grants by Program, Fiscal Years 1966–70 (in Thousands of Dollars)*

	Fiscal Year					
Program	1966	1967	1968	1969	1970	5-year totals
Architecture	—	28	815	327	348	1,770
Costume Design	—	13	—	—	—	13
Dance	605	177	624	642	1,751	3,799
Education	77	893	182	526	1,240	2,918
Folk Art	—	—	—	—	—	40
Literature	87	737	579	332	513	2,248
Museum	54	—	—	—	—	54
Music	184	654	1,115	862	2,525	5,379
Public Media	91	788	2,904	222	195	4,200
Special Projects	—	318	603	470	506	1,896
Theater	877	1,008	1,394	1,008	2,891	7,177
Visual Arts	511	736	569	337	970	3,123
Federal/State Partnership	—	1,988	1,847	1,606	1,964	7,405
Total	2,485	7,632	10,670	6,331	12,903	40,021

Note: Because of rounding, detail may not add to totals.
Source: Compiled from NEA *Annual Reports.*

successful in soliciting public support; in 1971–74, dance and theater received only 15 percent of NEA allocations. The decade or so prior to 1965 was marked by the emergence of new, high-quality regional resident theater groups, new nonprofit theater companies in New York, new dance companies, and major efforts by some slightly older theater and dance groups to expand their seasons and their touring efforts. Nearly all such organizations had almost continual financial problems. Naturally, when NEA arrived on the scene, they turned to NEA. Just as naturally, NEA, as a newly formed agency with necessarily limited ability to begin a fully elaborated program of grants to all art forms, devoted large shares of its funds to them.

In the 1971–74 period, music emerged as by far the largest of the NEA programs, accounting for more than 26 percent of all grant dollars. Most of the music program's outlays took the form of

Table 4-4. *Changes in NEA Program Emphasis, 1966–70 and 1971–74 (Dollar Amounts in Thousands)*

| | Fiscal years 1966–70 | | Fiscal years 1971–74 | |
| | Amount of grants | Percent of total | Amount of grants | Percent of total |
Program				
Architecture	1,770	4.4	6,730	4.3
Dance	3,799	9.5	10,220	6.5
Education[a]	2,918	7.3	8,827	5.6
Expansion Arts	—	—	8,068	5.2
Literature	2,248	5.6	2,886	1.8
Museum	54	0.1	18,742	12.0
Music	5,379	13.4	41,433	26.5
Public Media	4,200	10.5	10,693	6.8
Special Projects	1,936[b]	4.8	3,094	2.0
Theater	7,177	17.9	13,010	8.3
Visual Arts	3,135[c]	7.8	5,809	3.7
Federal/State Partnership	7,405	18.5	27,055	17.3
Total	40,021	100.0	156,566	100.0

Note: Because of rounding, detail may not add to totals.
[a]Includes Artists-in-Schools. [b]Includes $39,500 for folk art in 1967. [c]Includes $12,500 for costume design in 1967.
Source: Based on Tables 4-2 and 4-3.

grants to symphony orchestras and opera companies. Prior to 1970, many of these institutions hesitated to apply for public funds. (See Table 4-3.) Symphony orchestras and opera companies are among the oldest nonprofit arts organizations, and some of them have substantial endowments and long histories of generous private support. Because of that history, the boards and managers of the major music organizations were reluctant converts to the notion that direct public subsidy for the arts was necessary and proper. Although the program formally provides only matching grants defraying half or less than half of the costs of specified programs, in practice the grants serve as "general support"; most good-sized symphony or opera companies can easily isolate from their general budgets sets of activities whose costs far exceed whatever ceiling NEA has placed that year on grants to orchestral or opera organizations. (Since 1970, both the ceiling amount for such grants and the number of organizations aided have risen.)

In its first five years, NEA made virtually no grants to museums. Like the symphonies and opera companies, many art museums are long established, relatively well endowed, and governed by conservative boards that were initially suspicious of public subsidy. Until confronted with the economic reverses of the late 1960s and early 1970s – declining values of endowments, rapid inflation in costs, difficulties in private fund raising – museums were not, in general, active as claimants for public funds. But in the 1971–74 period, the endowment's museum grants rose precipitously, amounting to 12 percent of all allocated funds for this period, and making museums the second largest of NEA's formal programs.[21]

In 1971, the endowment established its Expansion Arts Program as part of its efforts to increase the availability of the arts. The Expansion Arts Program's "specific responsibility lies with neighborhood and community-based programs, where citizens have the opportunity for significant input, involvement, and direction regarding artistic, administrative, and developmental policy." It supports activities such as arts-exposure programs, community cultural centers, instruction and training, neighborhood arts services, special summer projects, and tour events (by assisting sponsors of regional arts events to import artists of outstanding quality from surrounding states). With the expansion of the museums program, the initiation of expansion arts, and the vastly increased share of funds devoted to music, nearly all the other programs inevitably received smaller shares of the total pie in the 1971–74 period than in the 1966–70 period. Yet, with one exception, the programs whose shares of the NEA budget declined actually received many more dollars from NEA because NEA's total appropriation rose sharply.

The exception is the literature program, for which grant funds rose only modestly (by about one-fourth) between 1966–70 and 1971–74. For several reasons, NEA has found it difficult to put large amounts of public subsidy into the literary arts. Except for film and broadcasting, literature is in the commercial, or for-profit, sector of the economy to a greater extent than other art forms. Literary artists work largely on their own rather than through organizations with heavy operating expenses. The nonprofit organizations that may be most important for certain literary activities are the universities, but universities receive considerable federal aid from other sources: the endowment for the humanities, the Department of Health, Education, and Welfare (HEW), or the federal science agencies.

The visual arts, broadly defined to include art museums and architecture as well as the formal NEA Visual Arts Program, occupy an intermediate position between the performing arts and literature.

Both institutions, such as museums, and creative individuals working on their own are important to the production of the visual arts. The Humanities Endowment and other federal agencies provide some support to both.[22] In 1971–74, the visual arts in this broad definition absorbed about one-fifth of total NEA grant funds and 29 percent of the funds granted by the eight programs linked to specified art forms; literature received only 2 percent of these funds.[23]

Since fiscal 1974, NEA has marginally increased its emphasis on education, expansion arts, and public media and substantially strengthened its special projects program.[24] The federal/state partnership program also is absorbing a larger share of total funds. But by and large, Table 4-2 appears to be a valid description of NEA's current programs.

NEA's Purposes

In recent years, NEA has presented in its annual appropriations submissions to congressional committees information organized by objective as well as by program. Although the published annual reports through fiscal 1974 were not organized in this fashion, I have categorized the reported grants for fiscal 1971–74 by purpose as well as programs.[25] Appendix C, Appendix D, and Tables 4-5 and 4-6 present the data on which this analysis is based.

Table 4-5. *NEA Grants by Purpose, Fiscal Years 1971–74 (in Thousands of Dollars)*

	Fiscal year				
Purpose	1971	1972	1973	1974	4-year totals[a]
Institutional aid	7,563	13,667	16,017	25,158	62,406
Aid to individuals channeled through institutions		2,171	2,833	3,856	9,301
Direct aid to individuals	378	685	1,900	2,691	5,653
Commissioning, production, and research awards	1,078	2,695	2,773	5,171	11,717
Grants for public education, awareness, and outreach	1,906	5,475	8,930	14,517	30,829
Grants for general programs (including Federal/State Partnership)	6,030	7,552	8,664	14,415	36,660
Total	17,397	32,244	41,118	65,808	156,566

Note: Because of rounding, detail may not add to totals.
[a] See Appendix 4-B and 4-C for detailed data and explanation of categories.

Table 4-6. NEA Grants by Purpose and Program, Total for Fiscal Years 1971–74 (in Thousands of Dollars)

Program[a]	Institutional aid	Aid to individuals (indirect)	Direct aid to individuals	Commissioning, production, research	Public education and outreach	General programs	All purposes[b]
Architecture	1,033	—	30	1,053	4,514	100	6,730
Dance	1,835	94	646	1,276	5,530	839	10,220
Education	—	—	189	123	717	272	1,301
Artists-in-Schools	—	—	—	—	7,526	—	7,526
Expansion arts	—	—	—	—	7,936	132	8,068
Literature	—	782	971	908	—	225	2,886
Museum	12,030	3,859	411	—	2,124	317	18,742
Music	33,731	2,925	820	396	1,420	2,141	41,433
Public media	4,904	828	587	3,848	—	526	10,693
Special projects	143	45	—	—	—	2,906	3,094
Theater	8,729	191	—	1,618	501	1,971	13,010
Visual arts	—	577	2,000	2,495	561	176	5,809
Federal/State Partnership	—	—	—	—	—	27,055	27,055
All programs	62,406	9,301	5,653	11,717	30,829	36,660	156,566

Note: Because of rounding, detail may not add to totals.

[a]See Appendix 4-B and 4-C for detailed and year-by-year data, sources, and explanation of categories. [b]Activities whose program location within NEA changed during the period have been classified on the basis of their fiscal 1974 location.

I have identified six major categories of support; in the various tables they are referred to as "purposes":

> Grants to institutions to assist them in carrying out activities that are central to their missions. Despite NEA's protestations, these grants amount to general support of the recipient institutions.
>
> Grants to institutions that are earmarked in such a way that they can be said to aid individual artists and arts professionals. Examples of such grants are institutional training activities and the museum purchase plan, which assists in the purchase of works by living American artists. To be sure, the institutional recipients benefit from such grants, but individual artists ultimately appear to receive most of the funds and benefits.
>
> Direct grants to individual artists and arts professionals — mostly fellowships.
>
> Grants that support the production of art, either by specific commissioning of works or by awards for experimentation, research, and documentation. In a sense, fellowship awards to individuals also are production grants because fellowship recipients are expected to do artistic work during the period they hold the award. (The endowment does not make study grants.) Assistance to literary magazines and small presses also falls into this category because its purpose is to facilitate the publication of new literary works.
>
> Grants whose purpose is mainly to educate the general public about the arts, to make people more aware of the arts, or to reach audiences not reached by more conventional means.[26]
>
> Miscellaneous grants for what the NEA annual reports list as "general programs"; the most important items in this category are block grants to the state arts councils.

Table 4-5 shows the grants by these six purposes for the four-year period 1971–74, by years; Table 4-6 shows how program and purpose relate to each other for the four years combined. In the 1971–74 period, roughly one-sixth of the total grant funds were devoted to assistance, direct or indirect, to individuals and to the direct support of artistic production; two-fifths to institutional support; one-fifth for public education, awareness, and efforts to attract new audiences; and close to one-fourth for general programs, primarily the federal/state partnership. Anecdotal evidence suggests that the state arts councils spend the bulk of their NEA grant funds on public education, awareness, and new audiences.[27]

During the four-year period, institutional aid declined slightly as a percentage of the total, and assistance to individuals and artistic production rose slightly. Public education and general programs grants together continued to receive about the same share of NEA funds, but NEA increased its own direct spending for public education activities much more rapidly than grants to state arts councils. In all categories actual dollar spending increased considerably.

Most grant funds dispensed under the four NEA programs that are not linked to specified art forms are classified in Table 4-6 as public education or general programs grants. The performing-arts programs, especially music and theater, make most of their grants as institutional aid, which accounted for 65 percent of total grant funds for the four programs in the 1971–74 period. More than half the dance program grant money went for touring, classified here as "public education," and a considerable share of public media program grants were for production purposes. The museum program is dominated by institutional aid, the architecture program by public education and awareness activities, and the literature and visual arts programs by aid to individuals and for production purposes.

The four stated objectives of NEA can be linked to the rigorous analytical arguments for government subsidy of the arts. For example, the objective of wider availability is consistent with government efforts to overcome income barriers to access to the arts, to overcome the high costs of informing people about the arts, and to offset the market pressures to provide the arts on a highly centralized basis. The problem of information cost, the centralizing tendency, and the Baumol-Bowen thesis (where it is truly applicable) justify intervening to strengthen cultural organizations. Concern for future generations ("positive externalities") justifies subsidy to preserve the cultural heritage. The theoretical arguments concerning income distribution, public goods elements, interdependence among art forms, information costs, and the thin markets for some art forms justify subsidies to encourage the creative development of talented individuals.

Table 4-7 classifies NEA grant expenditures for the fiscal 1971–74 period by the four major objectives, taking off from the classification by purpose in Tables 4-5 and 4-6. All outlays for public education and for general programs can be considered as making the arts more widely available (NEA objective I in Table 4-7); most

Table 4-7. *NEA Grants by Purpose and NEA Objectives, Total for Fiscal Years 1971–74 (in Thousands of Dollars)*

	Objective[b]				
Purpose[a]	I	II	III	IV	All objectives
Institutional aid[c]	—	43,684	18,722	—	62,406
Aid to individuals (indirect)[d]	—	3,720	—	5,581	9,301
Direct aid to individuals	—	—	—	5,653	5,653
Commissioning, production, research[e]	—	—	5,859	5,859	11,717
Public education, awareness, and outreach	30,829	—	—	—	30,829
General programs	36,660	—	—	—	36,660
Total	67,489	47,404	24,580	17,093	156,566

Note: Because of rounding, detail may not add to totals.
[a]Data on grants by purpose from Appendixes 4-B and 4-C and Tables 4-5 and 4-6. [b]Objectives are as follows:
  I – to make the arts more widely available
  II – to strengthen cultural organizations
  III – to preserve our cultural heritage for present and future generations
  IV – to encourage the creative development of talented individuals
The assignment of grants by objective is by the author; see notes *c, d,* and *e.* [c]70% assigned to objective II, 30% to objective III. [d]40% assigned to objective II, 60% to objective IV. [e]50% assigned to objective III, 50% to objective IV.

of the federal/state partnership money appears to have been used, ultimately, to further this objective. All direct grants to individuals; most outlays for aid to individuals channeled through institutions; and half of commissioning, production, and research awards may be classified as encouraging the creative development of individual artists. The remaining outlays may be classified as strengthening cultural organizations as such (objective II) or preserving the cultural heritage (objective III).

Most of the funds classified as "institutional aid" in Table 4-7 went to orchestras, opera companies, and theater companies. (See Table 4-6.) These expenditures seem almost entirely designed to bolster those organizations as such (objective II). Institutional aid to museums and the American Film Institute (the bulk of public media in Table 4-6) was mostly connected with conservation and similar activities that seem closely tied to objective III. Aid to individuals channeled through museums included a substantial amount of money for the training of staff and the hiring of visiting specialists; this aid seems more closely connected to objective II than to encouraging the creative development of talented individuals (objective IV. On the other hand, grants to independent schools of music, also listed as indirect aid to individuals, are clearly tied to objective IV. Commissioning, production, and research awards in architecture were largely for academic research; these awards were classified under objective II, whereas visual arts grants for works of art in public places were classified under objective IV.

The spending patterns suggest that wider availability, which accounted for 43 percent of all NEA grants in the 1971–74 period, has been NEA's priority. But these figures include grants made from the Treasury Fund, which provides matching funds for contributions from private donors; these grants do not reflect NEA's own priorities but rather those of the contributors. Most Treasury Fund grants to institutions apparently are intended to further objectives II and III. For the fiscal years 1975 and 1976 – excluding Treasury Fund grants – NEA planned to assign more than 50 percent of the money to the objective of wider availability.[28]

Wider availability is *not* the primary policy objective of the British Arts Council. But ours is a very large country geographically, with strong egalitarian and antielitist traditions. In congressional committee hearings on NEA authorizations and appropriations, the endowment's area of greatest vulnerability is its support of established artistic institutions and of activities concentrated in New York.[29] It was inevitable that the political price of large-scale federal support of the arts in the United States would be an overriding emphasis on wider availability. Moreover, the theoretical arguments for public support justify the objective of wider availability on grounds of income distribution, economies of scale in production, and the need for subsidized exposure of both potential consumers and potential producers to the arts to overcome their lack of knowledge of the arts, a lack of knowledge that could preclude their ever becoming consumers or producers. The disadvantage of efforts to promote wider availability is that they may expose a wider audience to amateur, low-quality, or even wholly nonartistic activities, instead of making high-quality art more widely available.

The second NEA objective, the strengthening of cultural organizations, has been NEA's second most important objective in practice, consuming 30 percent of NEA funds in the 1971–74 time period. Public support to strengthen artistic organizations as such by subsidizing performances and other artistic activities outside the traditional locations can be justified as part of the effort to overcome information cost problems and the centralizing forces in the arts. Considerations of income distribution also may justify public support for institutions so that they can present free or partially subsidized performances. But the most widely used argument for supporting institutions as such is probably the Baumol-Bowen thesis regarding relative productivity and cost trends, even though the applicability of this thesis has proved to be limited.

The endowment has accorded relatively low priority to experimentation, the avant-garde, and the wholly new in artistic production at fully professional levels.[30] A very small fraction of the grants under NEA objective II, a somewhat larger portion of those classed under objective III (especially the commissioning and production awards), and the bulk of the awards under objective IV – perhaps one-sixth of NEA grant funds in all – can be characterized as experimental.

Other Federal Government Programs

The federal government has clearly made NEA its "chosen instrument" for promoting the arts. But in the American governmental system, public agencies that are chosen instruments seldom have exclusive jurisdiction in the fields in which they operate. For example, the actions of government agencies primarily concerned with parks, housing, and education often have powerful indirect (and, sometimes, not so indirect) consequences for the financial state of the arts. It is very difficult to trace and quantify these actions in any systematic fashion.[31] However, a number of federal agencies other than NEA have direct, substantial, and more or less measurable ties to the arts. The most important of these agencies are the National Endowment for the Humanities, the Corporation for Public Broadcasting, and the Smithsonian Institution (whose organizational umbrella covers the National Gallery of Art).

The principal purpose of the National Endowment for the Humanities (NEH) is to encourage the "understanding and use of humanistic knowledge at all levels and to relate the study of humanities to public awareness and to national concerns."[32] The humanities, as defined by NEH, include the fine arts; this inclusion is commonly accepted in American intellectual and academic life. Thus, NEA and NEH have overlapping jurisdictions, although NEA is supposed to support actual artistic production, while NEH supports the scholarly and educational side of the arts (and the other humanities). In theory, NEH does not offer support for creative, original works in the arts or for performance or training in the arts but for theoretical, historical, and critical studies in the arts and for projects relating art appreciation to other fields of the humanities.

But the distinctions are not all that clear-cut. After all, NEA makes a major effort to promote public education in the arts and gives substantial financial support to art museums, institutions that are far more concerned with the history, criticism, and appreciation of the visual arts than with the creation of new works of art. For its part, NEH also supports art museums, makes grants for film and television production, finances performances of Shakespearean plays, and supports writers' workshops. In general, NEH supports older, more historical versions of NEA-type activities. For example, the largest grant NEH has given for television production was a $2.5 million grant to New York's WNET/13 in fiscal 1974 to help finance the production of "The Adams Chronicles." One of the largest of the museum grants, amounting to $428,000, supported a centenary exhibition of Impressionism, mounted by the Metropolitan Museum of Art. In 1975, NEH supported the American tour of Britain's Royal Shakespeare Company and, in 1973, it helped finance the Oregon Shakespeare Festival. But NEA, too, has supported the production of plays and films with historical themes, Shakespearean performances, and exhibitions of paintings that are by no means contemporary.

Table 4–8 presents NEH program expenditures for fiscal years 1970–74; the table presents 1974 data separately because in that year NEH shifted its emphasis substantially in favor of its Division of Public Programs; it maintained this new emphasis in fiscal 1975 and 1976 and is likely to strengthen it in the next few years in response to congressional pressure.[33]

The Division of Public Programs supports projects to make the humanities available to the general adult population that is not in school. For example, the division provides "media grants" for film and television projects based upon humanistic knowledge and involving direct collaboration between outstanding humanities scholars and media professionals. In fiscal years 1970–74, NEH made grants totaling $10.2 million for films and television, $6.1 million in fiscal 1974 (including the $2.5 million for "The Adams Chroni-

Table 4–8. *National Endowment for the Humanities, Program Funding by Division, Fiscal Years 1970–74 (in Thousands of Dollars)*

Division	Fiscal years 1970–74 combined	Fiscal year 1974
Public Programs	38,362	19,060
Education Programs	52,076	17,083
Fellowship Grants	24,369	7,537
Research Grants	35,603	13,686
Planning and Development	6,975	2,876
Total	157,385	60,244

Note: Because of rounding, detail may not add to totals.
Source: Based on NEH *Annual Reports* for fiscal years 1970 through 1974.

cles"). The division's Museums and Historical Societies Program supports interpretative exhibitions, community education projects, and museum personnel development; grants to museums in the 1970–74 period totaled $5.4 million ($2.9 million in fiscal 1974), of which somewhat under one-half went to art museums.

The artistic components of the spending of the other NEH divisions are smaller and less obvious. It appears that only small portions of the grant funds provided through the Division of Education Programs, which serves educational institutions at all levels, involve the arts, although this division does finance performances of plays and provides some support for art museums. In elementary and secondary education, the division provides the bulk of its support to projects integrating the creative arts with the humanities. Fellowship grants support individual humanists in their work as scholars, teachers, and interpreters of the humanities. If literary scholarship and criticism are regarded as essential contributions to the literary arts, then a significant portion of expenditures for the fellowship grants should be considered support of the arts. The division also provides research grants for (among other things) the development of research tools like bibliographies, guides and catalogues, and the editing of literary papers and works, which fall into the same category. A detailed examination of NEH grants suggests that roughly 20 percent of NEH program expenditures in fiscal 1974 (and perhaps slightly more in subsequent fiscal years) can be construed as federal government support of the arts.

The Corporation for Public Broadcasting (CPB) was established under Title II of the Public Broadcasting Act of 1967. The corpora-

Table 4-9. *Corporation for Public Broadcasting, Budgetary History, Fiscal 1967–75 (in Millions of Dollars)*

Fiscal year	Federal government funds	Private contributions
1967–69	5.0	2.8
1970	15.0	1.2
1971	23.7	5.1
1972	35.2	5.6
1973	35.0	4.0
1974	47.9	5.6
1975	62.0	5.0[a]

[a] Estimated.

Sources: 1967–74, CPB *Annual Reports* for 1973 and 1974; 1975, *The Budget of the United States Government, Fiscal Year 1976, Appendix,* p. 867.

tion is governed by a fifteen-member board of directors appointed by the President. The act authorizes CPB to make funds available to local stations; to establish interconnection services for television and radio; and to assist public television and radio through such activities as audience research, professional training, and experiments with new technology.

A stipulated percentage of the federal appropriation (41 percent in fiscal 1975) is distributed directly to the 400-plus public broadcasting stations as a form of "block grant," in furtherance of CPB's first objective, which is to strengthen local stations. In addition, CPB makes grants to local stations and the Public Broadcasting System to produce programs; CPB does not produce programs itself.

The corporation has had a more troubled budgetary history than NEA or NEH (see Table 4-9). It has had only limited success in attracting private contributions, in part because CPB did not have an arrangement similar to the endowments' Treasury Fund, under which each dollar of private contributions caused the release of an *additional* dollar of federal funds, above and beyond the basic appropriation. In addition, the Nixon administration (which strongly supported NEA and NEH) was suspicious of public broadcasting for some time. It began to support CPB only after public-broadcasting supporters agreed to place less emphasis on network arrangements and more on direct support of local stations. Unlike the other performing arts in the United States, public broadcasting depends very heavily upon government financial support. In 1974, 48 percent of the income for public broadcasting came from state and local governments (including boards of education and state universities); 23 percent from federal funds; and only 29 percent from foundations, business, individual subscribers, and other private fund-raising activities.[34]

Since 1970, CPB and NEA have jointly funded a number of major arts programming projects, including "Theater in America" in 1973–74, "Dance in America" in 1974–75, and a "Filmmaker in Residence" program in 1973–75. On its own, CPB has assisted such widely distributed arts-related series as "Men Who Made the Movies," "Inside the Arts," "Book Beat," and "Composers' Forum" (on National Public Radio). It is not easy to determine what share of total CPB money actually supports the arts because so much of the expenditure is for support of local stations and support for interconnection services, rather than grants for specific programming that can be identified in CPB annual reports.[35] Dramatic, music, literary, and "entertainment" programming probably accounts for a minor share of total public broadcasting costs, but much of the money provided by state and local governments and individual private contributors (as well as significant portions of business and foundation support) is available for general operating expenses and the costs of news, public events, and school-related programming. I estimate that at least half of total CPB funding should be considered as support of the arts. If federal support declined, arts and arts-related programming would probably suffer heavily.

The Smithsonian Institution is another federal agency that provides some support for the arts. The National Gallery of Art, which is part of the Smithsonian, had an appropriation of $7 million in fiscal 1975. In addition, the Smithsonian runs a "History and Art Program" (total budget of nearly $10 million in fiscal 1975), and makes grants to art museums under its "National Museum Programs" (total budget, $5 million in fiscal 1975).

The Comprehensive Employment and Training Act of 1973 (CETA) provides grants to state and local governments exceeding $2 billion annually for, among other things, creation of public service jobs. Recently some of the recipient governments have used the federal money to employ people on projects in the arts. This program, widely publicized as a latter-day version of WPA Federal Project Number One, has the same motivation – job creation – as the WPA project. As of 1975, only a modest amount of CETA funds had been applied to arts projects, but in the summer of 1977, NEA identified 5,000 CETA positions allocated to the arts, representing about $40 million in annual salaries. In October 1977,

Table 4–10. *Estimated Federal Government Support of the Arts, Calendar 1975 (in Millions of Dollars)*

Agency[a]	Amount devoted to the arts
National Endowment for the Arts[b]	87.4
National Endowment for the Humanities[b,c]	17.3
Corporation for Public Broadcasting[d]	32.0
Smithsonian Institution (including National Gallery of Art)[e]	10.4
CETA[f]	10.0
Total	157.1

[a] Estimated by the author on the bases indicated below. In general, the starting point is the average of the fiscal 1975 and fiscal 1976 appropriations. [b] Includes appropriations from the Treasury Fund; excludes administrative expenses. [c] Estimated to be 20 percent of total appropriation; see text. [d] Estimated to be 50 percent of total appropriation; see text. [e] All of appropriation for National Gallery of Art plus 20 percent of appropriation for History and Art and National Museum Programs. [f] Very crudely estimated on the basis of scattered newspaper clippings.

another 500 CETA arts jobs were provided under a $6.4 million one-year grant to New York City.[36]

Table 4–10 provides crude estimates of total direct federal government support of the arts in calendar year 1975 by all these agencies. The total is just over $150 million. (The NEA figure, which is nearly 60 percent of the total, is *not* a crude estimate; hence it is most unlikely that the "true" total is less than $130 million or more than $170 million.) This figure has grown from less than $5 million in 1965 and roughly $30 million in calendar 1970. In 1977, the two endowments received sizeable increases in congressional appropriations and late in the year the President recommended a major increase in federal funding for public broadcasting. Thus, even though the rate of increase in federal support of the arts is now far less than in the 1965–75 decade, total federal support of the arts is likely to exceed $200 million and perhaps even $250 million by calendar 1980.

State Governments and the Arts

Prior to the 1960s, New York City provided a disorderly collection of subsidies for the maintenance and operation of arts buildings, and a small number of other state and local governments provided a scattering of subsidies to local performing-arts organizations or art museums.

For the most part, these state and local governments supported the arts much as other city or state agencies might have subsidized a new sports stadium, for reasons of local pride, local economic development, or the public image of elected officials. Such support was no more the product of a coherent arts policy than the stadium subsidy was part of a systematic sports policy.[37]

The creation of state councils on the arts marked the emergence of systematic public support at the nonfederal level. The first of the grant-making councils – even antedating NEA – was the New York State Council on the Arts.[38]

Like so much else that happened in New York between January 1959 and December 1973, the formation of the New York State Council on the Arts (NYSCA) can be attributed to one man, former Governor Nelson A. Rockefeller. As early as 1957, a Rockefeller gubernatorial campaign position paper proposed the creation of such an agency. In 1960, the second year of the Rockefeller administration, the state legislature created the council as a temporary commission, with a $50,000 appropriation. The governor appointed the council's fifteen members and chose Seymour H. Knox as chairman. Knox held that position for fifteen years; in 1975, he was succeeded by Joan K. Davidson (Governor Hugh Carey's selection), who was followed by Kitty Carlisle Hart in 1976.

During NYSCA's first five years, the council had relatively stable but modest funding (see Table 4-11) and equally modest programs: surveying the state's cultural resources, funding a touring and exhibition program, and offering technical assistance to arts organizations. Toward the end of this period, the council began to assist individual creative artists by supporting a composer's forum and a program of readings by poets in upstate colleges. But the touring program was the major effort; it absorbed nearly half of the total NYSCA appropriations for the first five years.[39] Initially, the council subsidized the touring organization directly and paid the artists' fees in full, but beginning in 1963, it required that a local sponsoring group contract with the arts organization and raise funds from private sources to match state support; thus NYSCA initiated the matching-fund mode of operations subsequently adopted by NEA as its standard grant procedure.[40]

In the latter half of the 1960s, NYSCA appropriations slowly increased, and the council adopted new programs – in 1966, mu-

Table 4-11. *Appropriations for the New York State Council on the Arts, Fiscal 1961–76 (in Thousands of Dollars)*

Fiscal year ending March 31	Amount
1961	50
1962	450
1963	560
1964	534
1965	562
1966	772
1967	1,504
1968	1,898
1969	2,492
1970	2,256
1971	20,148
1972	14,423
1973	16,325
1974	16,445
1975	35,653
1976	35,653

Sources: New York State Council on the Arts, *Annual Reports,* and the *Executive Budget of the State of New York,* various years.

seum, film, and poetry programs and, in 1968, a festival program, generally requiring matching of council funds from local private sources.

In 1969–70, the NYSCA appropriation was $2.2 million. The following year it was $20.2 million. In January 1970, the New York State legislature voted the additional appropriation of $18 million to provide "state financial assistance to non-profit cultural organizations . . . to help offset operating deficits," with the stated objective of affording "maximum encouragement and assistance for the maintenance and development of the public availability of the existing cultural resources of the state." The problem addressed by this legislation was the immediate financial difficulty of the major museums and performing-arts organizations. The council was empowered to provide recipient organizations not just with support for specific programs or new activities, but with general institutional support. The only legislative restriction was that recipient organizations could not reduce the amounts of money they raised from sources other than NYSCA during the year for which aid was provided.

Thus, almost overnight, the council shifted its emphasis from sponsorship of touring and other outreach activities, technical assistance, and marginal support for a limited number of existing organizations, to helping the major artistic and cultural institutions of the state to survive. This transformation did not occur in a vacuum, of course; NEA had been receiving larger and larger appropriations and did not intend to provide general institutional support at all. The division of labor seemed natural and appropriate: the federal agency would concentrate on supporting new departures in the arts, aiding individual artists, and increasing the geographic availability of the arts, especially in the underserved regions of the country; the New York State agency would rescue the established cultural institutions concentrated in New York, which – although part of the national heritage – were of obvious and direct concern primarily to New Yorkers. (In 1970, NEA had not yet become a source of institutional support for established organizations.)

Although in the next three years NYSCA received smaller appropriations than those for 1970–71,[41] they remained far above earlier levels, and the council continued to assist major cultural organizations. Table 4–12 shows the distribution of NYSCA grants by program during this period. Performing-arts programs accounted for close to half of total grant funds, and aid to museums (all types, not just art museums) accounted for one-fifth of the total. As in NEA, the visual arts account for only a small percentage of the total and literature an even smaller percentage, although literature's share of the council's funds has not been declining as sharply as its share of NEA funds. An analysis of NYSCA grants by purpose, paralleling the analysis of NEA grants, indicates that in 1973–74 the grant total of $15.1 million was distributed as follows: $11.1 million for institutional support; $1.6 million for aid to individuals, research, and commissioning of works; and $2.5 million for community and education projects.

In the early 1970s, the council developed the decentralized grant-making system it still uses. The council's own staff focuses primarily on assistance to institutions and provides grants to service organizations to "retail" NYSCA support. For example, the Gallery Association of New York State conducts a touring exhibition program, and the New York Foundation for the Arts administers the performing-arts touring and technical assistance programs. The film and video bureau of the foundation rents films and provides film

Table 4-12. *New York State Council on the Arts Grants by Program, Fiscal 1971–74 (in Thousands of Dollars)*

Program	Fiscal year				4-year totals
	1971	1972	1973	1974	
Dance	1,755	1,243	1,330	1,368	5,696
Music	3,746	2,300	2,655	2,561	11,262
Theater	1,594	1,225	1,325	1,551	5,695
Film and Television-Media	1,366	1,130	1,135	1,089	4,720
Presenting Organizations	—	603	945	1,145	2,693
Architecture	—	—	—	328	328
Museum	4,012	2,775	3,000	2,879	12,666
Visual Arts*a*	855	700	725	685	2,965
Literature	184	265	261	331	1,041
Art Service Organizations*b*	986	1,069	1,533	1,592	5,180
Special Programs	2,024	1,790	1,815	1,598	7,227
Library Resources	2,300	—	—	—	2,300
Total*c*	18,822	13,100	14,724	15,127	61,773

*a*The program title was Visual Arts Community Projects until 1973–74, when it was retitled Visual Arts Services. *b*Includes Touring, a separate program in 1970–71, and Technical Assistance, a separate program in 1970–71 and 1971–72. *c*This table does not include administrative expenses of the council, which account for most of the difference between the grant totals shown here and the appropriations shown in Table 4-11. *Source:* From New York State Council on the Arts, *Annual Reports,* 1970–71 through 1973–74.

lecturers to schools, libraries, and film societies. Poets and Writers administers the readings and residency program for writers, and the Media Equipment Resource Center (MERC) of Young Filmakers lends film equipment and provides editing and studio facilities for nonprofit organizations free of charge. The Committee for the Visual Arts administers a visiting artist program for NYSCA. Similarly, service organizations administer the poets-in-schools project, assistance to literary magazines and small presses, and a program of fellowships for individual artists. NYSCA aid to producing organizations, most of which is for staff salaries, enables these intermediaries to operate programs in behalf of the council.

Early in 1973, a temporary State Commission on Cultural Resources, chaired by an influential Republican state senator, completed its work and recommended a very wide range of state government steps to assist and support the arts and culture.[42] In December 1973, Governor Rockefeller resigned. Malcolm Wilson, who served out the remainder of Rockefeller's term, proposed to raise NYSCA's budget appropriation for 1974–75 to $30.5 million, exclusive of administrative expenses. The arts establishment in New York lobbied with great vigor for Wilson's proposal. The umbrella lobbying organization, Concerned Citizens for the Arts of New York State,[43] based its plea on the operating deficits of arts organizations in New York. It was estimated that in 1973–74 the 836 arts organizations receiving NYSCA grants had operating expenses of $268 million and income from all sources other than NYSCA of $227.8 million, leaving a shortfall of $40.2 million, of which NYSCA aid covered only $14.9 million.[44] Even the proposed $30.5-million NYSCA appropriation would, at best, merely alleviate the crisis.

The lobbying proved successful. The basic NYSCA appropriation for 1974–75 was actually more than 10 percent *above* the governor's request. But this quantum leap in appropriations was not an unalloyed victory for the arts lobbyists. State appropriations fell back slightly in 1975–76 and, because of the state's financial crisis, even more in 1976–77. Moreover, the 1974 act and its 1975 successor earmarked some funds and otherwise restricted NYSCA's discretionary grant-making powers. The 1974 act required that the council make not less than 50 percent of its grants to "primary organizations," defined as:

> those eligible arts organizations . . . who by the quality of their arts services, their stature as arts institutions on a state or national level, or by the importance of their contribution to the arts discipline in which they specialize are particularly important to the cultural life of New York State and the loss of which or the diminution of whose services would in the opinion of the Council, constitute a serious artistic loss to the people of the state.[45]

It also required that NYSCA spend at least seventy-five cents per capita in each of the state's sixty-two counties. The 1975 legislation earmarked specific sums totaling nearly $1.2 million for a Bicentennial Barge, an "Artpark" near Buffalo, and a community-planning assistance center in western New York. Now that it appeared to be rich, NYSCA became an easy mark for legislators with causes somehow related to the arts.

The geographic-distribution requirement, which originated in both the general populist maxim that arts money should be democratically distributed (this maxim also has produced a requirement that 20 percent of NEA grant funds be distributed to the states, mostly as block grants) and specific complaints from legislators that their individual constituencies were being slighted, created major substantive and administrative problems. It is possible for a county without a sizable city or college town to house no professional-level arts activities at all; unless NYSCA can use its funds to finance touring companies or exhibition visits, poetry readings, and similar "imported" activities, its grants are likely to be used for amateur, even hobbyist artistic activities.[46]

In terms of dollars, the sparsely populated, largely rural counties are minor problems for NYSCA, simply because their populations are so small. The geographic requirement is more difficult to satisfy in some of the more densely populated counties. Within metropolitan areas, arts activities tend to be concentrated in the central parts of the central cities; in the surrounding suburban areas, even those that have large resident populations, professional arts activities are hard to find. Thus, the council has found it difficult to meet the per capita distribution requirement for the outlying boroughs of New York City, for some of the large suburban counties near New York City, and for a few of the suburban counties adjacent to upstate metropolitan areas. But such counties are very well represented in the state legislature, and they provided much of the political impetus behind the imposition of the per capita distribution requirement.

If local governments actively promoted the arts within their jurisdictions, state government funds could supplement local government support of already established activities. In July 1974, NYSCA compared county government support of the arts for the fifty-seven counties outside New York City with NYSCA allocations for 1974–75 under the per capita requirement. Table 4–13 shows that of the total NYSCA grants that could be assigned to any one county, 52 percent went to Manhattan organizations and activities and another 17 percent to other New York boroughs. New York City government support for the arts was more than twice the amount of NYSCA grants assigned to New York City recipients and activities.[47]

The other fifty-seven counties received $9.5 million in NYSCA allocations (31 percent of the NYSCA total), and only $3.8 million – two-fifths as much as NYSCA provided – in county government appropriations. By and large, the suburban counties around New York (and these include the richest counties, in per capita personal income, in the United States) put up very little of their own money

Table 4-13. *NYSCA Grants by Location, 1974–75, and County Appropriations for the Arts (in Thousands of Dollars)*

Area	No. of counties in group	NYSCA grants[a]	County appropriations[b]
Manhattan	1	16,136	[c]
Other New York City boroughs	4	5,402	[c]
New York City suburbs	5	2,657	522
Major upstate urban counties	5	3,418	2,836
Other responding counties	44	3,307	408
Nonrespondents	3	90	—
Total	62	31,010[d]	3,766

[a]Grants credited against the seventy-five cents per capita requirement (see text). [b]Appropriations for cultural activities other than libraries; some counties reported 1973 or 1974 rather than 1975 data. [c]New York City expenditures for cultural activities in 1974–75 totalled roughly $50 million, more than double NYSCA grants assigned to New York City activities. [d]In addition, $3.1 million was spent for statewide activities, not assignable to any one county.
Source: Based on council survey reported in Nathan Weber, "County Funding of the Arts in New York State," NYSCA, July 1974.

for the arts. Westchester was among twenty counties in the state that appropriated no local money at all in support of the arts. Only eight counties, including four of the five "major upstate urban counties" shown in Table 4-13, supported the arts in amounts that were as much as one-half the NYSCA allocations. Two of these four spent about as much from their own funds as NYSCA provides from state funds. The relationship between NYSCA grants and local government financial effort in New York State is rather similar to that between NEA grants and state government efforts nationwide. Political support for local subsidies to the arts appears to be limited; eagerness for painless funding from a higher level of government appears to be boundless.

In 1974–75, the first year of the geographic distribution requirement, actual payment of council grants was subject to lengthy delays (payment also had been delayed in earlier years) while council personnel verified the compliance of grant recipients with this and other statutory requirements. Many grants for the fiscal year beginning April 1, 1974, were not made until January 1975; meanwhile, a number of grantees had to resort to short-term bank borrowing at the high interest rates then prevailing. This was especially true of the various service organizations that NYSCA relies upon to retail its grant funds. Some of these organizations are financed entirely from NYSCA (and, in some cases, NEA) grants; some were newly created to serve the council and had no reserve funds to absorb delays. Moreover, the service organizations themselves had serious administrative problems with the per capita requirement because they had to set up systems allocating their own activities and spending by county.[48] At least one such organization had to hire an additional staff member solely for this purpose.[49]

The second major restriction imposed by the 1974 act, namely that the council allocate at least 50 percent of its funds to "primary organizations," imposed less of a substantive problem (but an equally serious administrative problem). In 1973–74, the council had used over 70 percent of its funds for institutional support, much of this for organizations that would be classified as primary under any reasonable set of guidelines. These organizations also had provided the main push behind the doubling in the NYSCA appropriation. Concerned Citizens asserted that twenty-eight of the largest such organizations had a combined deficit after state aid of nearly $13 million in 1973–74;[50] NYSCA could easily satisfy the 50 percent requirement just by deficit-elimination grants to these few organizations.

The council dealt with the problem by making a list of seventy-two primary organizations – most of them museums[51] and well-established performing-arts organizations (see Table 4-14) – for 1974–75 grants. In the following year, it added forty-five more organizations to the list, provoking vigorous protests from the arts establishment. Most of the additions were nonmuseum visual-arts groups, film and television organizations, and organizations concerned with literature (Table 4-14). Many were outside New York City, and a fair proportion were oriented to minority groups; most were rather new organizations. The establishment organizations, whose lobbying had played a major role in increasing the council's appropriations in both 1970 and 1974, felt betrayed by their own creature.

In fact, in the doubling of NYSCA funds in 1974–75, the major organizations had done very well. All the NYSCA programs shown in Table 4-12 (except the discontinued library program) were funded at much higher dollar levels in 1974–75 than they had been earlier. The increases were exceptionally large for museums and the major performing-arts groups, although relatively small for visual arts, literature, film and television media, art service organizations, and special programs, all of which involve smaller artistic organizations and/or individual artists. One of the smallest increases

The Subsidized Muse

Table 4-14. NYSCA *"Primary Organizations" by Type, 1974–75 and 1975–76*

	Number of organizations	
Type	1974–75	1975–76
Art museums	10	10
Other visual arts	1	13
Dance	9	12
Opera	2	3
Other music	15	19
Television and film	2	12
Performing-arts centers	4	4
Literature	1	5
Subtotal, arts	57	95
Other museums, botanical gardens, zoos, and other nonartistic cultural institutions	15	22
Total	72[a]	117

[a]These organizations received $17.9 million of the $33.9 million in council grants actually made in 1974–75.
Source: NYSCA releases.

was for the program of fellowships for individual artists administered by Creative Artists Public Service (CAPS), an art service organization established by the council.

Because of the subsequent expansion of the list of primary organizations and the cutbacks in total NYSCA funding (and the even more severe cutbacks in New York City government support of major cultural institutions in response to the fiscal crisis after mid–1975), 1974–75 may well mark the high point – for some years to come – in state and city government subsidy of major New York institutions. If so, and if NEA support rises at the moderate rate now in prospect, those institutions must either increase their earned income and private support very substantially or operate at fixed levels of dollar expenditure, whatever the rate of inflation in costs.

Despite its seniority among instruments of public support of the arts in the United States and its role as a model for both NEA and the arts councils of the other states, NYSCA has not yet solved most of the major and obvious problems that confront all government arts foundations. It has not resolved the conflict between the huge financial requirements of the major institutions on the one hand and, on the other, the desire to support individual artists, new organizations, new art forms, and more participatory art experiences. It has not dealt effectively with the political pressure for geographic dispersion of public funds where such pressure is, in fact, inconsistent with enhancing the accessibility and availability of the arts. It has not made firm decisions about the scope of activities that a government arts foundation should support. Should such an institution concern itself with the design of public buildings, graphic design in the operations of ordinary government agencies, and urban planning? Should it finance arts education and arts-related social service activities? Should it provide funds for zoos, botanical gardens, and nonarts museums? (Many state arts councils, including NYSCA, support such institutions.) How far should it go in supporting activities that are clearly amateur in nature?

Administering an arts agency is difficult, and administratively NYSCA has been far from successful. A big grant-making program must rely on the artistic judgment of professionals, but artistic professionals are not notoriously skilled as administrators, and many of the most highly qualified professionals are likely to be grant applicants. NYSCA has "solved" the conflict-of-interest problem by ignoring it. And NYSCA's decentralized system of grant making has not worked well in all cases. In addition, NYSCA faces a special problem that few arts councils outside New York confront: NYSCA is not supposed to support the non-New York activities of New York institutions. But – to take the extreme case – what is the dividing line between "local" and "national" for the Metropolitan Opera?

In 1975, a self-study commissioned by the council and undertaken by a special committee chaired by council member Edward M. Kresky, addressed many of these issues.[52] The Kresky Report looked skeptically on the nonartistic and educational activities of the council; recommended easing the statutory per capita distribution and primary organizations requirements; and, among other things, called for an overhaul of the council's administrative, reporting, and accountability procedures. Some of the administrative recommendations of the Kresky Report have been implemented and the per capita distribution requirement has been lowered from seventy-five to fifty cents.

State Arts Councils and NEA

Prior to 1967, when NEA began making block grants to the state arts councils, only twenty-two states appropriated any funds at all to a

Table 4–15. *Legislative Appropriations for the Arts, for States and Other Areas, Selected Fiscal Years, 1966–75 (Dollar Amounts in Thousands)*

Area	Fiscal year			
	1966	1970	1971	1975
States				
Total appropriations	1,271	5,993	25,047	55,005
New York appropriations	766	2,256	20,133	35,653
All other state appropriations	505[a]	3,737	4,914	19,352
Number of states with any appropriation	22	44	46	50
Other areas				
Total appropriations	915	1,677	1,853	3,892
Puerto Rico appropriations	915	1,491	1,682	3,605
Other areas[b] appropriations	—	186	171	287
Total funds	2,186	7,670	26,900	58,896
New York as % of:				
All states	60	38	80	65
Total	35	29	75	61
New York and Puerto Rico as % of total	77	49	82	67

Note: Because of rounding, detail may not add to totals.
[a]Excludes appropriation for Virginia State Museum (at that time serving as the official arts council) of $478,445, nearly all of which was for the museum per se. [b]District of Columbia, American Samoa, Guam, and the Virgin Islands.
Source: Associated Councils of the Arts.

state arts agency, and the combined appropriations in the twenty-one states other than New York amounted to only $505,000, hardly enough to support a single full-time staff member in each of the states (see Table 4–15). By 1972, each of the fifty states (as well as the District of Columbia, Puerto Rico, and three U.S. overseas jurisdictions) had arts councils receiving both NEA money and appropriations of state funds. With a few exceptions, these state arts councils resulted not from an autonomous rise of interest in patronizing the arts on the part of state governments but from the availability of NEA funds for the purpose.

In fiscal 1967, each state was awarded a block grant of $50,000; beginning in fiscal 1971, the grants began to grow larger, reaching $205,000 in fiscal 1976. Each state arts agency is entitled to this amount upon submission of a plan for the use of the grant money. Prior to fiscal 1974, the block grants were the sum total of NEA's federal/state partnership program, but beginning in that year, the endowment began making awards to the state arts agencies for a variety of special projects, above and beyond the block grants. In addition, NEA increasingly has been delegating the operation of specified programs, notably the artists-in-schools and coordinated-residency dance-touring programs, to the state agencies. By 1974, of its total $65.8 million program expenditures, NEA was paying out more than $13 million in the form of grants to state arts agencies; the block grants accounted for $7.5 million of this amount.

Table 4-15 indicates the responses of state legislatures to NEA's initiatives. In the early years, that response was very sluggish, except in New York and Puerto Rico, which have consistently dominated the statistics on nonfederal public funding of the arts in this country.[53] It was not until 1974 that total state appropriations, exclusive of New York, came close to equaling total NEA grants to the state agencies. State funding increased substantially in fiscal 1974 and 1975, but even in fiscal 1975, only seven states (New York aside) appropriated as much as $1 million and only five others appropriated amounts in the $500,000 to $999,000 range. The remaining thirty-seven states appropriated a total of $5.6 million among them, an average of $151,000 each, in a year when the NEA block grant was $200,000.[54]

Appendix E summarizes the reported activities of thirty-nine of the state arts councils. The modest levels of funding in most states limit the typical state arts agency to operating the NEA-delegated programs, supporting some touring, and utilizing the block grant and state funds mostly for a variety of public education, awareness, and outreach activities. The states with larger appropriations tend to support festivals and ticket-subsidy schemes and may provide grants to a small number of individual artists, but very few state agencies are sufficiently well funded to play a significant role in the support of the major or "primary" institutions.[55] In most of the United States, the alleged intensity of local pride in the orchestra, opera company, art museum, or resident theater company does not manifest itself in initiatives on the part of state or local politicians to commit state or local funds to the institution's support. For the most part, local pride is compatible with letting NEA bear the burden of providing public funds for the support of the primary institutions.[56]

One of the activities of state arts councils that makes use of both federal and state government funds but does not show up in Appendix E is lobbying for additional federal funds. A fair proportion of the limited staff time available to the characteristic small-state arts agency is devoted to lobbying. With NEA financing, the Louis Harris organization's National Research Center of the Arts has conducted a series of studies of cultural resources and the arts industry in individual states. All these studies have the same conclusions: the arts audience is increasing; the arts are an important industry in the state; cultural institutions are facing ever-widening "income gaps"; and therefore, more federal money is needed. Q.E.D.

For most state agencies, lobbying for more federal money probably appears to be the most sensible use of staff time and money simply because federal money is so important relative to state appropriations. As late as fiscal 1975, only twenty-four states had appropriations exceeding the $200,000 NEA block grant; in seventeen states, the appropriations were less than $100,000, one-half the block grant (including two states with appropriations of $10,000 and $5,100 respectively). But even these numbers understate the widespread failure of state governments to come close to matching federal funds.

In twenty-nine states in 1974, NEA provided 80 percent or more of combined federal and state funds for the arts (see Table 4–16). One-half of NEA spending allocable by state occurred in these states, whose legislatures were not willing to provide even so much as one state dollar for every four NEA dollars. Missouri and West Virginia came close to matching NEA's contribution. Only New York more than matched NEA funds. Table 4–16 suggests that the large states, in general, do not provide significantly more money for the arts than the small ones. (Seven of the ten most populous states are in the NEA 70-percent-and-more class; Texas is in the 90-to-94-percent class.) Nor is state government spending for the arts strongly related to differences in per capita personal income.[57]

In short, the conventional objective factors that analysts use in the study of differentials in state and local government expenditure patterns – size of state, degree of urbanization, level of income, and wealth – do not account for the differences in state-government funding for the arts. Presumably, therefore, these differences arise from politicians' perceptions of differences in tastes among the populations of the several states. And presumably, voters in most states do *not* value the benefits that the arts produce within that state highly enough to put up more than a small fraction of the total public subsidy.

If NEA's grants to state arts agencies were intended to promote

Table 4-16. *State Appropriations for the Arts and NEA Allocations, Fiscal 1974 (Dollar Amounts in Millions)*

States grouped by NEA allocation as % of combined state and NEA funds	No. of states	State funds	NEA allocations	Combined funds	NEA %[a]
95% or more	5	0.1	1.7	1.8	96%
90–94%	9	0.6	7.5	8.2	92
80–89%	15	3.3	16.7	20.0	84
70–79%	13	4.1	11.0	15.1	73
60–69%	5	2.4	4.3	6.7	64
50–59%	2	1.0	1.2	2.2	57
Total, excluding New York	49	11.5	42.5	53.9	79
New York	1	16.4	9.2	25.7	36
Total, 50 states	50	27.9	51.7	79.6	65

Note: Because of rounding, detail may not add to totals.
[a]Calculated from unrounded data.
Source: State data, Associated Councils of the Arts; NEA data from NEA reports and documents.

activities of national scope, it would not be reasonable to expect taxpayers to favor additional local support for such activities. But the purpose of NEA's block grants is to support highly localized activities, even though such activities are held in such low esteem in most state budget decision making, that they are undertaken only because the federal government provides "free" money to pay for them.

If state funding remains at the prevalent low levels, NEA's noble effort to develop effective state counterparts may be judged to have failed in most of the country. The state arts councils may be regarded as costly sops for congressmen determined to spread federal largesse widely and thinly, and as a means of creating a nationwide corps of lobbyists for NEA.

Local Government Efforts

Useful data on the state of the arts are hard to come by, in general, but data on the overall extent of local government support of the arts in the United States are simply nonexistent. Most reports by federal and state agencies on the finances of local governments do not show support of the arts as a distinct category but lump such

Table 4-17. *Selected Data on Local Government Support of the Arts (in Millions of Dollars)*

Location and type of recipient organization	Fiscal year	Amount
Nationwide data:		
Art museums[a]	1971–72	20.6
Major nonprofit performing arts organizations[b]	1973–74	3.2
Data for states, counties and cities:		
California – performing arts, art museums, visual arts, and arts service organizations[c]	1973–74	16.6
New York City – performing arts, art museums, concert halls, visual arts, and art service organizations[d]	1974–75	12.5
New York State, upstate counties – various arts organizations[e]	various years, 1973–75	2.6
New York State – performing and visual arts and museums (including nonarts museums)[f]	1970–71	15.5
Baltimore metropolitan area – 11 art museums, performing arts organizations and arts institutes[g]	1972–73	1.0
Massachusetts – city government support to 8 cultural organizations[h]	1973	0.6
Philadelphia – city government support of performing and "nonperforming" arts[i]	1973–74	6.5

[a]National Endowment for the Arts, *Museums USA,* 1974. Data apply to 340 art museums (6 percent of which are operated by local governments), with a total income in 1971–72 of $158 million. [b]Unpublished data from the Ford Foundation for 153 organizations with a total operating income of $194 million. [c]California Arts Commission, *The Nonprofit Arts Industry in California,* 1975. Data apply to 471 nonprofit organizations with budgets of $5,000 or more and total income of $79 million. [d]*Report of the Mayor's Committee on Cultural Policy,* October 15, 1976. Includes city government grants to arts organizations and city government direct budget allocations for operation, maintenance, and construction of buildings and facilities for the arts. Total budget allocations for all cultural institutions, including nonarts museums and the like were close to $75 million; actual expenditures were approximately $50 million (much of the capital budget allocation available was not spent during the year). [e]Based on the NYSCA survey reported in Table 4-13, but excluding appropriations for science and history museums and organizations. [f]National Research Center of the Arts, Inc., *A Study of the Non-Profit Arts and Cultural Industry of New York State,* 1972. Data apply to 568 organizations with total income of $169 million, including a sizeable number of nonart museums. [g]David Cwi and Albert Diehl, *In Search of a Regional Policy for the Arts:* Phase I, Joint Committee on Cultural Resources, Baltimore, 1975. The data appear to cover the total arts effort of Baltimore area local governments. [h]Massachusetts Governor's Task Forces on the Arts and Humanities, *The Arts: A Priority for Investment,* 1973. The data represent the total involvement of all Massachusetts local governments in the arts in 1973. [i]Greater Philadelphia Cultural Alliance, *An Introduction to the Economics of Philadelphia's Cultural Organizations,* 1975. The organizations covered had total income of $23.6 million.

expenditures with "parks and recreation" or "all other."[58] The available data include fragments for particular cities or states and bits of information on particular art forms on a nationwide basis. Unfortunately, the bits and pieces tend to be contradictory because definitions and concepts differ considerably.

Table 4-17 presents data drawn from a number of the better-known recent studies. These data suggest that city and county governments are reasonably generous supporters of their local art museums; in 1971–72, they provided about 13 percent of total income of all U.S. art museums. Data for California, New York, and a scattering of individual cities,[59] suggest that by 1975, local government support of art museums may very well have reached $40 million. Local government support for other arts activities, outside of California and New York City, is small in absolute dollars and tiny as a percentage of the total budgets of arts organizations. And even in those few places with an active tradition of supporting the performing arts, such as Philadelphia, New York, and the California cities, local government support is a very modest factor in the finances of performing arts organizations.

Apparently, art museums are considered important to a city's image, enhancing its attractiveness to residents, visitors, and business firms. No other art forms seem to inspire local tax efforts. The absence of adequate statistics makes it difficult even to guess as to recent trends in local government support of the arts. But it is probable that the situation may be rather bleak. The low level of government support may reflect a general unwillingness on the part of local electorates in all but a very few cities to sacrifice anything much in behalf of locally produced and consumed arts.

I have estimated (Table 4-10) that total federal government spending in support of the arts in calendar 1975 amounted to roughly $150 million, and that total state government appropriations for arts councils in fiscal 1975 amounted to about $55 million (Table 4-15). Although some of that money went to nonarts cultural organizations, a number of states also made line-item appropriations to favored arts organizations. Probably, total state government support for the arts as such in calendar 1975 was in the $60- to $65-million range. I estimate that local governments probably spent, in combination, about the same amount, two-thirds of it for art museums.[60] Thus, I estimate total public support of the arts in the United States at just under $300 million, with state and local governments spending rather less than the federal government, despite the obviously localized nature of arts in general.[61]

5

The Effects of Public Support
on the Arts

Students of public policy may use any or all of three approaches to
determine the effects of a given subsidy on its recipients. The most
conventional method for appraising the effect of public policy decisions in the United States is to examine the statistical relations
between changes in various types of activities and changes in the
amount of public money provided over time. The arts compete for
public funds with other programs whose consequences are ap-
praised in this fashion. But comprehensive data on the arts, even for
a single year, can be assembled only by using crude estimating
techniques. Usable and reliable data that span a period of years are
available only for a few segments of the arts "industry," but such
time-series data are essential for this kind of appraisal. In order to
say anything about the effects of an increase in public support for a
given type of artistic endeavor from $2 million in year one to, say,
$5 million in year five, we need comparable data on the overall
finances, work force, and artistic output of that art form in both
year one and year five.

Moreover, quite apart from the data problems, government has
been providing direct support for the arts in this country for less
than a decade – and the rate of increase in subsidy has been enormous.[1] Statistical analyses of changes over time for very brief periods, especially when there have been extremely large changes in the
causative variable, are notoriously unreliable. Therefore, the statistical analysis in this chapter is fragmentary and not intended to be
more than tentative.

Another approach is to ask a large number of organizations about
their perceptions of the effects of subsidy on their own activities, by
means of questionnaires. The National Research Center of the Arts,
Inc. and other survey research institutions have made extensive use
of this approach to determine the effects of arts subsidies. But the
responding organizations have had a strong incentive to provide
answers consistent with the propositions that (1) subsidy has been

beneficial and (2) a lot more is urgently needed. Hence, the results of such surveys must be considered suspect, as self-serving, until and unless they can be confirmed by data obtained at other times or in other ways. In time, repeat and follow-up surveys may either substantiate or discredit the results of the currently available one-time surveys.

A third approach is to collect a fairly small number of systematic case studies of artistic organizations and/or anecdotes about specific organizations, individuals, and cases assembled from personal contacts, newspaper clippings, and similar sources.[2] The obvious flaw in this approach is that it is necessarily unrepresentative. The bulk of this chapter consists of reports on the experience of a small number of grant-aided organizations. Although I have selected these case studies to encompass a number of different art forms and a wide range of organizational sizes, they are not intended to be representative; I have used them simply for lack of anything better. In some instances, clearly different conclusions have emerged from the case and statistical approaches I have used. For example, my statistical analysis suggests that the increase in government support of theaters during the period in question (1965–66 to 1973–74) did not lead to significant increases in output measured by performances but did result in very large wage increases. Yet the two theaters in our sample of case studies appear to have been able to increase considerably the number of performances and productions on the basis of government support. Because the two approaches are so different and each has serious weaknesses, such divergent findings cannot be fully reconciled, but it would be dishonest to withhold them.

Statistical Evidence: The Performing Arts

The limited time-series data that exist for the arts are confined to the performing arts and museums. All these data have serious deficiencies, but the surveys of the major performing arts organizations done by the Ford Foundation, providing annual data for the period from 1965–66 to 1973–74, contain enough continuity, comparability, and statistical quality control to merit analysis.[3]

The Ford surveys cover professional nonprofit companies in five performing arts forms: the resident theater, opera, symphony orchestra, ballet, and modern dance. The initial study, published by the foundation in 1974,[4] covered 166 companies with annual bud-

Table 5-1. *Census of Business and Ford Foundation Data on the Nonprofit Performing Arts, 1972 (Dollar Amounts in Millions)*

Establishments, receipts, and expenditures[a]	*Census of Business* Cal. 1972[b]	Ford Foundation 1971–72 season[c]
Number of establishments/organizations	747	153
Total receipts/total operating income	$238.1	$155.1
Operating receipts/earned income[d]	162.6	92.5
Receipts from admission/ticket income	128.9	60.4
Nonoperating receipts/unearned income	75.7	62.5
Government contributions[d]	15.8	8.1
Total costs of operations/total operating expenditures	258.2	159.4
Cost of personnel/total salaries, fee, and fringe benefits	172.9	115.5

[a]The first caption shown for each line is that used in the *Census of Business* and the second in the Ford Foundation surveys. The definitions, however, are virtually identical. [b]U.S. Bureau of the Census, *Census of Selected Service Industries, 1972, Subject Series, Miscellaneous Subjects,* SC72-S-8 (Washington, 1975), Table 21. Includes amounts for nonprofit organizations under headings "producers of legitimate theater" and "symphony orchestras, other classical music, and dance groups." [c]Unpublished tabulations provided by the Ford Foundation. [d]In both surveys, government payments to cover the cost of specified services are supposed to be reported as operating receipts or earned income, and government contributions should include only general support grants. However, actual reporting by respondents clearly deviates from these instructions.

gets of $100,000 and over, for the years from 1965–66 to 1970–71. The foundation estimated that this group represented at least 90 percent of the finances of *all* unequivocally professional nonprofit organizations in these art forms in 1970–71.[5] The follow-up surveys for the years 1970–71 through 1973–74 included a slightly smaller sample, 153 organizations in these art forms. The total operating expenditures of the new sample of 153 were 93 percent of total operating expenditures of the old sample of 166, for 1970–71, so that the new sample includes more than five-sixths of all professional nonprofit performing organizations in the five fields covered. Despite the differences in the two samples, together they provide data for nine years, at least on rates of change over the period if not on absolute dollar amounts.[6]

Recently, the U.S. Census Bureau published some tabulations of data on the performing arts collected in the course of the quinquennial *Census of Business.* This census covers retail and wholesale trade and selected service industries, including performing-arts organizations, both commercial and nonprofit, that customarily charge admission fees. Table 5-1 compares *Census of Business* data for calendar year 1972 for 747 nonprofit establishments to data for the Ford sample for the 1971–72 season. In dollar terms, the Ford sample accounted for roughly 60 percent of most of the income and expenditure items of the groups included in the *Census of Business,* a rather smaller percentage of government contributions (for the reason explained in the footnotes to Table 5-1, this comparison is peculiarly unreliable), and a substantially higher share of "unearned income," private and public contributions, and grants and endowment earnings.

The reason why the Ford Foundation sample has such a large share of unearned income is that fully professional symphony orchestras are virtually the only nonprofit performing arts organizations with significant endowment earnings, and the Ford sample includes nearly all symphony orchestras with endowment earnings. The sample is dominated by larger and older performing-arts organizations; such organizations are much more successful in generating contributions from individuals than are smaller and newer organizations. The *Census of Business* clearly includes many very small organizations.[7] Aside from differences in sheer size, the two sources differ in coverage because the census does not impose any test of professionalism and requires only that admission fees be charged (and many avowedly amateur performing arts groups charge admission in order to cover costs of the hall, ticket and program printing, and advertising). And because the census covers *all* classical music groups, it includes ensembles other than symphony orchestras.

The organizations in the Ford sample evidently account for a very large share of total direct public support for the types of artistic activities included in the Ford study, or at least did so in 1971–72, as Table 5-2 indicates. In that year, NEA and state arts council grants to theater, opera, symphony, and dance companies totaled an estimated $18 million. Other public agencies provided $4.3 million to symphony orchestras (this was mainly from local governments), and local governments provided $1.1 million (not shown in Table 5-2) to the theater, opera, and dance companies in the Ford sample. At that time, the 153 organizations received $23.3 million in income from government sources.

Table 5-3 shows the changes in the composition of income of the organizations in the Ford sample by category and as a group.[8]

Table 5-2. *Income from Government Sources for the Performing Arts in 1971–72, Ford Foundation Panel and Other Data (Dollar Amounts in Thousands)*

Type of income and source	Amount
(1) Ford Foundation survey of 153 major organizations: theater, opera, symphony, and dance companies[a]	
Services income from government sources	9,577
Government grants	13,765
Total (rounded)	23,343
(2) NEA grants to theater, opera, orchestra, and dance companies[b]	11,638
(3) New York State Council on the Arts grants under theater, music, and dance programs[c]	4,768
(4) Estimated grants to major performing arts forms by other state arts councils[d]	1,500
(5) Income from government sources of 90 "major" and "metropolitan" symphony orchestras *other* than NEA and state arts councils[e]	4,347
(6) Total of (2), (3), (4), and (5)	22,253

[a]From unpublished tabulations supplied by the Ford Foundation. [b]From Appendix 4-B; includes direct grants to orchestras, opera companies, and professional resident companies in theater and dance, grants for dance touring and dance and theater production grants. [c]From Table 4-12; roughly another $1 million was granted to presenting organizations for touring performances, but much of this probably did not appear in the accounts of the performing-arts organizations as government-source income, but instead as services income from private sources (the presenting organizations). [d]In 1971–72, legislative appropriations to state arts councils except that of New York totalled $5.4 million. The discussion of state arts council programming in Chapter 4 suggests that non-New York councils did not devote major shares of their funds to the four types of performing arts included in the Ford Foundation survey; the figure used here is a very crude estimate. [e]From the annual surveys of the American Symphony Orchestra League; 75 percent of the amount shown here came from local government sources and the rest from Federal agencies other than NEA, state line-item appropriations and similar sources.

Table 5-3 divides the income sources of performing-arts organizations into three major categories: government sources; the various types of earned income (other than from government sources); and unearned income (other than government grants). For all the categories other than dance companies, and for the entire sample, in-

Table 5-3. *Percent Distribution of Total Operating Income by Source, 1965–66 and 1973–74, for Performing Arts Organizations in the Ford Foundation Surveys*

Source of income	Theater companies		Metropolitan Opera		Other operas		Symphonies		Dance companies		All, except Metropolitan Opera	
	1965–66	1973–74	1965–66	1973–74	1965–66	1973–74	1965–66	1973–74	1965–66	1973–74	1965–66	1973–74
Government sources[a]	4	13	b	5	2	10	5	15	11	11	5	13
Ticket income	68	52	52	44	50	40	38	30	42	27	44	35
Services income, nongovt.	1	2	11	11	3	5	9	9	8	19	7	9
Recordings, radio, TV, films	—	b	3	2	—	b	3	2	b	2	2	2
Nonperformance earned income[c]	6	7	5	10	5	3	11	5	5	6	9	5
Other unearned income[d]	21	26	28	28	39	41	33	40	34	34	33	37
Total	100	100	100	100	100	100	100	100	100	100	100	100
Number of organizations covered	27	31	1	1	30	28	91	78	17	15	165	152

Note: Because of rounding, detail may not add to 100 percent.
[a]Includes services income from government sources and government grants. [b]Less than ½ of 1 percent. [c]Income from performance of other groups, school income, and receipts from concessions, program advertising, facilities rentals, etc. [d]Unearned income other than government grants, that is, individual, business, and foundation contributions and grants and endowment earnings.

come from government sources rose greatly as a percentage of total income.[9] Excluding the Metropolitan Opera, government support, which had provided less than 5 percent of total income for most of the categories in 1965–66, provided at least one-tenth of income for all the categories in 1973–74.

Table 5-3 alone does not provide convincing evidence of the effects of the vast increase in government support on other sources of income, but it is suggestive in several respects. First, it is not consistent with the proposition that increased government support in effect substituted for private contributions and grants that might otherwise have been forthcoming. For the sample as a whole and for theaters, symphony orchestras, and operas other than the Met, both unearned income from private sources and income from government sources simultaneously increased as proportions of total operating income.

The increase in unearned income from private sources was very largely a consequence of increases in the income shares coming from gifts from individuals, corporations, and local foundations. By and large, the role of the national foundations was smaller (relatively) in 1973–74 than it was in 1965–66. For theaters, national foundation grants provided 5.1 percent of total income in 1965–66, and 8.1 percent in 1973–74. But for all the other groups, especially the Met and the dance companies – and for the sample as a whole – national foundation grants declined as percentages of total income. The swing in national foundation grants cannot be ascribed to attitudes toward private philanthropy in general but was largely the result of specific policy decisions by the largest of the national foundations, Ford.

Second, earned income from nongovernment sources declined as a percentage of the total for all categories except dance,[10] suggesting that increased government support (and increased private giving) helped keep ticket prices lower than they might otherwise have been. The percentages of total income derived from tickets declined significantly. For the most part, the other types of earned income from private sources, including nongovernmental services and recordings, radio, television, and films, either did not decline or actually increased as percentages of the total. The income share represented by "nonperformance earned income" for symphony orchestras declined significantly, as a result, apparently, of an absolute dollar reduction in income for symphony orchestras from rentals of their halls for performances of other groups. The decline in income from this source in turn seems due to widespread increases in the length of the home orchestras' main seasons, reducing the availability of the symphony halls for performances of other groups.

It must be pointed out that conclusions about the effects of increased public support based solely on income shares are not terribly convincing. Theoretically, increases in government subsidy for any given service can reduce the prices at which the service is offered to the public, increase the volume of service provided, bid up wages and other operating costs, or merely substitute for subsidy from another source without having much impact on prices, output, or costs.

A formally correct analysis of the effects of a subsidy consists of a set of multiple-regression equations in which each variable is examined while the others are held constant. Unfortunately, the Ford time series does not contain enough observations to support statistically reliable conclusions from such a procedure, nor are all of the required types of data available in the Ford survey or other sources. Therefore, what follows is an impressionistic and piecemeal treatment that may well be accused of ignoring the possibility of interactions among the various possible effects.[11] I have examined ticket prices, ticketed attendance, ticket income, and wage costs in three categories – theater, opera, and symphonies – whose predominant activity is performance at productions to which admissions are paid.

Table 5-4 presents a greatly oversimplified model of the economics of the performing arts in the absence of subsidy, public or private. On the supply side, between calendar 1965 and calendar 1973, average wage and salary earnings for all U.S. industries increased by 59.5 percent;[12] hence, according to the Baumol-Bowen thesis, the "expected" wage increase in the performing arts and the expected increase in ticket prices between the 1965–66 and 1973–74 seasons were also close to 59.5 percent. Baumol and Bowen concluded that consumer expenditures for the performing arts tend to increase proportionately with personal income over time. Earlier in this book, I reported the results of a recalculation of the types of data, based on revised data series, that they used; for the 1960–75 period, it appears that the increase in consumer expenditures was somewhat less than proportional to the increase in personal income, but the evident error in the underlying data for earlier years in this period causes an understatement of the degree of "income elasticity." Thus, the presumption that the demand for the live performing arts rises proportionately with income seems, for present purposes, a safe one.

I have also noted that consumer spending for the performing arts

Table 5-4. *An Oversimplified Model of the Economics of a Performing-Arts Industry Dependent Entirely upon Box Office Admissions, 1965–66 to 1973–74 Percent Changes*

Economic variable	Explanation of change[a]	Percent change
(1) Wage rates	U.S. wage level	59.5
(2) Production costs	Wage rates	59.5
(3) Ticket prices	Production costs	59.5
(4) Personal income, U.S.	—	95.8
(5) Price level, U.S.	—	40.8
(6) Relative price of tickets	(3) relative to (5)	13.3
(7) Effect of relative price increase on consumer demand	(6) × − 0.25	−3.3
(8) Consumer demand for admissions	(4) modified by (7)	89.3
(9) Ticketed attendance	[1+(8)] ÷ [1+(3)]	18.7

[a]See text for further explanation.
Source: All general economic data for the U.S. apply to the change between calendar 1965 and calendar 1973 and are derived from the *Statistical Abstract of the United States, 1975.*

Table 5-5. *Percent Increases in Economic Variables, 1965–66 to 1973–74, for Selected Groups of Performing-Arts Organizations Included in the Ford Foundation Surveys*

Economic variable	Theaters	Operas (excl. Metropolitan)	Symphonies
(1) Total personnel costs	141.6	160.8	135.1
(2) Performances	11.1	64.0	79.7
(3) Personnel costs per performance[a]	91.8	59.0	30.8
(4) Ticket income	101.4	114.4	80.0
(5) Ticketed attendance	38.1	48.3	17.8
(6) Average ticket price[b]	46.0	43.5	52.8
(7) Income from government sources	718.3	1,897.2	534.5

[a]In concept, (1) ÷ (2), but calculated directly from survey data. [b]In concept, (4) ÷ (5), but calculated directly from survey data.
Source: Calculated from Ford Foundation data by linking percentage increases for the 1965–66 to 1970–71 and 1970–71 to 1973–74 periods.

appears to be sensitive to the relative price of tickets, although only moderately so. Between calendar 1965 and calendar 1973, personal income in the United States rose by 95.8 percent, and the general price level (the *Consumer Price Index*) rose by 40.8 percent. The expected rise in ticket prices, as suggested above, was 59.5 percent. In relative terms, the expected rise was 13.3 percent.[13] Combining the effects of both personal income and relative price increases (the latter depressed demand by 3.3 percent below what would be expected on the basis of income alone), the expected rise in consumer spending for admission to the performing arts during this period works out to 89.3 percent.[14] Given the rise of 59.5 percent in ticket prices, the implication is that paid attendance had an expected rise of 18.7 percent (Table 5-4).

Table 5-5 shows the percentage changes in similar economic variables actually recorded for the performing-arts organizations in the Ford Foundation surveys. Although not identical with those in Table 5-4, the variables are the closest approximations available. In particular, variable (3) of Table 5-5, personnel costs per performance, is an inadequate measure of wage costs, but its inadequacy is mitigated by the hypothesis that productivity in the performing arts is constant, while productivity in the rest of the economy increases. If this figure is an adequate measure of wage rates, then wage rates may have risen far more than expected (Table 5-4) for theaters, about the same for operas, and less than expected for symphony orchestras. In all three cases, ticket prices rose less than expected – but more than the *Consumer Price Index*. Ticket income, the measure of consumer demand, exceeded expected levels for theaters and operas but fell short for symphonies. Attendance increases greatly exceeded the expected levels for theaters and operas and approximately equaled expected levels for symphonies.

All three types of arts organizations received large increases in government funds during this period, but evidently public subsidy had quite different effects on each.[15] Public subsidy made it possible for theater companies to increase wages far more rapidly than wages increased in the rest of the economy – indeed, the total dollar value of those "excess" wage increases was nearly equal to the $2.7 million increase in income from government sources during these years – while keeping the increase in average ticket prices quite low, relative to the *Consumer Price Index,* thus facilitating a sizable increase in attendance. Had the theater companies found it necessary to raise ticket prices in proportion to the increase in wage costs per performance, according to our model, attendance would have declined significantly. But the "output" of the theater companies increased importantly during this period in only one dimension— attendance. The number of performances increased very modestly, as line (2) of Table 5-5 shows. According to Ford data not presented in the table, the number of productions increased even more modestly, and the number of artists on season contract (a figure that might be considered an indicator of quality) hardly at all.

The opera companies in the survey did not make wage increases—in terms of personnel costs per performance—in excess of those in the economy at large, but the number of performances increased very substantially and the number of performing artists very little; hence, average annual earnings per artist increased substantially more than average annual earnings elsewhere in the economy. The infusion of public funds enabled the companies to keep ticket-price increases down, and attendance increased more for opera companies than for the other categories. The number of productions did not rise significantly; however, the opera companies presented substantially more performances of each production. So public subsidy can be said to have contributed to longer seasons, more nearly full-time employment for opera-company personnel, and significant audience expansion.

During the period covered in the Ford surveys, numerous major symphony orchestras extended their seasons to close to a year-round basis and considerably increased the number of performances per year. Wage costs per performance rose only modestly, but for the larger symphonies with many full-time musicians who live mainly on their orchestra salaries, the true measure of wage costs is the average annual salary, which clearly rose substantially during this period. Public subsidy seems to have had little other effect on the symphony orchestras. It did little to hold ticket prices down or to encourage more paid attendance. Much of the subsidy was explicitly intended to support contracted (rather than ticketed) performances, including free or low-priced performances in schools, parks, and other public places. The number of ticketed performances increased only modestly during these years, while the number of contracted performances more than doubled. In 1973–74, the surveyed organizations gave 1.5 times as many contracted as ticketed performances (the reverse of the relationship in 1965–66).

The finances and activities of symphony orchestras during this period were greatly affected by an external financial event of significantly greater dollar magnitude than the rise in government support. In 1966, the Ford Foundaton announced a massive grant program, designed to effect a long-term improvement in the finances of American symphony orchestras, primarily by increasing their endowment funds.[16] The program involved, at the outset, sixty-one orchestras, sixty of which were to receive, on June 30, 1976, endowment funds totaling $58.75 million, if the orchestras complied with certain conditions and raised additional matching endowment funds totaling $86.4 million by June 30, 1971 (all but a few were successful in raising these funds).

Between 1966 and 1971, the orchestras were paid expendable grants for current operating purposes (essentially, to offset the diversion of their fund-raising efforts from covering current deficits to matching the Ford endowment grant), totaling $17.3 million; some also received developmental grants for special projects. They also were free to use the income from both the Ford endowment grant and the matching endowment funds generated for current operating purposes during this period.

Ford's direct operating grants averaged more than $4 million annually over the five-year period, and by 1969–70, the income from the Ford and matching endowment funds was greater than income from all other endowment funds for the eighty "major" and "metropolitan" orchestras included in the survey done by the American Symphony Orchestra League (ASOL) for that year. In effect, the Ford program led to a more than doubling of symphony orchestra endowment income. In 1969–70, total government support amounted to $4.7 million.[17] Ford operating grants were $4.3 million, and income from the Ford and matching endowment funds was $3.9 million. All other private-source unearned income was $22.4 million. Together, the Ford program provided about 23 percent of all income from sources other than nongovernmental earned income, while government support provided only 13 percent.[18]

The Ford Foundation staff had devised this program in the hope that it would result in longer seasons, larger audiences, more and new orchestral services, and higher incomes for musicians. These conditions would enable musicians to devote more of their time to symphonic work, make music a more attractive career for talented young people, and ultimately enhance the quality of artistic production in this form. Table 5-5 shows that between 1965 and 1974 seasons increased in length, audiences increased, new services were provided, and musicians' income climbed sharply. Indeed, it appears that the announcement of the Ford program strongly bolstered the already rising militance among orchestra musicians.

In *Orpheus in the New World,* Philip Hart points out that militance was on the increase well before 1965[19] but that in the mid-1960s the gap between expenditures and earned income widened sharply as a result of fairly rapid increases in the salaries of artistic personnel.[20] There is clear evidence that "the mere prospect of the Ford Foundation grants in 1966 greatly stimulated the demands of [the] players in their desire to assure themselves of their share of the bounty."[21] Clearly, the Ford money did not create the militance, but it did enable the militant musicians to press their demands successfully. And of course, the foundation had *intended* its grants to result in higher earnings for musicians.

After 1970–71, Ford officially terminated its expendable grant program, although the increased endowment earnings generated by the program continued to benefit the orchestras.[22] But by 1970–71 government support for symphony orchestras was growing rapidly. The National Endowment for the Arts (NEA) orchestra program had started in 1969–70, involved fifty orchestras by 1970–71, and continued to grow in both dollar amount and number of orchestras in the ensuing years. During this period, state arts councils also became a significant source of orchestra support. In 1970–71, total government support, of all types, to the ASOL major and metropolitan orchestras was $7.8 million. In 1973–74, it was $15.2 million, of which $5.4 million was provided by NEA, $2.9 million by state arts councils, and $6.9 million by other public sources, mainly local governments. In the aggregate, the orchestras ran "bottom-line" deficits after 1970–71. Anticipation of the release of the Ford endowment funds (totaling nearly $150 million, including the matching funds) after June 30, 1976, may have generated a certain willingness to invade capital or run up bank debt. Thus, the results shown in Table 5-5 are traceable to the combination of Ford Foundation money (especially in the 1966 to 1971 period) and the rise in government support (especially after 1970).

Although the increase in public subsidy may not be responsible for all the changes in the fortunes or experiences of the arts organizations covered by Table 5-5, public subsidy seems to have: made possible very large increases in earnings of artistic and supporting personnel (in the case of operas and symphonies, mostly by increasing the number of performances); facilitated audience access to the performing arts (in the symphony case, to performances other than the regular ticketed ones); and fostered some increase in output in terms of the number of opera and symphony performances. Subsidy did *not* do much to increase the number of theater and opera productions, nor did it help the symphony orchestras much with ticket prices.

Although NEA has sought to increase the amount of employment of individual artists by making it possible for the companies that employ them to have longer seasons, the endowment has never explicitly indicated that increasing artists' earnings is one of its objectives. If increasing the wage rates, per week or per performance, of artists relative to the rest of the working population is *not* an intended outcome of a subsidy program but occurs nonetheless, that result might be considered a failure in the program. Public subsidy to the organizations in the Ford survey must be counted generally successful, but alternative subsidy policies might have elicited similar increases in production and attendance at lower public costs, especially in the case of the theater companies.

Now, the preceding statistical analysis has at least three major and obvious flaws. First, it relies on limited data and a greatly oversimplified model of what might have occurred without subsidy. Second, it implicitly assumes that each of the Ford survey groups of organizations is insulated from the others and from the rest of the performing arts. In fact, live performing-arts groups in any given city compete with one another to some extent both within and among art forms, for audiences. For example, nonprofit resident theater competes with commercial theater, and symphony orchestras compete with performances by nonorchestral ensembles. All the live performing arts compete with film and the electronic media. And some groups compete with others for artistic personnel. Thus, the analysis may overstate the positive effects of increased government subsidy if, in fact, the groups in the Ford sample increased their attendance and output at the expense of less-subsidized artistic competitors. On the other hand, the analysis may understate these positive effects if (improbably) audience expansion for the organizations surveyed also expanded audiences for other, less-subsidized competitors.[23]

The available data do not permit convincing assessment of the extent to which these "spill-overs" occurred in the 1965–66 to 1973–74 period. For many years, *Variety* has published statistics on the gross receipts of two major sectors of the commercial theater, the Broadway stage and "the road," touring performances of Broadway-type productions. The *Variety* statistics show that gross receipts of Broadway and the road combined were very little higher in the 1973–74 season than they were in 1965–66. In some of the intervening years, the increase over 1965–66 was only 15 percent. Our simple model, in Table 5-4, predicts an increase of roughly 90 percent; thus, subsidy to nonprofit resident theater companies may appear to have diverted attendance from the commercial theater, especially road companies.

However, during this period, another sector of the commercial theater arose and began to flourish. By 1973–74, dinner theater was estimated to be generating gross receipts three times as high as those of the Broadway stage, with half of the dinner-theater gross receipts ascribed to the theatrical peformance (rather than the food).[24] If dinner theater is included in this analysis, little diversion of attendance appears to have taken place. Moreover, since 1973–74 Broadway has had a series of increasingly successful (in terms of gross receipts) seasons. Data for 1975–76 show the combined receipts of the commercial theater to be substantially *above* the results predicted by our simple model.

The National Income Accounts prepared by the U.S. Department of Commerce include annual estimates of personal consumption expenditures for admissions to "legitimate theaters and operas and entertainments of nonprofit institutions (except athletics)." This category is very broad but it is the only available source of aggregate time-series data on such consumption. If data on the organizations in the Ford surveys and the commercial theater are subtracted from these aggregates, the increase in expenditures for the remaining activities from 1965–66 to 1973–74 is slightly greater than 80 percent. This figure suggests that audiences have been diverted to some extent from unsubsidized to subsidized performances, but the difference is small and the data are too crude to be confidently relied on in this case.

A third major difficulty with the analysis of the Ford survey sample is that the averages can be very misleading. In particular, the extent of public support differs considerably among individual performing arts organizations. For example, although all the major orchestras in the ASOL survey received NEA grants in 1974–75 (and in fairly uniform amounts), some reported receiving no state arts-council support, and some reported receiving no local government support – and the amounts involved were far from uniform. Thus, the aggregate figures would not be adequately informative if in fact organizations getting little public subsidy experienced large changes in attendance, performances, and other variables, while the more heavily subsidized organizations experienced relatively small changes in these variables. The presence of such distortions can be detected only through examination of individual organizations receiving public funds.

Grant Recipients: Sixteen Cases

In the course of this study, I have examined the impact of public support on the fortunes of sixteen specific artistic organizations:[25] eight performing arts organizations, two each of four major types (symphony orchestras, opera, theater, and dance companies) selected, for logistical reasons, among those in the eastern United States; and eight service organizations, chosen because such organizations are the principal means used to channel public support to the literary and visual arts and also serve those forms of the performing arts that involve individual artists working on their own or in small groups rather than in large ensembles. The organizations examined comprise a highly unsystematic sampling of the hundreds of publicly aided organizations, but they include representatives of most of the major types of organizations assisted, art museums aside.

Directly or indirectly, the following questions were posed: What difference has the advent of large-scale public support made in the nature and scope of the organization's activities? (Sometimes the answer was that public support *created* the organization.) How would the organization respond to a significant reduction in public support? (Sometimes the answer was: by dying.) Alternatively, what are the specific things the organization would do if it could receive large increases in public support? Finally, quite apart from the dollar amount of public funds, how have the grant-making procedures as such affected the operations of these organizations? The purpose of these questions was to determine whether, for these particular organizations, subsidy had or had not been efficient in the sense of advancing some or all of the goals of public financial intervention commensurately with the dollars expended. Not surprisingly, directors and managers of some organizations found it harder to respond to such questions than did others. Typically, the larger and older organizations (whose officers had worried about their finances for a long time) and the literary service organizations (literary people are apt to be more articulate than others) were able to answer most directly.

Symphony Orchestras

Symphony orchestras are among the oldest of the nonprofit performing-art institutions in this country, and in terms of audience and expenditures, they remain much the largest. In 1972, the operating budgets of the ASOL major and metropolitan orchestras amounted to more than one-third of total operating costs for all the arts covered by the *Census of Business* data reported in Table 5-1; in the same year, symphony orchestras accounted for just under half of the total budgets of the organizations in the Ford survey. The symphony orchestra is also the prototypical art organization on which Baumol and Bowen based their thesis. Most other performing-art institutions can achieve some improvements in productivity and have done so, but for the symphony orchestra the opportunities for such gains are indeed limited. Because symphony orchestras are so vulnerable to the economic squeeze described by Baumol and Bowen, because they are old and numerous, and because their boards include many influential civic and business figures, the symphony orchestras played a major, and perhaps a decisive, role in pressing for the great leap upward in public support from the federal government and the state of New York in 1970 and 1971.

These organizations that sought public funds and the agencies of government that provided them did *not* seek to reform the structure of the symphony orchestra as an institution, to change its function, to create new orchestras, or to experiment with wholly different kinds of musical performance or the presentation of new music. Geographical distribution was not an important issue because by the mid-1960s nearly every American city of significant size had its own more or less professional orchestra. The repertoire of symphonic music is well established, and all sorts of incentives conspire to encourage orchestras to rely on this repertoire rather than, as in theater, dance, and films, to present new material. Moreover, to a considerable extent, the example of a relatively small number of important orchestras determines the directions of symphonic music, and public subsidy continues today to be relatively marginal in the budgets of these influential orchestras. The primary purpose of the public subsidies to orchestras, in the eyes of both grantors and recipients, was to cover operating deficits.

By any financial or economic measure, the Philadelphia Orchestra is the country's most successful symphony orchestra. Indeed, in 1974–75 the Philadelphia Orchestra, then celebrating its seventy-fifth anniversary, ended the season with a surplus. The financial history of the Philadelphia Orchestra Association has been anything but stormy. As Hart recalls, right after World War I the association conducted a major endowment campaign, and during the 1920s the orchestra operated at a surplus on the basis of earned income from performances, endowment earnings, and very small annual contri-

Table 5-6. *Percent Distribution of Symphony Orchestra Income, by Source, 1973–74*

Source of income	78 orchestras, Ford Foundation survey	29 "major" orchestras, ASOL survey	Philadelphia Orchestra
Nongovernmental earned income	46	46	66
(Recordings, TV, etc.)	(2)	(3)	(8)
Nongovernmental unearned income	40	41	27
(Endowment earnings)	(12)	(12)	(11)
Government sources	14	13	7
Total	100	100	100
Total, in thousands of dollars	92,985	83,175	4,854

Note: Because of rounding, detail may not add to totals.
Sources: Ford Foundation unpublished tabulations; American Symphony Orchestra League 1973–74 survey; Philadelphia Orchestra Association, *Annual Report 1973–74* and interview notes.

butions. By the end of the 1950s, the orchestra was still breaking even, although not running annual surpluses. In 1960–61 earned income accounted for 82 percent, endowment income for 9 percent, and annual contributions for the remaining 9 percent of the association's revenue.[26]

In recent years, as the orchestra has begun to receive government support and larger annual contributions, the share of revenue provided by nongovernmental earned income has declined somewhat. But as Table 5-6 shows the Philadelphia Orchestra continues to generate an extraordinarily large share of its revenue from earnings – including a substantial amount from recordings[27] – by the standards of other American symphony orchestras. Its relatively modest government support in 1974–75 included a $100,000 general support grant from the city of Philadelphia, a small state arts-council grant for youth concerts, and the maximum NEA grant under the orchestra program ($150,000 in 1976), ostensibly for specific projects but in practice for general support.[28] Although the association does more annual fund raising than in the past, it relies far less on annual contributions than other symphonies. As of 1975, it was receiving very little money from corporate contributions,[29] probably because, unlike most supplicants for corporate gifts, the Philadelphia Orchestra cannot demonstrate dire financial need in the form of large deficits.[30]

The Philadelphia Orchestra was the first in the country to operate on a truly year-round basis; in 1963 its representatives signed a union contract providing for fifty-two weeks of employment including thirty in Philadelphia at the Academy of Music; five in New York, Washington, and Baltimore; and ten at two summer programs, in Saratoga and at Robin Hood Dell. It is the world's most traveled orchestra and, by a wide margin, the most recorded of the American ensembles. Its heavy schedule of standard orchestral activities precludes any extensive outreach activities to new types of audiences or performances in new formats. The Philadelphia Orchestra remains in the concert hall, although for the country as a whole, "over 40 percent of symphony orchestra activity now takes place not in the concert hall but in schools, homes for the elderly, hospitals, parks and plazas, and even manufacturing plants and prisons."[31]

The orchestra established its fifty-two week season, its emphasis on standard orchestral activities, and its relatively conservative program content[32] before it began to receive public (and Ford Foundation) support. The new sources of funds cannot be held to have had significant effect on what the orchestra produces, nor can they be said to have resolved a financial crisis, because the Philadelphia Orchestra has not confronted one for many years. Even if the level of public subsidy were much lower, the orchestra's existence would not be in danger.[33]

The Ford Foundation grants and public subsidy may have increased musicians' wage scales,[34] but the Philadelphia Orchestra has traditionally paid and continues to pay its musicians more than any other orchestra in the world. Higher wage rates for musicians are not an explicit objective of public policy (although subsidy for other orchestras has been designed to extend musicians' employment to a year-round basis). The Philadelphia Orchestra's subsidy may have enabled the orchestra to hold down the prices of its best seats,[35] but that too hardly seems a particularly worthwhile use of public funds and most certainly is not an announced objective of any government funding agency.

In size and history, the Charlotte Symphony Orchestra is at the opposite end of the scale from Philadelphia's among professional-level American symphony orchestras. The Charlotte Symphony Orchestra was founded in 1932, but its budget did not reach

$100,000 until 1970–71; as a result, it did not receive NEA support until the following year and was not among the sixty-one orchestras in the Ford Foundation endowment and sustaining grant program begun in 1966. Its achievement of truly professional status is a recent event.

The development of the orchestra mirrors that of the Charlotte metropolitan area itself, which only recently has become large and affluent. With a mid-1974 population of 589,000, the Charlotte metropolitan area has since 1960 grown in population at a rate about twice that of the country as a whole. The in-migrants include executive and professional employees of new and expanding firms with regional offices' or headquarters in Charlotte. Since 1959, and especially in the early 1970s, per capita personal income in Charlotte has increased at a rate significantly greater than that for all U.S. metropolitan areas.[36] With more people, more income, and a more cosmopolitan tone, Charlotte has been ripe, in recent years, for the development of community-based professional arts organizations.

Unlike the Philadelphia Orchestra, which works a full schedule of rehearsals, performances, and recording sessions forty-five weeks a year, the Charlotte Symphony Orchestra in 1975–76 had a season of twelve performances in two local auditoriums with a combined capacity of roughly 25,000 for the twelve performances. Twenty-three of the orchestra's eighty members work on a full-season contract and also play in the chamber orchestra and in ensembles. Most orchestra members are music teachers in nearby schools or music students who are members of the Youth Symphony of the Carolinas, an organization sponsored by the Charlotte Symphony Orchestra.

In number of performances and listeners reached, the orchestra's activities in schools in the Charlotte area and in neighboring counties outrank the main season concerts. The orchestra has vigorously promoted its school activities, and all of its public funding including support from NEA, the state arts council, and the county school boards, is for school programs. The school programs account for most of the increase in the orchestra's total budget from $101,000 in 1970–71 to $428,000 in 1974–75.

In recent years, like other ASOL metropolitan orchestras, the Charlotte Symphony Orchestra has been receiving about one-fifth of its total income from public sources, but it receives more of its public support from local governments than do most ASOL orchestras, in part because of its school programs. The Charlotte Symphony Orchestra has a strong rival for state arts council support— the North Carolina Symphony Orchestra, a larger and more ambitious enterprise that tours the entire state and in 1975 received $800,000 in state arts council funds, whereas Charlotte received only $25,000. The North Carolina Symphony evidently is viewed as the state's "chosen instrument" for the presentation of symphonic music in North Carolina.

The Charlotte orchestra falls well below its ASOL counterparts in generating private-source unearned income. Its main-season audience appears relatively insensitive to ticket prices,[37] but quite sensitive to the scheduling of performances: Saturday evening performances are poorly attended. During the main season, the orchestra presents rather conventional symphonic music and builds programs around performances of internationally known guest soloists.

For the Charlotte Symphony Orchestra, the advent of public support on a relatively large scale directly financing the orchestra's activities in schools, has had two consequences: it has enabled the orchestra to reach new audiences (although orchestras in other parts of the country have long engaged in similar activities in schools); and it has permitted the orchestra to employ a cadre of musicians on a full-time basis, presumably raising the quality of all the orchestra's performances, in the schools and in the main-season concerts.

Unfortunately, increased public support of the Charlotte orchestra has not gone hand-in-glove with a big increase in private support, as it has for the performing arts more generally (see Table 5-3). The absence of private support is disappointing, given the newly rich character of the Charlotte area. Nor is it clear that the orchestra needed its relatively modest NEA and state arts-council support to achieve its program expansion or to reach new audiences to the extent that it has. Without federal and state money, the Charlotte Symphony Orchestra might have been compelled to be more aggressive in private fund raising, been able to make up the difference with local government money, or found ways to do even better at the box office. The North Carolina Symphony Orchestra might have given more performances in that part of the state. On balance, external (that is, federal and state) public funding of the Charlotte Symphony seems to have been a rather modest success, a marginal but not essential supplement to the aggressive support of the school programs by the area's local governments.

The impact of public support of the Charlotte Symphony is consistent, in general terms, with the results of the statistical analysis presented earlier in this chapter. The statistical material suggested that increased public support for symphony orchestras led to an increase in the number of performances outside the regular season and mostly outside the concert hall and an increase in annual earnings of musicians because of the increased number of performances. The Charlotte orchestra's performances increased, and its members' earnings rose, but mainly because of the county school boards; the external government support in a sense appears to have been a substitute for the private fund raising of other symphony orchestras. Both the Charlotte and the Philadelphia orchestras appear to have less than other symphony orchestras, statistically, to show for federal and state support. Perhaps the statistical results are misleading; perhaps case studies of other orchestras might show similar results. By themselves, the Philadelphia and Charlotte cases suggest that NEA support of virtually all professional symphony orchestras in the United States is not particularly well-conceived. Whatever the rationale for subsidy, there is no excuse for subsidy that makes no difference in the conduct or fortunes of the subsidy recipients.

Opera

Even more than the Philadelphia Orchestra, the Metropolitan Opera is venerable and preeminent among artistic organizations in this country and worldwide. But unlike the Philadelphia Orchestra, the Metropolitan Opera has been in dire financial straits for years. Time and again, the Met has come close to financial disaster because of economic depression, strikes, union contract settlements for which the Met had no money, the launching of unaffordable new ventures, or (in the mid-1960s) the move to a new opera house. Time and again, on the brink of disaster the Met has been rescued by radio-broadcasting contracts, Ford Foundation grants, fortuitous large bequests, spectacularly successful fund-raising drives, and, recently, large doses of federal and New York State government support.

The Met also differs from the Philadelphia Orchestra in its vigorous and multifaceted efforts to reach new audiences. It is striving to build – both for itself and for opera in general – the national constituency that the inherently expensive nature of grand opera and the very large size of the Met itself[38] require. It has been clear for years that New York City is too small a geographic base from which to draw private or government contributions and grants for the support of the world's largest and most costly performing-arts organization.

Table 5-7 sets forth the finances of the Met for the fifteen seasons ending with 1974–75. In ten of those fifteen years, operating expen-

Table 5-7. *Finances of the Metropolitan Opera, 1960–61 to 1974–75 (Dollar Amounts in Millions)*

| Year | Total operating expenditures | Total operating income | Percent distribution of operating income | | |
			Earned nongovt. sources	Unearned nongovt. sources	Govt. sources
1960–61	$7.2	$7.1	89	11	—
1961–62	7.1	7.1	87	13	—
1962–63	8.4	8.3	84	16	—
1963–64	8.9	8.7	82	18	—
1964–65	9.9	9.9	81	19	—
1965–66	15.8	15.3	72	28	a
1966–67	21.3	21.9	65	34	1
1967–68	16.9	17.6	75	22	2
1968–69	17.4	17.9	77	21	2
1969–70	16.0	14.6	69	29	2
1970–71	19.6	19.5	79	18	3
1971–72	22.2	21.2	75	23	2
1972–73	24.1	21.3	76	21	3
1973–74	24.6	24.1	68	28	5
1974–75	27.7	27.3	67	27	6

Note: Detail of percent distribution may not add to 100, because of rounding.
[a]Less than one-half of 1 perent.
Source: The classification is that used in the Ford Foundation surveys, and the data for 1965–66 through 1973–74 are from the Ford tabulations; they closely match data in Metropolitan Opera annual reports except that the annual reports round downwards in the historical tables. Data for earlier years are from Metropolitan Opera Association, *White Paper on the Metropolitan Opera,* June 1971, p. 19; 1974–75 data from the annual report for that year.

ditures exceeded income from all sources, unearned and earned. During the first half of the 1960s, the financial deficits were small or nonexistent; although operating costs increased steadily (in part because of a modest lengthening of the New York season), as Table 5-7 shows, private-source unearned income (including foundation grants) increased more than proportionately. But in 1965–66, the Met's operating expenditures rose sharply for two reasons: first, the Met moved from its old opera house to the new one in Lincoln Center, which has more (and better) seating capacity and far more space for stage, rehearsals, storage, and offices but far higher operating costs; and second, the Met launched a national touring company (which it was able to sustain for only two seasons). A substantial special grant from the Ford Foundation and very successful fund raising from individual donors[39] kept the deficit small in that year and permitted small surpluses in the following three years.

In 1969–70, a strike cut the number of performances at the Met by roughly one-third and reduced ticket income by $3.7 million, more than 40 percent. The strike also reduced operating costs by only $1.4 million, 8 percent lower than in the previous year. Between 1968–69 and 1969–70, the Met moved from a $504,000 surplus to a $1.4 million deficit. The strike had repercussions in subsequent years as well. For one thing, in order to settle the strike, the Met's representatives had agreed to contracts providing fifty-two weeks of employment for nearly all artistic and technical staff. Moreover, in the following year, individual contributions fell off sharply, an event most observers trace to the strike.

In addition, attendance – in the sense of percent of box office capacity actually sold – declined considerably. Although this decline is also generally ascribed to the effect of the strike on opera-going habits, it is more directly attributable to the 20 percent increase in ticket prices in the 1970–71 season, itself a consequence of the strike's impact on the Met's finances. In its first four years at Lincoln Center, the Met had been selling 96 percent or more of its box office capacity; in the five years after the strike, ticket sales ranged between 86 and 92 percent of capacity.[40] If the company had sold 95 percent of capacity in each of those five years, its combined deficit for the five years would have been only a little over $500,000 rather than $4.8 million.[41]

In each year since the 1969–70 strike, the Met has operated at a net deficit (see Table 5-7). By 1972–73, the deficit had reached $2.8 million, in part because of new union contracts signed in the summer and fall of 1972. The Met management responded with a general program of belt-tightening economies, cancellation of a scheduled new production of *Don Giovanni,* and elimination of special programs. Then, late in the 1972–73 season, the Met received its first general-support grant from a government arts agency.

Before 1966, the Met had received no direct government support. In that year, the City of New York began its annual grants to defray part of the costs of free concerts in the city's parks. The concerts are enormously popular; a single performance often attracts as many as 100,000 people.[42] The city government's grants for the park concerts have ranged from $89,000 to $225,000 for a single

Table 5-8. *Government Support for the Metropolitan Opera, 1965–66 to 1974–75 (in Thousands of Dollars)*

| Year | Total govt. funding | Support for services and special programs | General support | |
			NYSCA	NEA
1965–66	25	25	—	—
1966–67	100	100	—	—
1967–68	440	440	—	—
1968–69	310	310	—	—
1969–70	267	267	—	—
1970–71	599	599	—	—
1971–72	453	453	—	—
1972–73	659	509	150	—
1973–74	1,142	367	275	500
1974–75	1,740	240	1,000	500

Source: For sources, see Table 5-7. Amounts reported on the basis of the Met's fiscal year, which ends July 31; they differ from the amounts recorded in government reports, on the basis of the fiscal years of the respective grantor governments (June 30 for the Federal government and New York City; March 31 for New York State).

summer season, but this subsidy has never covered more than half the costs of the concerts; in 1970–71 and in 1973–74, grants from the New York State Council on the Arts (NYSCA) substantially covered the remainder of the costs, but in most years the Met has had to utilize funds raised from nongovernment sources to operate the program.

The Met also has received grants for other special programs and services. For three years, NYSCA provided an annual grant of $105,000 to cover part of the costs of the Metropolitan Opera Studio, a company of young singers that presented live opera performances in schools in New York State. This program was a casualty of the Met's financial difficulties at the end of the 1974–75 season. In 1971–72 and 1972–73, NEA, which had earlier provided some support for the short-lived national touring company, provided project support for student seats at regular Met performances as well as for the Met's "Look-ins," ninety-minute programs designed as an introduction to opera for children aged ten to fourteen, and the "Mini-Met" performances by a reduced company in a 299-seat theater at Lincoln Center. In 1972–73, NYSCA also supported the Mini-Met, but after that year the project became another fiscal casualty.

As Table 5-8 indicates, project support from government sources had reached $600,000 a year before 1973. In that year NYSCA made a $150,000 emergency assistance grant to the Met. In 1973–74 and 1974–75, both NYSCA and NEA provided the Met with general support funds. With this substantial general support from government sources, program cutbacks, and very aggessive fund raising from private sources,[43] the Met was able to reduce its overall financial deficit from the horrendous $2.8 million in 1972–73 to roughly $500,000 in 1973–74 and $400,000 in 1974–75.

Although every year the Met has lost money on nearly all its special programs, including its annual spring tour outside New York, this aggressive constituency building – along with equally aggressive efforts to use the electronic media (starting in the 1930s with radio broadcasts) to reach a wider audience – may have played an important role in securing the general public support the Met has obtained recently. However, even at the 1974–75 level, public subsidy is clearly not a complete solution to the Met's financial problems. With the 1975–76 season approaching, the Met confronted such dismal prospects that the management entered labor negotiations in the summer of 1975 calling for both a substantial wage cut *and* a reduction in the length of the season. The new contracts that emerged from these negotiations reduced the contractual season to forty-six weeks for singers and dancers and forty-four weeks for musicians.[44]

The Met has never has a substantial endowment; in its private fund-raising efforts, it has concentrated on getting current gifts to cover annual operating deficits and capital gifts and bequests to finance new productions and special programs or to provide relief of the current budget. Years of deficit operations have depleted the Met's capital, and in 1975, its last major asset, the site of the old opera house, was sold, in part to pay off short-term indebtedness. By the end of the 1974–75 fiscal year, the Met had $3.8 million in funds functioning as endowment, a $28 million budget, and a history of net annual deficits as high as $2.8 million. Thus, the Met cannot look to depletion of capital as a significant source of financial sustenance.

Unlike many other arts organizations and the Met itself at times in the past, the Met has a management that appears to be making realistic and vigorous efforts to close the financial gap. For example, for the 1975–76 season, the Met undertook the most aggressive subscription campaign in its history to increase the percentage of capacity sold and substantially increased its ticket price differentials. Following the example of European opera houses, the Met raised the top ticket prices for especially popular operas (from twenty-five dollars to thirty-five dollars), but continued to sell the cheapest seats for less than four dollars. The price differentiation was not a great success, but the management deserves credit for making the attempt, and in any case 94 percent of capacity was sold for the (shortened) 1975–76 main season in New York, compared to 86 percent in the preceding year. The increase in attendane was in part the result of the subscription campaign, which made available to people under the age of thirty-five a "Met Sampler" subscription-series package including reduced-price orchestra seats for three standard performances, libretti for each opera, a trial subscription to *Opera News,* and a backstage tour.

Other recent efforts to close the financial gap include new ventures in recording and television, efforts to increase rental income from the opera house (especially in the summer months, when the other facilities at Lincoln Center are thriving but the Metropolitan Opera House is dark much of the time),[45] and, in July 1976, the launching of the Metropolitan Opera Ballet Ensemble, a fourteen-dancer troupe from within the company's twenty-nine-member ballet company that will perform during the weeks cut from the schedule under the 1975 union contracts. Given the precarious financial state of most dance groups, it is not self-evident that this venture can contribute to the closing of the gap.

The Met's financial problems cannot be traced to managerial sloth, lethargic fund raising, unwillingness to invade capital, or any of the other all-too-common characteristics of venerable nonprofit organizations; the basic difficulty is the inherently high cost of presenting high-quality grand opera. The essence of grand opera is opulence – the operas themselves call for large choruses and ballet companies, full orchestras, elaborate sets, and lavish costumes. An element of this opulence is high-priced "superstar" soloists, who can earn fees in excess of $4,000 per performance.[46] At some performances, the soloists' fees exceed the combined salaries of the orchestra and ballet. But an attempt to cut costs by declining to bid for the stars would significantly change the Met's standing among the world's opera companies and conceivably cost even more money in foregone box office income and private contributions.[47] To be sure, opera companies can present standard-repertoire operas in nontraditional ways that are less opulent and less costly, just as some theater troupes present Shakespeare's plays in abridged form with smaller casts, starkly simple sets, and relatively inexpensive stylized costumes. But surely the objective of preserving the cultural heritage justifies maintaining a relatively small number of stellar-quality opera companies that present grand opera in the traditional and costly mode.

The Metropolitan Opera is one of perhaps a half-dozen such companies in the world today, the only one in this hemisphere and, arguably, the best in the world. It is, in two senses, the United States counterpart to the Royal Shakespeare Company: our premier national theater and our entry in an art form in which we do as well as or better than anyone else. The evidence of the past fifteen years indicates that the Met cannot be supported at the box office or on the basis of the box office plus private contributions.[48] If it is to survive, it will require government support on a large scale.

But this support cannot be justified as building audiences, educating the young, or making grand opera accessible to people with low incomes. No matter how vigorously reduced-price ticket schemes, special youth programs, or media exposure are promoted, the typical audience for grand-opera live performances at the Metropolitan Opera House will remain relatively small[49] and (as long as there is any real effort to defray a significant part of the Met's costs from box office receipts) relatively affluent. The decision to subsidize the Met from public funds must be based on a straightforward "merit-goods" argument: the Met is a good thing that should be perpetuated and can be perpetuated only with fairly large amounts of public subsidy.[50]

Experience in other countries suggests that opera companies can absorb huge amounts of public subsidy effortlessly – by using a bigger chorus, ballet corps, orchestra, or backstage staff, by performing more different operas within a season (with fewer performances of each one), or by putting on more new productions each season.[51] Although at its current level subsidy to the Met is unlikely to have such results, it will have to be adjusted over the next few years.[52] Ideally, the subsidy should further the objective of preserving first-quality grand opera without reducing incentives to economize or be inventive in generating other types of revenue and contributions.

A relatively new phenomenon in the United States is the resident and fully professional regional opera company that has high standards for performance and stresses innovation in the form of new operas or the performance of older ones that are seldom seen and heard. Opera in the provinces in the United States is by no means a new thing; in the nineteenth century, touring performances by European troupes or imported soloists reached towns of quite modest size. But like the regional and touring theater performances of that era, the opera performances more often than not were of very poor quality; in the first quarter of the twentieth century, the touring groups succumbed to competiton from films.

The Baltimore Opera Company is now twenty-five years old. Its artistic director is Rosa Ponselle, and its orchestra is the Baltimore Symphony. The company sells out all performances on a subscription basis before the season opens. Its silver jubilee season in 1975–76 included the world premiere of a new American opera, *Ines de Castro,* a presentation of the Santa Fe Opera Company in its revival of Offenbach's *La Grande Duchesse de Gerolstein,* and a production of Donizetti's *Maria Stuarda,* an anything but hackneyed program; the company staged three performances of each of these three productions. The company has a five-year growth plan under which it will increase its presentations from nine to twenty in the 1980–81 season. The company recruits star performers from the Met, Europe, and elsewhere as soloists, directors, and conductors.

In 1973, the Baltimore Opera Company established as a touring mechanism the Eastern Opera Company, which now tours Maryland schools for five weeks each year. Frequently, an opera performed in a school (or elsewhere outside an opera house) is nothing more than a concert given by a handful of singers with piano accompaniment. The Eastern Opera Company attempts to offer schoolchildren a more authentic and complete opera experience. It presents fully staged one-act operas, and it has developed an ingenious method for doing so economically. Because the major cost item in touring is the orchestra, the Eastern Opera does not take an orchestra on tour. Instead, it tapes an orchestra and conductor in performance of the opera's music in advance, and videotapes the conductor. At the school, the singers perform in costume, with sets, accompanied by the music tapes played on sound systems; the videotape of the conductor is played on a television set installed on stage to direct the singers.

The regional opera companies, and their central organization, Opera America (founded in 1970; its president from 1970 to 1975 was the general manager of the Baltimore Opera Company, Robert Collinge) are a hotbed of productivity-improving schemes. Opera America administers a scenery and costumes cooperative, a lending library of opera scores, and a job bank for opera artists, with yearly national auditions of singers before an audience of opera company directors. Opera America strongly pushes sharing of productions among companies, like Baltimore's presentation of the Santa Fe production of *La Grande Duchesse de Gerolstein*.[53] Collinge himself was instrumental in the design of the Ford Foundation's "cash reserve grants" to opera companies as well as NEA's grant program for singers and internship program for young administrators, stage directors, stage managers, designers, rehearsal pianists, and coaches.

In its 1973 and 1974 fiscal years, the Baltimore Opera Company received about 15 percent of its total income from government sources, rather more than other opera companies, and about 40 percent from nongovernment earned income, rather less than other opera companies except the Met (see Table 5-3). It receives modest grants from the city of Baltimore and extremely small amounts from the state arts council; NEA is its public mainstay. It has had fairly generous Ford Foundation support for some years and does vigorous private fund raising locally. In its silver jubilee year, it was particularly involved in fund-raising efforts, inspired by the need to pay the high costs of producing the new opera, *Ines de Castro* (for which federal bicentennial funds had been promised but were not forthcoming).

The vigor and magnitude of the Baltimore Opera Company's private fund raising suggest that public support has not been essential to its survival or to the scale and number of its main-season performances. Public support has, however, enabled the Baltimore Opera to do main-season programming of very high quality and commensurate cost, providing, like the Met, a merit good; and it has financed innovative outreach activities, via the Eastern Opera Company. These activities also justify the subsidy: opera is inherently so expensive that low income is an especially serious barrier to access; moreover, because opera is perhaps more of an acquired taste than most of the performing-arts forms, failure to expose the young to it can permanently narrow audiences (and deny opportunity to potential performers); finally, it is difficult, because of both high costs and low demand, to present opera to audiences, young or old, outside the largest of cities. The strong management of the Baltimore Opera has made it a worthy and effective vehicle for the achievement of those public goals. The statistical data on the performing arts indicate that public support had a more pronounced effect on the output (measured by performances, ticket income, and ticketed attendance) of the regional opera companies than that of the other performing arts analyzed. Public support seems to have had precisely this effect on the Baltimore Opera Company.

Theater

Until relatively recently, the non-Broadway professional theater in the United States was dominated by touring companies of Broadway shows and summer stock; some of these troupes were of high quality, but they usually presented only the most conventional fare. Nonprofit professional companies, if not artistically weak, were very weak in financial resources. But, during the past quarter-century, the nonprofit resident professional theater, mostly (but not entirely) outside New York, has flowered.[54] At first this flowering was aided by substantial foundation assistance; more recently, the infusion of public support has become important in making the nonprofit resident theater not merely *the* serious alternative to road companies and summer stock for non–New York theatergoers but also a major source of innovation in the American theater.

Among the most successful and earliest permanent theater companies established outside New York is the Arena Stage, created in 1950 by Zelda Fichandler. Located in Washington, D.C., Arena Stage is actually two theaters: the Arena, seating 811, and the smaller Kreeger Theater, seating 500. The company presents new American plays, new American playwrights, premieres of important European plays, plays from the past restaged and reinterpreted, and plays from the commercial theater that have failed and can be given new life. The Arena also operates the Living Stage, a separate improvisational company for children that tours Washington, D.C., and other cities without charge, offering training workshops for the community and apprentice experience for university and professional-school students.

From 1950 to 1955, Arena presented its productions in an old movie house seating 247 people around a central stage. In 1956, the theater was closed for a year until a more suitable structure could be found. From 1957 to 1960, an abandoned brewery, which the acting company nicknamed the Old Vat, served as Arena's 500-seat theater. The present 811-seat theater, designed by Harry Weese, was built in 1960 at a cost of over $1 million, the bulk of which ultimately came from Ford Foundation grants. During the 1960s, Arena's subscription rolls increased, and the theater was filled to 90–95 percent of capacity. Another Ford Foundation grant of $800,000 and a $250,000 gift from David Lloyd Kreeger, as well as other foundation and private support, financed construction of the 500-seat, $1.5 million Kreeger Theater, which adjoins the Arena structure and was completed in 1971.

The two theaters run productions simultaneously throughout the September–July season: eight productions at the Arena and four or five at the Kreeger. The company presents its plays in short, regularly scheduled runs rather than in an expensive rolling-repertory system that would require two or more different productions each week. By producing plays in both houses simultaneously, the company achieves some of the creative and aesthetic benefits of a rolling-repertory system without its staging costs. Arena Stage tries to maintain a permanent acting company of about fifteen actors, supplementing them with outside artists when necessary. The world premieres of *The Great White Hope* and *Raisin* took place at the Arena, and the entire cast of the former accompanied that play to its Broadway run.

Arena's vehicle for community service is the Living Stage, which developed out of a pilot theater-in-education program into a full range of improvisational theater activities. Today, the Living Stage offers workshops in the performing arts for children and adults, teacher-training sessions for public and private school systems, and free theater for inner-city youth.

During Arena's first fifteen years, it was able to exist on income from its box office receipts and relatively modest gifts from individual donors. By 1965, however, Arena was aggressively and successfully seeking foundation grants both to support its current operations and to finance building projects. The Ford Foundation has been an especially generous benefactor; over the years, Ford has given Arena $3 million, $1.6 million in capital grants.[55]

Despite this heavy foundation support and, more recently, NEA support, Arena relies more heavily on box office receipts than most nonprofit theaters (see Table 5-9). Arena has a longer and fuller season than most other nonprofit theaters. (In 1973–74, performances of *Raisin* extended to late July.) Its reliance on government support, 12 percent in 1973–74, is characteristic of theater companies, but NEA has been its only significant government benefactor.[56] Arena receives much less local private support than most other theaters. In 1973–74, Arena received less than 9 percent of its income from individuals, corporations, local foundations, and United Fund drives, while the other thirty-one theaters in the Ford Foundation group received 18 percent of their total income from such sources.[57] Arena receives virtually no corporate support.

Washington's Kennedy Center for the Performing Arts is a vigorous and successful competitor with Arena for private funds and accounts, in part, for Arena's failure to obtain much local private

Table 5-9. *Percent Distribution of Income of Nonprofit Professional Theater Companies, by Source, 1973–74*

Source of income	31 theaters, Ford Foundation survey	Arena Stage, Washington	Trinity Square, Providence
Nongovernmental earned income	61	71	53
Nongovernmental unearned income	26	17	24
Government sources	13	12	23
(NEA)	(6)	(12)	(11)
Total	100	100	100

Sources: Ford Foundation unpublished tabulations; Washington Drama Society, Inc., *Financial Report, June 30, 1974; The Rhode Islander: The Providence Sunday Journal Magazine,* October 7, 1973 (data on the *budget* for 1973–74, not actual results); and interview notes.

support. The Kennedy Center surpasses Arena too, in ability to raise capital funds from foreign governments and businesses. More important, Arena is wary about local private support. Zelda Fichandler considers community residents the most conservative of benefactors and those most likely to be hostile to controversial and experimental theater:

> I am not very strong on community giving, except perhaps when it represents only a small percentage of the total. I think we could well do without the hand that rocks the cradle, for the hand that rocks the cradle will also want to raise it in a vote and mix into the pie with it . . . . So, then let the money be given at a distance, once removed, and let it be awarded by a jury of one's peers. Let the audience be the only judge.[58]

The impact of substantial national foundation support over a decade and, recently, significant NEA support is fairly obvious: Arena has become a major force in American theater. The company is substantially housed, operates a very full season, employs about one hundred people year-round, does a great deal of new production, and, directly or indirectly, provides training for the theater. It is in the community outreach and education business although only marginally; its main services are to its audiences in the two theaters and to the theater as an art form. With additional public support, Arena would change its ativities but not in fundamental ways: it would increase the size of the permanent acting company, increase rehearsal time, rent additional storage space for props and costumes, and tour in the United States. With less public support, it would (presumably) have to cut back those of its activities least well supported at the box office and perhaps overcome its squeamishness about raising money from those grubby hands that rock the cradle.

Clearly, NEA support for Arena has little to do with the objective of wider availability; the affluent residents of Washington's suburbs are not so culturally deprived or isolated as to require federal subsidy. The grants to Arena further other objectives: strengthening cultural organizations as such and fostering the development of actors, diretors, playwrights, and those engaged in other theater arts and crafts. In terms of economic efficiency, public subsidy is justified to the extent that it supports Arena's experimental activities. Zelda Fichandler herself regards Arena as a straightforward merit-good case, a means of supporting high-quality performance in the theater. But the Metropolitan Opera Company is unique, whereas the United States contains a fair number of Arena-type companies, all of them good things, too. It is very difficult to determine the "proper" level of public support to which each of them is entitled.

Until recently, the essential financial ingredient in Arena's existence and flowering has not been public subsidy but foundation support. If the major foundations do actually withdraw from the support of theater – as some have threatened to do[59] – Arena will face a difficult future. Presumably, it will seek more NEA support, not for new departures but to replace foundation support for its current operations.

A smaller and newer enterprise than Arena, the Trinity Square Repertory Company of Providence, Rhode Island, has achieved considerable national acclaim, in part because of its very highly regarded appearances on public television's "Theater in America" series. Founded in 1964, Trinity has become celebrated for its production of imaginative new plays and its innovative staging techniques. In 1973, Trinity moved into its present home, a two-theater complex constructed within the old Majestic Theater, formerly a vaudeville house and movie palace. The larger of the two theaters, the 800-seat Lederer, may be the most flexible in this country, if not the world. Aside from a small balcony, the Lederer is essentially a large empty box in which seating, stage, and everything else can be and is rearranged to suit the requirements of each new production.[60]

Trinity did not spring from native roots in Providence but rather was located there as a deliberate act, to establish a regional theater in New England and to reach audiences not familiar with new theater techniques. Adrian Hall, Trinity's founder and artistic director, had the opportunity to locate the theater in New York, and Trinity's productions probably would have been better patronized and more solidly financed if he had done so.

Trinity embarked on efforts to reach and educate new audiences very soon after it was founded. In 1965, a Rockefeller Foundation grant supported Trinity's presentation of twenty performances of *Twelfth Night* for local high school students. In the following year, a three-year grant of more than $500,000 from NEA and the U.S. Office of Education launched the "Project Discovery" program, which is still in operation. Initially, Trinity confined itself to conservative programming in a large auditorium in downtown Providence, to audiences of high school students from across the state, more than 90 percent of whom had never previously attended a live professional theater performance. In recent years, it has become bolder and now routinely presents highly unconventional programs and staging.

In 1966, NEA and the Office of Education also made Project Discovery type grants to theaters in New Orleans and Los Angeles. Neither of the latter programs long survived the expiration of federal funding. But when Trinity's federal Project Discovery grant expired, the state of Rhode Island, local school boards, and private contributions supplied funds to keep the program alive. Today, in addition to live presentations (forty performances in 1974–75), the program provides study materials, tapes, records, and filmstrips based on the productions to schools and public libraries in Rhode Island and conducts workshops for students at Trinity's theater and in the schools.

As Table 5-9 shows, Trinity receives relatively little of its income from box office and similar sources. Trinity has had difficulty in filling the Lederer Theater for weekday evening performances.[61] In the summer of 1974, Trinity spent six weeks in Boston in an effort to bring its productions to the attention of people living in the Boston area who might occasionally make the one-hour trip to see a Trinity performance. The company also tours nationally each year, but it remains considerably short of the fifty-two-week season that Arena very nearly achieves.

Like the Arena, Trinity is not very successful in generating local private gifts but quite successful in attracting grants from national foundations. Aside from the substantial support it receives from the state government and local school boards for Project Discovery, Trinity has little other local government support.

Like Arena, Trinity receives heavy NEA support.[62] In fact, Trinity owes its emergence as a bright star in the American theater firmament to a high degree of public subsidy. Public television has made it possible for Trinity to become a national cultural resource. But Trinity's difficulties in attracting local support at the box office or in contributions raise a troublesome public-policy question; Trinity is supposed to be first of all a regional theater, but the region displays a good deal of indifference to it. This local indifference does not justify allowing Trinity to perish or even to be cut back. Because of Project Discovery, Trinity scores high in terms of the NEA wider-availability objective and even higher than Arena as an experimental theater. Perhaps the appropriate solution is to promote even more nationwide exposure for Trinity, via touring and public television, so that the rest of the country can benefit more from the generous federal subsidy it has been providing.

The records of both Arena and Trinity are somewhat at variance with the statistics for theaters discussed earlier and presented in Table 5-5. Both theaters have substantially increased the number of their performances over time and in other ways have exceeded the statistical averages shown in Table 5-4. The obvious effects of public support on what Arena and, especially, Trinity produce are inconsistent with the figures in Table 5-5, which suggest that in most nonprofit theater companies subsidy has served mainly to increase actors' salaries. These inconsistencies suggest, as in the case of symphony orchestras, that NEA's policy of subsidizing virtually all professional nonprofit theater companies more or less indiscriminately is a questionable use of public funds.

Dance

The New York City Ballet is the country's largest ballet company (in 1973–74, it accounted for roughly one-fourth of the combined operating expenses of the ten ballet companies included in the Ford survey). Founded in 1948 by Lincoln Kirstein and George Balanchine, it operates as a constituent unit of City Center of Music and Drama, Inc. Since 1964, it has performed at the New York State Theater in Lincoln Center; the other principal occupant of the State Theater is the New York City Opera, which is also the other main City Center constituent.

The New York City Ballet originated in the School of American

Ballet, founded by Kirstein and Balanchine in 1934 and still operated by them as a separate entity. Nearly all the New York City
Ballet's dancers (seventy-five out of eighty-five in 1975) are trained
at the school. Unlike classical ballet troupes in the past, the New
York City Ballet does not rely on a star-dancer system; like modern
dance groups, it relies very heavily on a "star" choreographer/
leader, George Balanchine. This dependence raises a basic question
about the ability of the New York City Ballet to function artistically in the long run. The company's financial condition, although
of secondary importance, is a more immediate concern.

The company's fall and spring seasons in New York at Lincoln
Center total twenty-three weeks. The entire company tours for an
average of nine weeks each year, including a month in residence at
the Saratoga Summer Festival, a week at Wolf Trap Farm Park in
Virginia, and two weeks during the winter at the Kennedy Center
in Washington. During its Lincoln Center season, the company
saves on production costs by scheduling its ballets in groups. It may
perform a given ballet three times in one week and not at all again
during the remainder of the season. In accord with the historic
policy of City Center, the company keeps its ticket prices within a
relatively narrow range; in 1975, the top price for both subscription
and nonsubscription seats was $9.95, a low price by New York
performing arts standards.

Scheduling ballets in groups probably works to discourage subscription attendance, on balance, because prospective subscribers
who cannot attend at all in a given week must miss one ballet
entirely. Low top prices should increase ticket sales. In fact, during
the New York season, the company obtains only 25 percent of its
audience from subscription sales (in contrast, most symphony orchestras and opera companies and some regional theater groups
obtain 75 percent or more of their admission receipts from subscription sales), and it seldom fills the 2,779-seat State Theater. In 1973,
it sold only 55 percent of capacity. During the New York season,
the company faces strong competition for the dance audience in
New York from a number of other dance companies. In fact, the
company's parent organization, City Center, has frequently com-
peted with its own constituent, presenting performances of the Joffrey Ballet, the American Ballet Theatre, and the Alvin Ailey Dance
Theater at the old City Center Theater on 55th Street while the
New York City Ballet was in residence at Lincoln Center. Few
dance companies perform in New York for more than one week at
a time. Thus, some observers believe, New York dance audiences

attend the short-stay competing performances for fear of missing them and assume that they will have other chances to "catch" the New York City Ballet.

Still, for a dance company, the New York City Ballet covers a unusually large share of its operating expenditures from earned income from nongovernment sources. In 1973–74, earned income covered 51 percent of the operating expenses of the nine other ballet companies and 60 percent of the expenses of the five modern dance companies in the Ford survey; it covered 70 percent of the New York City Ballet's expenses. In that year, the company's operating expenses were about $4.6 million, and public support amounted to $549,000, of which $138,000 came from the City of New York in the form of payment of operating and maintenance expenses for the State Theater,[63] $146,000 from NEA for touring and new productions, and $265,000 from NYSCA, mostly as general support. Contributions from individuals, corporations, and small foundations (including the New York City Ballet's allocated share of the annual fund drives conducted by Lincoln Center and City Center) in 1973–74 approximately equaled government support.

The biggest factor in the finances of the New York City Ballet, as for so many other performing arts organizations, especially in dance, has been the Ford Foundation. Ford had provided substantial grant and loan assistance to both the New York City Ballet and the New York City Opera prior to 1974, but in that year, it made large grants to both organizations, to be paid out over a seven-year period, provided that the company raised matching funds and met other requirements. The New York City Ballet grant amounted to $3.2 million; the grant erases a $1.4 million deficit accumulated prior to 1974,[64] forgives a previous Ford loan of $500,000 that would have been repayable in 1976 and 1977, establishes a $1 million cash reserve, and provides $300,000 for general operating expense.

The great bulk of the New York City Ballet's unearned income, whether from public or private sources, has been unrestricted as to purpose: in 1973–74, only one-sixth of that income (exclusive of the $1.4 million deficit-erasing Ford grant) was for specified purposes: touring and new productions. The rise in public funding has financed some touring but most of the public subsidy has financed the long New York season, new productions, and fairly substantial increases in compensation for performers. The 1970 union contract increased dancers' salaries by 50 percent, and the contract settling the 1973 one-month strike provided another generous settlement. A reduction in public or private unearned income very likely would limit the number of new productions and/or reduce the length of the New York season. It also might cause a cutback in touring, but such a cutback would not significantly reduce the exposure of new audiences to ballet because the company does not tour small or remote places where the population is starved for the live performing arts but rather places that are already relatively richly supplied. Thus, public support for the New York City Ballet does not further the objective of wider availability.

Public support has obviously been useful in increasing artistic quality by providing a longer season for artists and by financing new productions. But the substantial foundation and government support received by the New York City Ballet, as well as a number of other professional dance companies, may have caused a more rapid increase in the number of dance performances than in the size of the dance audience. The use of public funds to cover the deficits of symphony orchestras, opera companies, and theater companies (like Arena) that play to nearly full houses but still are unable to cover expenses is quite different from the use of such funds for a ballet company that plays to a half-empty house in a city well supplied with other dance performances, nearly all of which also are government subsidized.

Relative to theater and the other performing arts, ballet is still an "infant industry" in this country, an art form to which most people have never been exposed, and one that requires subsidized production if it is ever to reach a critical mass of audience. As such it may be entitled to subsidy, especially when houses are half-empty. But the New York City Ballet itself does not qualify for a subsidy on this basis. This infant is more than forty years old, and ballet is hardly exotic or unfamiliar in New York. The New York City Ballet aparently does not draw full houses in New York not because it is unfamiliar but because it has too much competition.[65] So long a season is not necessarily essential to achieve the merit-goods standard of high artistic quality; its principal effect apparently is to raise artists' earnings and encourage their unions to demand inflationary settlements (even, at the price – as in 1976–77 – of a strike that very nearly canceled the entire season).

The Paul Taylor Dance Company was founded in 1955 by Paul Taylor, who had previously earned acclaim in the field of modern dance as a soloist and choreographer. When NEA launched its Coordinated Dance Residency Touring Program in 1968, the Paul Taylor Company was one of the four original groups included, and it has participated in the NEA touring program each year since then. In addition, since 1960, the company has toured abroad, usually under the sponsorship of the State Department and often with foundation support.[66] Although it is New York-based, the Paul Taylor Company in recent years has performed in New York for only two weeks each year, one week in fall or winter and a second in late spring. Unlike the New York City Ballet, which spends twenty-three weeks at Lincoln Center, the Paul Taylor Company usually spends twenty-three weeks a year on tour.

The company is composed of eleven dancers and one understudy and has thirty dances in its repertoire. Taylor usually composes two new works each year for presentation during the brief Broadway season. He has often presented his company on both commercial and public television, and the documentary, "Paul Taylor: An Artist and His Work," has had numerous public-television showings. During the 1974–75 season, the company toured in eleven states, usually for a two-and-a-half-day presentation at each stop, and it was in residence for seven weeks during the summer at the Center for Music, Drama and Art in Lake Placid, New York. During the summer residency and while on tour, the group not only performs nightly but offers lecture-demonstrations, master classes, and open rehearsals.

Recently, about three-fourths of the company's income has come from performances (mainly in the form of contract fees from sponsors of touring performances), an unusually high percentage for modern dance companies. But the nonprofit organizations that sponsor company touring performances are themselves frequently subsidized by NEA directly, by NEA through state arts councils, and with state and local government funds, so that the books of the company–like the books of most dance groups–understate the extent of dependence on government funds and, by implication, overstate the dependence on box office income.[67]

Together, NEA, mainly supporting new productions, and NYSCA have financed about 20 percent of the company's budget; private gifts provide only about 5 percent of the total. The unearned one-fourth of the company's income essentially finances part of the deficit that the company incurs for its brief New York season. If the Taylor Company had more direct public support, it would perform more in New York; the dancers would like to lengthen the New York season because they live in New York and consider the New York dance audience the most challenging. But adding two weeks to the 1975–76 New York season would have increased the company's total budget (above the 1975–76 level) by nearly one-fourth and, despite the sellout crowds the company usually gets in New York, would not have brought in an equivalent amount in ticket sales.

In fact, by the end of the 1975–76 season, the deficits stemming even from a two-week New York season had so undermined the company's finances that its continued existence was threatened. The company's Argentinian impresario, who was on the verge of bankruptcy himself, unexpectedly canceled a six-week South American tour, planned a year earlier and designed to recoup some of the losses on the June 1976 New York season. In September 1976, the company announced that it was "disbanding indefinitely." Two weeks later, a rescue effort to continue the troupe was announced. This effort included a one-week season in Washington in November 1976 opening with a gala benefit, an NEA emergency "challenge grant," pledges by corporations made through the National Corporate Fund for Dance, and a reconstruction of the company's board of directors. The Washington season yielded $20,000 net, part of the $52,000 necessary to match on a three-to-one basis, the $17,500 NEA challenge grant.[68]

The dance touring that NEA has promoted since 1968 has helped to develop audiences for the dance in general and provided needed exposure for lesser-known dance companies. Touring has provided the Paul Taylor Company's dancers with additional employment and has strengthened the company in that sense. But the company hardly needs exposure. It is well-known, regarded as one of America's very best dance groups, and guided by a leader who is widely recognized as highly creative. However, even if the Paul Taylor Company itself is well established, modern dance outside New York City has enough of the qualities of an infant industry to justify NEA's efforts to expose new audiences outside New York to the best in modern dance.

The policy perspective of public subsidy for the dance clearly differs from that of public subsidy for some other performing-art institutions, notably the resident theater. In dance, the artistic resource is deemed worthy of support only if there is an enormous amount of touring; in theater, the resource is deemed worthy of support if it simply carries on at its home base. Perhaps a more nearly intermediate position for public policy would be appropriate for both. Subsidies for touring or other forms of exposure to new and wider audiences are easy to justify, perhaps more for an infant industry like modern dance than for experimental theater, but this difference is one of degree, not kind. Support of modern dance at its home base, as well as support of a theater company like Trinity Square, can be justified because of the experimental nature of the activity and on merit-goods grounds. It is not self-evident that one art form is distinctly more meritorious than the other.

Art Service Organizations[69]

Art service organizations were functioning in the United States long before government began providing significant financial support for the arts. Some organizations, such as ASOL, founded in 1942 (or Opera America, founded in 1970), were established to serve the common interests of arts institutions of a given type. Some, particularly outside the performing arts, provide a variety of services ranging from emergency financial aid to assistance in selling artistic output to artists working on their own or in small, precariously financed and managed groups. Some are avowedly educational in purpose, designed to bring the arts to new audiences or to involve people in the arts as active participants. And some combine these objectives.

One of the country's oldest nonprofit presenting arts organizations is Young Audiences, Inc. Since 1950, it has been presenting musical performances for school-age children, mostly in elementary schools, and today it has forty local chapters in thirty-four states. In 1975, Young Audiences presented performances in 4,500 schools, utilizing the services of 1,500 artists, with a total attendance of more than 3 million children. The programs consist of ensemble performances, usually by musicians in local orchestras, including some spoken description of the piece of music, the instrument, the composer, and the like.

Until recently, nearly all Young Audiences recitals were more or less isolated two-hour episodes, not preceded or followed up by related work in the school itself. In 1971, NEA and the Sears Roebuck Foundation contracted with the J. R. Taft Corporation to conduct an evaluation of the Young Audiences program. This study found that the recitals had relatively little impact on their young audiences; few children remembered the melody, who the musician was, or the name of the piece.[70] Subsequently, Young Audiences has moved toward what it calls "intensity programs." It assigns an ensemble group to a given school for two or three months; during this time the ensemble presents between six and sixteen performances for a limited student audience whose membership remains the same for the entire residency period. The performances are followed by workshops and classroom demonstrations in a format that permits direct interactions among students, artists, and teachers.[71]

From its earliest days, Young Audiences has been popular among private benefactors. It has received substantial support from national and local foundations. In 1974–75, eighty-five corporations contributed funds. Music world notables regularly participate in the annual Young Audience Week, the organization's main function for fund raising from individuals. The largest nongovernmental contributor has been the Music Performance Trust Fund, an organization established by the musicians' union some years ago, financed from royalties on the performance of recorded music, for the purpose of paying fees to union musicians at free performances.[72]

In 1975, close to one-half of the total Young Audiences budget of more than $2 million came from public funds. About $500,000 was put up by local school boards (some of this money was raised by parent-teacher associations), and $250,000 was granted by NEA. Some local chapters receive support from the U.S. Office of Education, and many are assisted by state arts councils.

Young Audiences obviously can use additional public support: for expansion in general and to increase the number of season-long ensemble-in-residency programs. Just as obviously, Young Audiences is one of those "safe" institutions that has little difficulty in obtaining private and local public support. The grants it has received from NEA have not clearly been essential to its operations (given the substantial public support from other agencies) or had lasting educational and audience-expanding effects. Certainly, the mission of Young Audiences is a proper object of public support. But if NEA support is largely a substitute for other forms of private and public support that might have been forthcoming in the absence of NEA grants, or—still more—if Young Audiences programs have not been very effective in building audiences, then public support that is warranted in concept has been wasteful in practice.

Affiliate Artists, Inc., also is devoted to bringing the performing arts to new audiences—adults in this case. It was founded in 1966 in the belief that

> the young professional performer is a powerful and barely tapped resource, not only to extend the support base for the arts, but to enhance the quality of life in America by taking his talent to where millions of people conventionally congregate— which is not in the concert hall.[73]

An equally important objective is to fill "the vacuum America has thus far offered the artists between formal training and full mastery of his instrument"[74] by offering young artists opportunities for intensive performing experience.

The performers – mostly singers and instrumentalists, but also conductors, dancers, and actors – are placed in communities for residencies totaling eight weeks a year. Each of the fifty-plus Affiliate Artist appointments (there were forty-nine in 1974 and fifty-five in 1975) is separately financed by a corporation, foundation, or public agency together with a local presenting institution – a college; a state, regional, or local arts council; a performing-arts organization or art festival; or a church or civic group. In 1975, each appointment cost $12,000, $10,000 contributed by the sponsor and $2,000 by the presenter, with the artist receiving $7,000 and the rest used for travel, administrative, and promotional costs.

The Affiliate Artist is selected by the presenter from a list supplied by Affiliate Artists after auditions. In the course of four two-week visits to his community, the artist averages eighty informal performances in a wide variety of settings ranging from schools, libraries, and churches to factories and shopping centers. The program emphasizes meetings with local residents and breaking down the formal barriers between artist and audience. In the early years, nearly all of the presenting organizations were colleges, but recently, most have been other types of organizations.[75]

In 1974, with the support of the Exxon Corporation and NEA, Affiliate Artists launched a young conductors program, placing younger conductors with leading orchestras for an entire year, to fill a gap in the career path between intermediate conducting and national recognition. The plan is to extend this model to programs for promising young choreographers and theater directors.

Affiliate Artists' principal public benefactor is NEA, which functions both as a cosponsor of individual artists and as a source of grants to support the organization's programs, providing about one-fifth of Affiliate Artists' budget. State and local arts agencies provide smaller amounts as presenters and, in a few cases, as sponsors. Foundations (notably, the Sears Roebuck Foundation) and corporations also provide substanial support both for sponsorships and for general operating expenses, often on a continuing basis rather than as one-time grants. Continuing corporate sponsorships especially enable the company to identify with the specific appointment and take pride in it.

The organization has grown gradually, adding to the number of appointments and expanding the scope of its programs only as financing, particularly from private sources, has been assured. The organization has found public funds valuable, not only for the money itself but also as a seal of approval that facilitates private-sector fund raising. Today, the NEA grants, especially those for overhead expenses, seem essential to maintain the present level of operations.

Affiliate Artists' impact on adult audiences is difficult to evaluate, but the organization clearly serves to assist talented young artists already launched in their careers, affording them performance opportunities that are neither one-night stands nor lengthy residencies isolated from the main centers of artistic activity, and providing them with a modicum of financial security. In the performing arts, it is not easy to design ways of assisting individual artists (as opposed to arts organizations). The Affiliate Artists approach appears to be an ingenious solution to that problem. Both merit-goods grounds and market-failure arguments justify public subsidy to break bottlenecks in the development of the career of talented young artists. The NEA grants to Affiliate Artists appear to have been a sensible use of public funds.

In the middle and late 1960s, the City of New York, like large-city governments elsewhere, mounted a number of small summer programs under the general rubric of "culture and recreation" to benefit young people in low-income areas. One of these programs was the production of films by Lower East Side teenagers to be shown on the city government's "Moviebus." This program was the seed from which Young Filmakers Foundation, Inc., was generated, in 1968. Subsequently, Young Filmakers expanded its range of film and television media services and its target population, which now includes both individuals of all ages and nonprofit arts organizations.

Its Media Equipment Resource Center (MERC) lends film, video, and sound equipment to users throughout New York State for periods up to six months at no charge. In 1974–75, nearly 500 individual artists and nonprofit organizations received equipment loans with an estimated dollar value (at commercial rental rates) of nearly $600,000. In addition, MERC offers in-house studio, editing, dubbing, and equipment-maintenance services to filmmakers. In 1974–75, 259 artists and organizations used such services; the estimated commercial value of these free in-house services was more than $200,000. Recipients of MERC equipment loans and in-house services distributed their films via public access cable and, occasionally, broadcast television; educational organizations; and presentations in theaters, galleries, and festivals. In addition, theater and dance groups produced media works for incorporation in live performances and used MERC's facilities to document their live work for analysis or the historical record.

In January 1972, Young Filmakers instituted a Media Teacher Training (MTT) program to instruct educators in the teaching of media-use skills to elementary and high school students, as well as to community groups. MTT operates teaching workshops on a contractual basis on the premises of interested schools and organizations. The workshops vary in length from one-day preliminary introductions to intensive sessions. During 1974–75, more than 1,000 New York State teachers, librarians, recreation workers, and filmmakers received training or retraining under MTT's program, which charges a fee based on the participant's ability to pay. In addition to these training workshops, Young Filmakers provides teacher-placement consultation and media program design for schools throughout the United States.

Young Filmakers directly interacts with its Lower East Side neighborhood through Community-Action-Newsreel, a media production and training center offering television-studio production courses and producing new films and videotapes on such subjects as community/police relations, drug addiction, and problems of the aged, as well as coverage of cultural entertainment developed by local black, Puerto Rican, and Chinese artists. These productions have been aired on commercial and public television stations. Members of minority groups and women are given priority as applicants for C-A-N training, which will soon include a course in television script writing.

In 1975, the U.S. Office of Education contracted with Young Filmakers for the production of ten half-hour television programs on Caribbean-Hispanic Americans, for a junior high school-age audience. Young Filmakers also was the recipient of a Ford Foundation research grant for a study of the relation of filmmaking to cognitive and perceptual development in children and youth.

In 1974–75, public funds provided the great bulk of the Young Filmakers' budget of nearly $430,000. NYSCA is the program's major public benefactor, providing about 40 percent of the budget in 1974–75 and considerably higher percentages in earlier years. Young Filmakers has received small NEA grants under the Expansion Arts and Public Media programs and small amounts of city government support. Recently, the Office of Education contract has been the major source of federal government money.

Like other NYSCA grant recipients, Young Filmakers is required to account for the expenditures of its NYSCA grant on a county-by-county basis as a result of the legislative requirement that NYSCA expend at least 50 cents per capita in each of the state's counties. The MERC equipment loan program is one of the few NYSCA grant recipients that operates statewide. Accounting for MERC's activities on a county-by-county basis has proven onerous.

Unlike Young Audiences and Affiliate Artists, which are only marginally dependent on public support and receive most of their money from private sources, Young Filmakers would not have come into existence or developed successfully without public support; its most important activity, MERC, has been almost totally sustained by public funds. The activities of Young Filmakers, particularly MERC, are a clear-cut instance of highly efficient public subsidy; the subsidy provides services whose value, on the basis of demonstrable quantitative measures, substantially exceeds the costs of the subsidy to the taxpayer.[76] Government support has enabled individual artists and small nonprofit organizations to produce films to which the high cost of equipment and studio facilities and the lack of technical expertise might otherwise pose insurmountable barriers. In a sense, government support has been instrumental in the realization of economies of scale – one of the classical arguments for government intervention in any field of activity. And the able and imaginative principals in Young Filmakers seem to be continually finding new opportunities to realize economies of scale and otherwise provide a large amount of service for each dollar of subsidy.

Poets and Writers, Inc., is an example of the heavy reliance the New York State Council on the Arts places on art service organizations in its grant programs. Poets and Writers was created to serve NYSCA's poetry program, and most of its activities continue to be in New York State, although NYSCA is no longer its sole source of funds. Until 1975, Poets and Writers administered NEA's Poets-in-Schools program in New York, which is now under the direction of a new service organization.

Poets and Writers' primary responsibility is the administration of a statewide Visiting Writers Program which makes grants to nonprofit organizations and schools interested in sponsoring readings, workshops, and residencies for poets, writers, and playwrights. The sponsoring institution is responsible for most of the program's expenses; Poets and Writers limits its contribution to a portion of the poet's or writer's fee, which can range from $100 to $1,000. In 1973–74, 209 sponsors received aid for presentations by 337 different writers.

With NEA assistance, Poets and Writers also publishes biennial directories of American poets and fiction writers as well as a bimonthly information newsletter. *The Directory of American Poets,* 1975 edition, contained the names, addresses, and brief resumes of more than 1,500 poets as well as a listing of over 450 organizations that have sponsored readings and workshops. A special service section of the volume provided such information as a list of bookstores that stock poetry and literary magazines; a listing of anthologies, films, and videotapes of contemporary authors; names of literary organizations and publications useful to writers; and a checklist for sponsors of readings and workshops. *The Directory of American Fiction Writers* includes similar information of use to prose writers. The newsletter, *CODA,* acts as a supplement to these publications, providing practical information on book fairs, copyright decisions, tax information, and deadlines for public and foundation grant applications; it also provides information on such subjects as how to get one's first book published, approaching foundations, and establishing a small press. In addition, *CODA* includes a listing of poets and authors available for readings, and descriptions of residency and reading programs assisted by Poets and Writers' funds.

Poets and Writers has used NEA funds to tape readings by poets for use on National Public Radio. In 1973–74, Poets and Writers received a grant from the U.S. Office of Education under the Manpower Development and Training Act to train unemployed and underemployed poets to work in the Poets-in-Schools programs. In that year, government support provided 86 percent of the organization's $223,000 budget. The major share of public funds, 48 percent of the total budget, came from NYSCA. The only private support received by the program was a single foundation grant of $20,000, to satisfy NEA's matching requirement for the Poets-in-Schools grant, and less than $12,000 in income from sales of the *Directory* and interest earnings. But Poets and Writers' accounts do not include nearly $95,000 in matching funds, in the form of authors' fees paid by local schools and nonprofit sponsoring organizations, generated by the activities of Poets and Writers. In 1973–74, in effect, federal and New York State grants totaling about $192,000 provided and stimulated a total of $182,000 in fees to poets and writers; covered the administrative costs of the residency, readings, and training activities; and paid most of the costs of the *Directory, CODA,* and the radio tapes.

Poets and Writers is clearly a creature of the major public arts-funding agencies, not an independent entity with some record of being able to attract private money in some quantity that is marginally assisted with public money. For such an organization, the general requirement that each government grant be matched by funds from another source seems inappropriate and potentially hazardous. Presumably, NEA and NYSCA will recognize the de facto status of, and continue to support, Poets and Writers as an organization serving artists in a field that receives rather modest public support and providing them with both services and income rather inexpensively.

The rationale for using public money to provide earned income for literary artists like poets is based on the notion that this artistic activity is meritorious and requires support because its market is so small. Because the market is so limited and the earnings of so many literary artists so low, the informative and other services provided by Poets and Writers – which, like the activities of Young Filmakers, amount to realizing economies of scale – cannot be sold on a self-supporting basis to the consumers of these services. That is, the services of the *Directory* and *CODA* are not regularly provided by commercial organizations because such organizations could not sell them in sufficient quantity at prices high enough to cover their costs. Thus, the public funds used to support Poets and Writers do not substitute for market processes (or, since the organization has proved unable to attract private gifts, for privately raised funds). To the extent that literature is deemed to merit a subsidy designed to elicit artistic output beyond that generated by the ordinary commercial process, public support of Poets and Writers seems warranted.

Like Poets and Writers, the Coordinating Council of Literary Magazines (CCLM) is very much a creature of the government arts funding agencies rather than an independent entity with a significant private-support base. It was founded in 1967 by a group of writers and editors concerned for the future of noncommercial literary magazines, whose financial health, always fragile, seemed to be getting even more precarious. At that time, the recently established NEA had decided to subsidize literary magazines. In 1970, NYSCA also decided to subsidize literary magazines based in New York State, but in the state alone, hundreds of magazines were likely to apply for support. The government agencies therefore turned to CCLM as a medium through which "wholesale" blocks of government subsidy of literary magazines could be "retailed" to the applicants.

Today, CCLM is a membership organization with more than 300 magazines as members. Its elected grants committees decide on annual grants, which generally range between $250 and $3,000, for general support, payments to authors, or other specified needs. To be eligible for a grant, a magazine must have been published for at least a year and have put out, during that time, at least three issues, focusing on creative and critical writing. Scholarly magazines and those that concentrate on current events or social and political issues ordinarily do not qualify for support.

This retailing of subsidy to individual magazines remains CCLM's major function, but in addition CCLM has taken on activities akin to those of Young Filmakers, centrally organizing and providing services that are costly when done by individual magazines, thus realizing economies of scale in such areas as low-cost magazine production, graphic design and promotion, and subscription and distribution matters. In 1971, CCLM established a Print Center in New York (subsequently spun off to an independent organization that receives direct support from NYSCA), offering low-cost printing facilities to individual magazines.[77] In 1974, a similar Print Center was opened in California. Aided by a substantial Ford Foundation grant to improve the distribution of small magazines, CCLM is developing a library subscription system and increasing the visibility of small magazines through activities at exhibitions and book fairs and advertising in commercial publications. Seminars, workshops, and other forms of technical assistance to the staffs of small magazines conducted since 1970, are part of the distribution project.

Prior to receiving the Ford grant, CCLM obtained about three-fourths of its budget from public sources, with NEA the predominant contributor. Nearly all of the remainder represented matching funds raised by the magazines themselves, not private-sector contributions to CCLM. Apart from the Ford grant, CCLM has had little success in raising money from nongovernment sources. Thus, public support has served to *create* CCLM, not merely to permit its expansion, and the withdrawal of public support would lead to its demise.

In 1976, NEA's Literature Panel, judging CCLM's administrative costs to be excessive, suggested that NEA withdraw support from CCLM and economize (thereby freeing up money for additional grants in literature) by taking on the retailing function itself. Fortunately, this proposal has not been implemented. It might have freed a modest amount of money for grants simply because NEA's administrative costs (prior to fiscal 1978) came from a separate appropriation for that purpose (to the National Foundation for the Arts and Humanities, the umbrella organization). But it is inconceivable that NEA or any other federal agency could administer the program more cheaply than CCLM. (For one thing, federal salaries are far higher than those paid by CCLM.) Thus, the real result would be an increase in total public costs for the activity. Moreover, the public would not obviously benefit from the participation of the Literature Panel itself in the contention-ridden business of making large numbers of decisions on very small grants.

The justification for public subsidy for CCLM is almost identical with that for Poets and Writers. The fostering of literary magazines is a merit-good, and CCLM's provision of services and facilities amounts to realizing economies of scale. But NEA's Literature Panel has showed more concern for spurious economies than for the fundamental question of whether and how much literary magazines should be encouraged, by whatever means. This episode raises doubts about the quality of decision making by NEA panels.

Much of the original impetus for the establishment of CCLM came from fears for the survival of such artistically well-established but financially shaky literary magazines as *Partisan Review*. But increasingly, with NEA encouragement, CCLM has used its funds to foster the emergence of new magazines that are of very marginal literary quality in many cases and function on such a small scale that they can benefit substantially from a grant of $1,000 or $2,000. This use of funds has become somewhat controversial.

Policy makers dealing with subsidies in many areas encounter conflict between spreading subsidy thinly over a large number of recipients and concentrating it on a few, between using public funds to encourage expansion and participation and using them to preserve the better-established entities. In the arts alone, such conflicts arise among opera, theater, and orchestra companies no less than among literary magazines.[78] But the conflicts are especially sharp among literary magazines here because the total public funding available for them is so limited.

Another membership organization, one that long antedates the advent of public support of the arts and that often has championed the individual literary artist *against* governments, is the P.E.N. American Center. Founded in 1922, it is a constituent unit of International P.E.N., a worldwide association of poets, playwrights, essayists, editors, and novelists, the basic goal of which is "to promote and maintain friendship and intellectual cooperation among men and women of letters in all countries, in the interests of literature, the exchange of ideas, freedom of expression, and good will." Membership in P.E.N. is by invitation only, and invitations are extended only to published writers and editors of demonstrated accomplishments. In 1975, P.E.N. had approximately 1,500 American members.

The organization maintains an emergency fund for needy writers and sponsors workshops for beginning writers in underprivileged areas, lectures by and receptions for visiting foreign authors, an annual P.E.N. translation prize, a prison writers' competition, reduced-rate health insurance for writers, aid to refugee writers, and book exhibits. In addition, P.E.N. publishes an occasional newsletter and two annuals listing American and foreign sources of grants and awards for writers. Both American P.E.N. and International P.E.N. are deeply involved in combating the censorship of literary works and seeking better protection of literary copyrights, as well as in organizing campaigns to petition East European, Latin American, and Asian countries to free imprisoned writers. As of 1975, P.E.N. had more than 400 names on its roster of imprisoned writers.

The American Center's various activities clearly are not of the educational outreach type. They are designed to promote literature generally but the welfare of professional writers more particularly. The results of a survey of P.E.N. members conducted in 1972 justify this concern for the economic welfare of individual writers, including the accomplished writers that comprise P.E.N.'s membership. Fewer than 40 percent of these professional writers reported had income – from all sources – in excess of $10,000 that year; only one-fourth received all their income from writing. Most depended heavily on earnings from teaching, lecturing, and employment in publishing, advertising, or television.

Since its inception, NEA has been making grants to American P.E.N. Recently, NEA and, in much smaller quantities, NYSCA have supplied roughly one-half of P.E.N.'s budget ($180,000 in 1976). The organization raises some money, with difficulty, from foundations, but most of its private-sector income comes from its own constituency in the form of dues, receipts from the sale of publications, contributions by its own more prosperous members, and some assistance from publishers, notably for translation prizes.

Public support has not changed P.E.N.'s mission or transformed the organization, but it has permitted American P.E.N. to expand its activities. Although NEA has encouraged and continues to encourage such expansion, and although P.E.N. has a list of projects it would like to undertake, P.E.N. has difficulty in raising matching funds and is afraid that hasty expansion would jeopardize its ability to continue to serve its writing constituency effectively and at low cost. Given P.E.N.'s long record of achievement, if NEA were to increase its commitment to literature, increased grants to P.E.N. – with some easing of the matching requirement – might be reasonably efficient. If literature is to be assisted on merit-goods grounds, P.E.N.'s activities and performance qualify it as a recipient of such assistance.

Like so many young artists in other fields – poets, writers, musicians, filmmakers – young visual artists have three kinds of needs that service organizations can supply: opportunities for earning more income, more chances to expose their work to audiences, and supporting facilities and services that are expensive for individuals operating on their own. The Committee for the Visual Arts (CVA) is a small, New York-based service organization founded in 1974, largely at NYSCA's urging, to meet all these needs. In 1974–75, $60,000 of its $85,000 budget came from NYSCA and another $15,000 from NEA. As of September 1975, the organization had made virtually no organized private fund-raising efforts.

The activity that CVA was originally organized to conduct is its Visiting Artists Program, under which nonprofit art and educational organizations in New York State sponsor lectures by visual artists and art critics, typically involving a speaker's fee of $150. CVA pays up to half the fee and travel expenses, and the sponsor defrays the other part of the costs; in 1973–74, fifty-six different organizations sponsored 140 lectures by artists and critics. Another form of financial support for artists is CVA's Emergency Materials Fund, which provides artists with up to $300 each for the purchase of materials for a commissioned work, or for transportation and related costs for an exhibition, when the commission or exhibition offer comes from a nonprofit sponsor.

The largest activity in CVA's budget is Artists' Space, a gallery for New York State artists who have no commercial gallery affiliation. Each month, a rotating election committee, itself chosen by polling as many as 650 artists, selects three artists to exhibit in the gallery. The gallery also is used for performing artists' presentations in the evenings, especially for the presentation of works by filmmakers and multimedia and video artists.

Another activity designed to assist "unknown" visual artists in gaining exposure is the Unaffiliated Artists File, a depository of slides of the work of New York State visual artists without commercial gallery connections. After three years of operation, the file has grown to include slides submitted by more than 500 persons. In addition, NEA supports CVA's National Registry of Public Art, which contains slides, photographs, and descriptive information about visual art in public places.

On the face of it, each of these activities is a useful and creative way to deal with real problems in the visual arts, and some of the programs obviously qualify for public subsidy under the economies of scale argument, if the visual arts in *some* form are deemed merit goods. But most of CVA's staff time is absorbed by activities that the organization itself considers to be its lowest priorities, notably the Emergency Materials Fund and the Unaffiliated Artists File. The file has grown to an unmanageable size in part because CVA imposes no professional or esthetic requirements on registrants; as a result, the file includes hobby painters along with serious, would-be professional artists.

Moreover, most of the things CVA does are not unique but to some extent duplicate services provided by others, sometimes without subsidy. Hard by CVA's gallery in the Soho district, young and relatively unknown artists are running a number of galleries as artists' cooperatives without public subsidy.[79] Many commercial galleries in Soho make their space available free of charge for evening performances. Creative Artists Public Service (CAPS), the organization NYSCA established to operate its program of direct grants to individual artists, maintains a file of artists who have been grant recipients, which, because it reflects some screening for quality, is probably more useful to organizers of exhibitions, critics, and collectors than CVA's file. It is difficult to justify public subsidy – even in small amounts – for things that are already being done, with or without subsidy, however worthwhile those things are in their own right.

The major nationwide service organization concerned with crafts and the "artist craftsman" is the American Crafts Council, founded in 1943. Some of the council's activities involve crafts as a medium of self-expression for ordinary people, but by and large they serve professional-level craftsmen functioning as artists. In 1956, the council founded the Museum of Contemporary Crafts in New York; it sends museum exhibitions to other cities and formerly operated a museum on the West Coast. It sponsors regional workshops, seminars, and lectures on crafts; it also runs a rental slide and film service and issues a number of publications, including the monthly *Craft Horizons,* directories of craft shops and courses, bibliographies of reference materials, lists of suppliers of crafts material, and a newsletter for crafts educators. Many of its services are directed to its more than 37,000 member-craftsmen; for example, they may use the New York headquarters as a depository for port-folios to be perused by potential clients and customers.

Until 1968, one benefactor, Aileen Wells, provided almost all of the council's income, aside from membership dues and earnings from the sale of services. In 1968, Mrs. Wells began to reduce her support; the council then began to seek foundation, corporate, and government support aggressively for the first time and to generate more earned income. But in recent years, the council has incurred large deficits and substantially depleted its capital, which is now near exhaustion.

The council's budget is in excess of $1 million annually. Earned income, notably from *Craft Horizons* and membership dues, covers well over half the budget. National foundations provide some sup-port. Government funds, amounting to roughly 10 percent of the budget, include a small general-support grant and a NYSCA grant earmarked for Museum of Contemporary Crafts staff salaries, a National Park Service contract for services connected with crafts programs in the national parks (for example, a program for the Gateway National Seashore in New York and New Jersey), and a similar contract with the U.S. Office of Education. A few state arts councils provide small grants to the council; and a larger number of state councils directly fund local crafts organizations.

Obviously, government support of the council has been much too small to have had a great impact on its activities, and general public support has been insufficient to overcome the council's mas-sive financial difficulties. Meanwhile, the "crafts industry" is boom-ing with evident growth in sales of the work of professional and semiprofessional craftsmen, great success for crafts fairs and shows, and vast expansion in the number of crafts hobbyists and the sales of books, kits, and supplies to them. The council must remain a nonprofit organization with tax exemption if it is to receive grants from foundations and NEA and contributions from corporations and individuals. But its status prevents it from taking full advantage of this boom. For example, its magazine, *Craft Horizons,* is limited in the amount of advertising it can sell. The council originated the Rhinebeck (New York) Crafts Fair as an educational venture some years ago, but it became so profitable that the council had to spin it off, making it a separate commercial corporation.

Perhaps both the council and the arts funding agencies would benefit from a basic reorganization in which the museum and a limited range of educational activities would retain nonprofit tax exempt status – and receive NEA, NYSCA, and foundation support – and the council's other services to craftsmen would be handled by a new membership corporation that could exploit the booming market for crafts and also contract with government agencies, like the Park Service and the Office of Education, to provide consulting services. Without such a reorganization, the American Crafts Council will require a very substantial increase in public subsidy in order to survive. And that increase is hard to justify for an organization that has opportunities to obtain additional earned income.

In fact, it is hard to justify *any* public subsidy for an activity that is commercially booming and about which people can learn (and in which they can participate as either consumers or producers) through numerous alternative – and unsubsidized – means. Crafts present no problem of access or availability, of economies of scale, of centralization, or of Baumol-Bowen cost-trends. The decision to subsidize the council seems to be the product of a particular chain of reasoning: the crafts are meritorious; the main service organization, the American Crafts Council, is pressed financially; hence, the council should receive public support. The amounts of money involved in such decisions are small, but however small, the funds assigned to NEA or NYSCA do not become the personal property of agency officials or panels to be spent carelessly.

Such conclusions as can be drawn as to the efficacy of public subsidy of the arts from these sixteen cases tend to reinforce the obvious: public subsidy is most likely to have impacts that are consistent with plausible public-policy goals if the recipient organizations are run by people who combine *both* artistic imagination *and* thoughtful management. The cases show that public subsidy has produced some splendid artistic outcomes but that it is also capable of having an impact that is close to invisible. And they do suggest some conclusions about the effects of public support in terms of its objectives. For example, public subsidy is justified to overcome the barriers to access to the arts that are associated with low incomes. Subsidy that results in lower ticket prices (Table 5-5 suggests that theater and opera companies generally raised ticket prices by less than expected percentages between 1965–66 and 1973–74, when public support was steeply rising), finances free performances (NYSCA and New York City support of Metropolitan Opera concert performances in the parks, city of Philadelphia support of the Robin Hood Dell concerts), or brings ensembles and artists to the schools (the Charlotte Symphony, Eastern Opera

Company of Maryland, Trinity Square, Young Audiences, Poets and Writers) can be construed as at least designed in part to further this objective.[80]

Subsidies are required simply to achieve an economically efficient allocation of resources if they generate important benefits external to the immediate producers and consumers of the arts. One source of external benefits is the interdependence among art forms, particularly musical arts. For example, Baltimore Opera musicians also play for the Baltimore Symphony and other nearby orchestras that do not provide full-time employment; thus, public support of the Baltimore Opera Company probably confers some benefits on consumers who attend the symphony but not the opera performances. Subsidies to the Charlotte Symphony Orchestra also enhance the peformances of the local opera company, but in this instance, the effectiveness of NEA grants has not been clearly established. Subsidies to the Philadelphia Orchestra, which provides its musicians with year-round employment, do not have such spillover effects. And, given the abundance of first-rank musicians and performance opportunities in New York, support of the New York City Ballet also is unlikely to generate spillovers of this type.

Another external benefit is that provided to future generations by the preservation of the great artistic works of the past, the nurturing and development of distinguished artistic organizations, and the production of new works of high quality. The activities of most of the major performing-arts organizations generate such benefits, but public subsidy does not invariably enhance their ability to do so. The subsidy for the Philadelphia Orchestra probably does not, that for the Metropolitan Opera almost certainly does.

Yet another external benefit comes from experimentation. Both Arena and, especially, Trinity Square; both the New York City Ballet and, especially, the Paul Taylor Dance Company, as well as the Baltimore Opera are experimental in the sense of taking the risks associated with putting on wholly new works. The Baltimore Opera and some of the service organizations, notably Affiliate Artists and Young Filmakers, are experimental in the sense of trying out new methods of providing services to artists or of artists.

Whatever purpose they may serve in other places, the arts surely have a significant positive effect on the economy of New York City, an external benefit that warrants part, perhaps most, of the New York City and NYSCA support of the major New York City performing-arts organizations and those service organizations that have a strong New York City orientation. The Met and the New

York City Ballet are clearly the prime contenders among our examples in this respect.

Economic efficiency also calls for subsidy when production costs have certain characteristics, one of which is declining unit costs as the scale of operations increases. Young Filmakers and the literary service organizations achieve economies of scale by the centralized provision of various types of services and facilities.

The high costs of providing information to potential audiences and artists about the nature of the arts call for subsidy of various touring, outreach, and educational activities, at least to the extent that such activities would not be undertaken without subsidy. Touring or other performances before new audiences can justify local government support of the Charlotte Symphony and state and NEA support of Trinity, the Eastern Opera Company of Maryland, and the Paul Taylor Dance Company. Support for the Paul Taylor Company also can be rationalized as supporting an infant industry. The information cost problem is a basis for support of Affiliate Artists and Poets and Writers. It also is applicable, in theory, to Young Audiences and the American Crafts Council, but in practice subsidy to these organizations is of questionable efficacy and/or necessity.

The claim of the arts to be so meritorious that they deserve subsidy to make them more widely available than market forces alone would make them obviously has special persuasiveness in connection with art forms for which market demand is especially small. Poetry, literary magazines, serious fiction in general, and many aspects of the visual arts satisfy this criterion, and the service organizations that work in these fields can base their claim for support on such grounds.

The merit-goods argument is also particularly forceful in light of the probability that without subsidy the arts would be even more concentrated than they are in a few large cities. The organizations that effectively combat the centralizing tendencies of the arts also deserve support on one of the economic efficiency grounds, overcoming high information costs.

Virtually all performing-arts organizations freely assert that the long-term cost trends forecast by the Baumol-Bowen thesis present them with serious problems. However, the financial difficulties of the performing-arts cases were not traceable to the Baumol-Bowen trends[81] but to unsuccessful ventures, a failure to develop expected support at the box office or elsewhere, a withdrawal of previously available support, or efforts to expand without either market or donor support visible. Nor did the granting agencies apparently base particular decisions on Baumol and Bowen's concerns, except in the case of the NEA Orchestra Program, which seems to be a direct response to the Baumol-Bowen thesis and whose support for the Philadelphia and Charlotte symphony orchestras seems respectively unnecessary and unwise.

6

Support for the Arts and
the Public Interest

At this point it is appropriate to ask whether large-scale public support for the arts has, by and large, been successful. The question, though, is a hard one to answer, mostly because of the lack of a universally acceptable set of criteria for measuring success. Even if the criteria suggested earlier in this book are accepted, they remain difficult to apply. It is far easier to describe the amount and extent of public subsidies and to present fragmentary data as well as some case studies on their impact. But even the latter material, which is not representative of the whole spectrum of activity in the arts benefiting from public subsidy, can support contradictory conclusions that emphasize the problems encountered in seeking to assess the role of public support for the arts.

Thus, the statistical analysis of symphony orchestras suggests that subsidy was of real consequence, while the case studies of orchestras suggest the opposite. Conversely, the statistical analysis of the nonprofit resident theaters as a group indicates that public support did little apart from raising labor costs, which was not the case for the two theaters in the case studies. Under the circumstances, evaluation of what direct, large-scale public support of the arts has wrought must be impressionistic.

Agencies funding the arts, whether public or private, do not make use of my criteria in making their own evaluations. Instead, they articulate objectives as NEA has done: increasing the availability of the arts to the entire population; strengthening cultural organizations, preserving the cultural heritage, and encouraging the creative development of talented individuals. Although it is more than a little arbitrary to assign specific grants to one or another of these objectives, as was done in Table 4–7, it appears that of the estimated total subsidies (from all levels of government) of just under $300 million in 1975, roughly three-eighths was provided primarily to increase the availability of the arts, about half to assist cultural organizations, and the remaining one-eighth to advance the cultural

155

legacy. NEA and the state arts councils (although not NYSCA) place relatively more emphasis on availability, but the largest part of state and local government support is for aid to organizations.

But the proposed criteria for public support are implicit in the operations of the funding agencies. In American society, economic and financial conditions depend largely upon voluntary private decisions, either in the marketplace, where money is exchanged for goods and services, or outside the market, where individuals and private organizations voluntarily contribute money for worthy purposes (encouraged by tax advantages). To a considerable extent, such private decisions further the objectives of public grants for the arts. But private decision making may fail to serve the public interest in the arts in any of several ways: first, the unequal distribution of income and wealth may inhibit the access of both consumers and potential producers to the arts; second, markets may not work well in the arts in a number of ways; third, even if markets worked reasonably well, those markets plus voluntary private gifts still might not provide enough for the arts. Each of these arguments can be deployed to justify government subsidy to increase access to the arts, strengthen cultural institutions, preserve the cultural heritage, and develop individual talents.

Public Support and Income Barriers

The income distribution argument has at least three distinguishable components that can be related to specific grant programs: first, in the absence of public subsidy, the arts tend to be provided in places that are remote, physically and/or psychologically, from many low-income people; they are generally provided in imposing structures in the central parts of our largest metropolitan areas. Second, location aside, admissions prices themselves may constitute a barrier to the availability of the arts. Third, the necessity of lengthy and costly training and the very modest earnings prospects of artists, at least in the early years of their careers, are more likely to deter talented youngsters from low-income families than those who can rely on family financial support from pursuing careers in the arts.

The government arts foundations devote a large – and apparently increasing – share of their resources to enhancing the availability of the arts.[1] In both intent and effect, such spending is a response to the unequal distribution of income. Much of it takes the form of subsidies to local cultural centers and arts groups operating in rural areas, small towns, and low-income inner-city neighborhoods within major metropolitan areas; to bring touring groups and exhibitions to smaller cities; and to bring individual artists or ensembles to dispersed sites throughout the country, including schools, via such programs as Artists-in-Schools, Young Audiences, and Affiliate Artists.

The rise in racial and ethnic self-consciousness and the acceptance of equality of opportunity as a priority of public policy have helped to produce programs that serve the purpose of increasing access by reaching out to low-income populations rather than merely to middle-income people who happen to live in places not well-served by major arts institutions. For example, in fiscal 1974, the Arts Exposure Program within NEA's Expansion Arts Program made seventy-three grants totalling $901,000. About one-third of this money went to New York City organizations, about one-third to organizations located in other major metropolitan centers, and the remaining one-third to organizations in smaller cities and towns and rural areas. All of the New York City grants were for activities located in minority-group inner-city areas or explicitly designed to reach low-income ethnic and racial minorities. Two-thirds of the grants to organizations located in other large cities financed similar activities, but most of the grants to organizations located outside the big cities did not. In this respect, the Arts Exposure Program reflects the priorities of the larger Expansion Arts Program, as well as the comparable activities of NYSCA and some of the other state arts councils.

In order to broaden access to the arts, the grant-making agencies have subsidized no-charge appearances by artists in schools, on the streets, and in other popular settings and the provision of services and facilities to aspiring artists. (Young Filmakers is an obvious example.) Public subsidy to symphony orchestras is associated with a large increase in the number of free and reduced-price orchestral performances in parks and other places. At least some opera companies (the Met in parks, the Baltimore Opera in schools) and some theater companies (Trinity Square in schools) have also utilized public funds in this way. In addition, where subsidy has helped keep ticket prices down for ordinary performances, it can be said to make the arts more accessible to people with moderate incomes.

Fellowships and similar grants of public support for individual artists are awarded through competitions in which talent is the main criterion. Although it is impossible to assess the extent to which such programs overcome income barriers to artistic careers, a large number of grantees are apparently minority-group members. Almost certainly significant numbers of these young artists come from low-income families; for such young people, public subsidy programs may make the difference betwen persisting in and abandoning artistic careers.

Clearly public funds have helped to lower income barriers to access to the arts. But much of the public money spent for the objectives of wider availability brings the arts to places and audiences that are by no means poor and to audiences that pay relatively stiff prices for access. For example, upper-, not lower-, income people comprise the audiences for the New York City Ballet at the Kennedy Center in Washington and the Saratoga Festival. Similarly, a fair number of art museums charge special admissions fees for the special exhibitions that account for about one-third of NEA grants to art museums.

Undoubtedly, the mean income of the audiences for free performances in parks and schools is well below that of the audiences in concert halls, opera houses, and theaters. But many of the people who attend the free performances would not attend regular performances, even if the ticket prices were not so high relative to their incomes. Many members of the free performance audience are deterred from attending regular performances by barriers of age or physical inconvenience. In fact, like much of the radio and television audience for the serious performing arts, many probably are middle-income people with a mild, rather than passionate, interest in the particular art form, not so much unwilling to part with the price of a ticket as unwilling to go to the trouble of making reservations long in advance and possibly traveling to a theater or concert hall in inclement weather. They find it much simpler to go to the park, on the spur of the moment, on a fine spring or summer evening.

The public funding agencies might increase, at least marginally, the income-distribution effects of their grants, for example, by sponsoring more "reverse touring"–the British practice of using public funds to bring low-income people to the arts (rather than bringing the arts to places where the audiences may turn out to be very affluent). The simplest form of support for reverse touring is the large-scale distribution of free tickets to regular performances. The public agencies also could make grants designed to encourage aggressive discrimination in ticket price policy, such as that of the New York Shakespeare Festival for its Central Park performances: selling every other row to contributors (at $5.00 or more a seat in 1975 and 1976), while keeping all other seats free.[2]

Subsidy to Offset Market Failure

The most general form of the market-failure argument for government action – in any field – is that private producers and consumers in market transactions make their decisions solely on the basis of costs and benefits to them and ignore costs and benefits to others, including society at large. For the most part, government support of the arts, occasioned by the need to cope with the earnings gaps of arts institutions, the necessity of more than a token season if professional quality is to be achieved, the hope that more exposure to the arts will build audiences and uncover hidden talent, or the desire to offset the unequal distribution of income, will yield – as a by-product – what is perhaps the most important form of benefits external to today's producers and consumers of the arts: the preservation, enhancement, and transmission of the artistic legacy for future generations. The intergenerational problem calls for additional government support of the arts only if there is some evidence that the legacy is in real danger for lack of funds.

A large fraction of total public subsidy is devoted to strengthening and preserving arts institutions. Despite long-term projections of financial disaster for the arts, most arts organizations are in relatively good financial condition, with a few exceptions, notably the Metropolitan Opera. On balance, therefore, at the current level, public subsidy does not seem so small as to threaten the preservation of the legacy for future generations. In fact – again with the notable exception of the Met – the overall artistic legacy may well be in better financial shape today than it has ever been.

Despite the large deficits widespread among arts organizations, the curtailment of museum hours, narrowly averted bankruptcies (like that of the Paul Taylor Dance Company), and the actual financial collapse of some artistic organizations, the total volume of high-quality artistic activities and institutions has greatly expanded in recent years. The artistic legacy that this generation will pass on to posterity has been vastly enriched, not diminished. Even though, in the process of expansion, some organizations have faced severe difficulties, it does not follow that the legacy is in financial danger. For example, the considerable increase in the number of ballet and dance performances in New York may make it very difficult for the New York City Ballet, despite its prestige, to fill its house for a long season at present. This difficulty reflects not imminent financial danger to the artistic legacy but the inherent unevenness of the expansion process. Art museums appear to have greater financial difficulties than other carriers of the artistic heritage, but even their difficulties are unevenly distributed and, in at least some cases, may reflect overly ambitious expansion plans.

Another justification for government intervention to secure external benefits is the inadequacy of the market as a means of eliciting innovation and experimentation in situations where the risk of failure is high and the opportunities for large monetary rewards for success very limited. Such situations prevail in some (but not all)[3] of the arts and provide a strong case for government subsidy to the avant-garde and the wholly new in artistic production. Roughly one-sixth of NEA grant funds can be characterized as supporting innovation and experimentation in the arts. Because of NEA (and, to a lesser extent, some of the other funding agencies), the financial resources available for innovation in the arts are greater than ever before in American history.

In most European countries, the major established arts organizations absorb the bulk of government arts subsidies, with little left for nonestablishment efforts. The United States – the citadel of capitalism and the giant enterprise in government, business, and charity – apparently devotes far more public money than does any other nation to innovation in the arts. It is fitting that the United States, as a rich country that has traditionally believed itself especially hospitable to the new and different, generously supports innovation.

Increasingly, lobbyists for more public support for the arts have argued that the arts yield an external benefit that is both visible and measurable: they help the local economy. In the summer of 1975, the Metropolitan Museum of Art sponsored a survey that indicated that half of the 85,000 weekly visitors to the museum in a typical summer week are not residents of New York City, and 27 percent live outside the metropolitan region. The museum outdraws such celebrated tourist attractions as the Statue of Liberty, the Empire State Building, and the United Nations. These nonresidents spend nearly $4 million a week in New York's hotels, restaurants, shops, and entertainment centers, a figure that the museum contrasts with the city government subsidy of $2.6 million for the 1975–76 fiscal year.[4] A NYSCA study of the 900 New York organizations that received NYSCA support during all three of the fiscal years ending in 1977 showed that they had total operating expenditures of $410 million in 1976–77 and a payroll of nearly $240 million and that they constituted one of the few growth industries in the state.[5]

Theoretically, support of the arts can benefit a local economy in a number of ways. The arts can provide a magnet for tourists, business conventions, and other visitors; but they are likely to perform this function only in a few, rather specialized places, such as New York City, where the arts comprise a major "industry," and certain summer resort areas, like Saratoga and Tanglewood. More generally, the availability of the arts can help a local economy by making the area a more attractive one in which to live and thus indirectly encouraging firms to locate plants and offices there. No doubt even a modest presence of the arts has this effect, but its economic consequences are likely to be trivial unless the artistic and cultural amenities of the area are among its most conspicuous characteristics and distinguish it from other competing areas. It is hard to believe that the presence of the Charlotte Symphony has much, if anything, to do with that area's booming economy.

Of course, federal and state government subsidy of a local arts organization benefits the local economy; any inflow of funds from an outside government, whether for a military-base payroll, revenue sharing, or a new post office, is similarly beneficial. Like foreign aid to a developing country, it helps the balance of payments. But a local government arts subsidy, in most places, is unlikely to have any discernible economic-development benefits, although it may be a good thing for other reasons.

In New York, the arts industry is so large that it not only is a drawing card for outsiders but also generates what urban economists call "agglomeration effects"; the primary arts activities require a wide range of supplying and supporting facilities and services, and the whole agglomeration over time has developed a specialized labor force to serve it. The benefits of agglomeration can be dissipated quickly if the total volume of arts activities slips below a critical point; therefore, the city and state governments have a real interest in providing enough subsidy to prevent any such slippage.

Information Costs and Wider Accessibility

Economists have long argued that market processes can have "optimal" results – in the sense of yielding the quantity and quality of goods and services that best reflect the sum total of the preferences of all the members of the society – only if consumers and producers have adequate information about all the relevant possibilities. But a taste for the arts is acquired largely through education and experience. Most people go through most of their lives with little or no exposure to most art forms. Artists are lost to the world because most children have no opportunity to experience at first-hand the art form for which some of them may have some innate bent and talent.

About $100 million of public funds are now being spent each year mainly to increase exposure to the arts (that is, in pursuit of the wider availability objective). Although this subsidy may not have measurably increased the permanent size of audiences for the arts or facilitated the discovery of youthful talent, it has clearly brought some experience of the arts to substantial numbers of people for whom the arts are an entirely new thing. In the last decade, hundreds of thousands if not millions of Americans have discovered through publicly supported programs some form of the arts and found it so fascinating that continuing experience with that art form – at some level – will be part of the rest of their lives. The emphasis of the public funding agencies on wider availability has made ordinary Americans more familiar and comfortable with the arts than their counterparts in other large countries seem to be. And this development may in time result in significant audience expansion.

But the record of public subsidy in reaching new audiences is mixed. Some of the subsidy – for example, for touring performances before college audiences – may amount to preaching to the converted. Some public grants – for example, for some programs in the schools – have been criticized as having only shallow and transitory impacts on audiences. And much public money, including a lot provided through state arts councils to community arts groups, supports participation in the arts at an amateur or hobby level that may not prepare audiences or artists for professional-quality work. Subsidies for nonprofessional participation in the arts may be warranted, but not as a device to correct this form of market failure.

Demand for the arts is such that without subsidy from private philanthropy and/or government grants, highly professional performances and exhibitions are likely to be highly concentrated in a relatively few large cities. At the very least, the season for a performing-arts organization outside the major cities will be very short if left to box office support. Moreover, the quality of performances will be higher, in general, the more steadily performers, supporting artists, and craftsmen can be employed in presenting such performances. If the local market and local private contributors can support only a handful of performances each year, then local professionals must devote most of their time to earning a living in other pursuits. By extending the period of employment, public subsidy for touring, additional performances at the home location, or ancillary services (like performances in schools) can raise the quality of artistic activity.

Public subsidy has substantially contributed to the lengthening of seasons in the performing arts. Over the last decade, many orchestras have become year-round operations, and opera companies as a group have had major increases in the number of performances. For example, the Baltimore Opera Company has effectively increased the length of its season greatly, through the operation of the Eastern Opera Theater. The Arena and Trinity companies also have lengthened seasons, and dance companies – largely through touring – have done likewise. In few cases has increased government support been the sole source of financing for the lengthening of seasons (the Ford Foundation's role has been vital in numerous cases). But if they had received less public support, most performing-arts organizations, aside from a few of the symphony orchestras, would have had shorter seasons and the arts would have been more centralized in both quality and quantity. In short, wider availability – whether it is viewed as a corrective to market failure or as supplying a merit-good – is an objective that public subsidy has been reasonably effective in pursuing.

Government intervention on merit-goods grounds can be justified whenever and wherever the demand for a given art form is very low. For example, the drastic shrinkage in the number of general magazines over the past thirty years has reduced the market for short stories to a fraction of what it had been from the mid-nineteenth to the mid-twentieth century. As Philip Hart and other critics of the symphony orchestra have pointed out, the orchestral repertoire is far less open to the work of contemporary composers than it was early in this century.[6]

Both NEA and NYSCA assist artists working in fields where markets are extremely limited by providing fellowships and by subsidizing service organizations that pay fees to artists and/or provide them with services. On the whole, those grants seem well conceived, but they involve only very small fractions of the NEA and NYSCA budgets, and these art forms have been relatively neglected in the expansion of the total amount of public subsidy in recent years. Moreover, NEA has not actively sought out opportunities to maximize the value of the limited expenditure for these purposes. For example, in the four fiscal years 1973–77, NEA made grants totaling $1.2 million to 363 composers and librettists, but after the premiere, artists still confront the problem of getting continued or repeat performances of new works. It was only in 1976 that

NEA took its first steps to address this problem.[7] Unlike some foundations, the endowment has not tied its support of orchestras to the performance of new works (for example, by providing guarantees of ticket receipts for such performances).

The Earnings Gap

The most common merit-goods argument for public intervention is, of course, the Baumol-Bowen thesis, which holds that the long-term financial viability of the major performing-arts institutions is questionable in the absence of increasing private contributions and government support. Undoubtedly, the form of art organization for which the thesis has the most applicability is the symphony orchestra because of the severe constraints on increasing its productivity, its limited opportunities for generating new sources of earned income to offset rising wage costs, and the evidence that demand for symphony orchestra tickets may be highly responsive to price increases. When ticket prices rise, some consumers can give up symphony performances for such alternatives as recordings and (in larger cities) concerts by soloists and chamber ensembles.[8]

Figure 6-1 depicts some trends in the finances of the ASOL major and metropolitan orchestras betwen 1969–70 and 1974–75. The gap between expenses and earned income from nongovernment sources did not increase disproportionately during this period; earned income rose about as rapidly, in percentage, as total expenditures. But in dollars, the earnings gap rose from $38.4 million to $66.5 million. Government support filled about 12 percent of this gap in 1969–70 and 27 percent in 1974–75. With less government support, a fair number of orchestras probably would have had to make some difficult adjustments, including substantially larger increases in ticket prices. Concern for income distribution justifies government support to moderate ticket price increases.

Most of the increase in government support for the symphony orchestras was ostensibly tied to specific projects, notably, more performances in schools, in parks, and elsewhere, and not explicitly designed to narrow the earnings gap. But, according to Philip Hart, beginning in the mid-1960s, the larger orchestras, under the pressure of musicians' militancy, negotiated contracts providing for longer seasons. They then inaugurated new services, such as free concerts, in order to provide musicians with the amount of employment required by the union contracts. Thus, with less government aid for the new services, the orchestras would have had larger

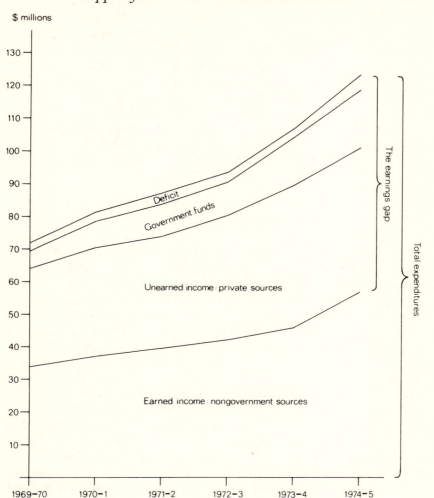

Figure 6-1. The Earnings Gap, 1969–70 to 1974–75, U.S. Major and Metropolitan Symphony Orchestras. *Source:* American Symphony Orchestra League annual tabulations.

deficits, not fewer services and lower expenditures.[9] On the other hand, with less government support, orchestra managers might have been more resistant to signing contracts that extended the seasons.

Thus, even symphony orchestras pose questions about the efficacy of and the need for the recent large increases in government support. In some cases, such as Philadelphia, increased government support has relieved the pressure for private fund raising and permitted the orchestra to leave untapped potential sources of private contributions. In more cases, increased public support served to increase the compensation of musicians (and nonartistic staff), mainly in the form of movement toward year-round seasons. The year-round season, as Hart points out, is not unequivocally a good thing, even from the standpoint of the policy objectives of improving the artistic standards of the institutions and fostering the careers of talented individuals. A fair number of musicians in the larger orchestras find that the year-round season hobbles them professionally by preventing them from engaging in outside musical activities that are more satisfying artistically.[10]

Merit-Goods in General

The Metropolitan Opera is a special case. Subsidy to the Met will not bring it to the poor, expand its audience, cause it to do radically different things, or realize scale economies. Moreover, the Met in fact has achieved what amount to productivity improvements and continues to do so and therefore does not fit the criteria of the Baumol-Bowen thesis. The Met's problem is not that its earnings gap will increase over time but that its earnings gap here and now is so large. The Met is not a victim of one or another form of market failure; a reasonably well-functioning market simply does not produce enough income to cover the costs of the art form the Met produces: a full season of first-quality grand opera. The case for public subsidy for the Met is simply that it is a good thing that cannot survive without subsidy – a pure merit-good.

Many advocates of public subsidy maintain that the arts in general fit this description. But the granting agencies have made an effort to utilize, as the basis for distribution, more narrowly defined objectives that are susceptible to reasoned arguments about purpose and efficacy. The funds generated by taxation are not being distributed casually by high-minded mandarins claiming to know what is best for a population that does not know what is best for itself. Nonetheless, the grant-making process has not been entirely free of fuzziness or of decisions to support applicants, regardless of the scope of their activities or the causes of their financial needs, simply because they are Good Things.

No doubt, the pressures for wide geographic dispersal of grants, lobbying of Establishment organizations (like the symphonies), and the use of specialist panels of reviewers of grant applications with built-in biases in favor of activities the panelists themselves are engaged in professionally are to blame in part for the deficiencies of agency decision making. But if they are to increase their effectiveness and cope with some of the serious difficulties of public support, the officials and council members who have been given so much discretion by the Congress and state legislatures need to define priorities more carefully and to avoid retreating into rhetoric.

Contradictions and Problems

A general rule of public finance, in a system that has several levels of government levying taxes and making decisions on how those taxes should be spent, is that the geographic area in which the benefits from a particular expenditure are realized should correspond roughly to the geographic area within which taxes are collected to finance that expenditure. The citizens of a locality should not bear the burden of a tax to finance benefits that will accrue largely to outsiders. Benefits that are widely distributed should be financed from taxes that also are widely distributed, otherwise local voters will probably provide less of the public service in question than the broader community would want. On the other hand, if taxpayers in a large area pay for very local benefits, local citizens may ask for and receive more of the service than they would be willing to pay for in taxation if they had to finance it themselves.

The geographic scope of the benefits that flow from most government activities cannot be defined precisely, and it may be particularly difficult to define for the arts. The nation's cultural heritage is made up of the collections of specific museums and the talents of artists working in specific places and organizations, which may or may not tour widely. And a grant for production of a play to be broadcast nationally on public television may strengthen the local theater company doing that play and thus generate local as well as national benefits. Because of its superior tax-collecting ability, the federal government must play an important role in public support of the arts, but in instances where the ratio of local or regional benefits to national benefits is high, local and state governments also should participate in the subsidy effort.

The federal role clearly should be dominant, perhaps even more so than it now is, for example, in supporting artistic innovation and experimentation, because the benefits of both successes and failures are nationwide. Similarly, because Americans are mobile, the career development of talented individuals is of national concern and properly a major NEA responsibility.[11] A small number of truly national arts institutions, notably the Metropolitan Opera, also have a special claim on national, as compared to state or local, public support. And where public subsidy is necessary to guarantee the preservation of the cultural heritage for future generations, the responsibility of providing such a subsidy clearly attaches to the federal government.

In the earlier years of public support of the arts, such nonfederal agencies as NYSCA supported major institutions in the absence of federal support. More recently, the balance has shifted. Increasingly, as the level of federal funding has risen, federal funds have supported quite localized arts activities, with little or no matching from local or state public funds. Not surprisingly, most state arts councils have very modest programs, involving the support – with their own and NEA money – of highly localized activities. Few play any role at all in the support of major arts institutions.

Local government support of the arts (art museums aside) also is minimal in all but a very few cities. And the data on local government matching of NYSCA funds in New York State counties are also bleak. Under congressional mandate, NEA seems to have been wasting federal money that could be better spent in support of activities that are more obviously of nationwide interest, such as stipends for individual artists and grants for innovation to people and groups in states that conspicuously fail to support the arts with their own money. The artist may be worthy, whatever the state government chooses not to do.

Moreover, even major arts institutions may not have an unequivocal claim to substantial NEA support if their own local and state governments abstain from supporting them. Those institutions that form part of the national cultural heritage also may generate local benefits. A sensible "hold-harmless" policy might be to tie *increases* in future NEA funding of specified major institutions to some degree of matching by state and local governments.[12]

Art in Everyday Life

Significant amounts of funds provided by the federal and state governments support amateur participation in the arts. In pursuit of wider availability, NEA and NYSCA explicitly seek not only to expose more people to first-hand experience with professional-level arts but also support amateur participation and assorted efforts to make art "a part of everyday life." Undeniably, the bulk of the benefits from the civic theater or amateur crafts workshop in a given community accrue to the residents of that community. If those residents are unwilling to bear the tax burden of paying for such benefits – as they generally seem to be – then federal and/or state support seems most improper.

A number of advocates of public support for the arts in general, in the United States and in other countries,[13] argue that the funds available for public support for the arts are so limited that professional-level activities need every penny of that money. They assume, explicitly or implicitly, that at an annual subsidy level of $300 million or so, the marginal social benefit from an additional dollar of public subsidy for professional activities greatly exceeds the marginal social benefit from that dollar devoted to amateur activities.

Supporting this assumption is the evidence that public subsidy is not really necessary to elicit more amateur participation. Observers of the art scene agree that amateur participation, both with and without subsidy, has been on the rise for some time, reflecting broad social and economic trends that include increased levels of educational attainment, higher personal incomes, diffusion of knowledge about the arts via television and films, and reductions in the relative costs of many of the supplies and much of the equipment necessary for amateur participation. In contrast, public subsidy *has* been essential for some major elements in the expansion in professional-level activities, such as the dance.

Some critics suggest that at some point total public subsidy for the arts might be high enough to include some support for the amateur sector. Others argue that public subsidy for the amateur would make no sense, save in political log-rolling terms, no matter how adequately the professional world of the arts is supported. They maintain that few of the theoretical arguments for public subsidy apply to amateur activities, even though such subsidies have income distribution effects (the flowering of amateur participation without subsidy is very much a middle-class phenomenon), and amateur participation probably leads to more sustained and devoted appreciation for the professional arts than characterizes the occasional television watcher of "Theater in America," or the spectator at a quartet performance in a shopping center, or the elementary school pupil listening to a poetry reading.

Some critics argue that by providing subsidy for amateur activities governments blur the distinction in quality between the amateur and the professional. In an egalitarian society, they assert, it is hard enough to foster artistic excellence – a rare and therefore seemingly elitist thing – without governments undermining the quest for excellence by bestowing their financial blessings on the ordinary. Moreover, they claim, support of amateur activities may so lower the standards of the public funding agencies that they may lose the ability to make hard-and-fast quality distinctions and slide into support of low-quality professional performance. They cite NEA's efforts to develop "indigenous cultural resources" as a case in point.

The principle that the arts should be a part of everyday life has resulted in the expenditure of some public money to support certain professional and amateur activities that introduce the arts to audiences that are essentially captive. A single recent issue of *The Cultural Post*[14] describes, approvingly, the operations of three such NEA-sponsored efforts: performances on city buses in Cincinnati, a 1973 laser-beam "sculpture" that lit up the night sky for miles over center-city Philadelphia, and a touring theater performance before a hostile, disorderly junior high school audience in Marion, Illinois. No doubt the "damage" done to the unwilling captives of these works of art is negligible, but the principle involved is no different from that which results in the installation of canned music systems in elevators, airplanes, and other public places.

Another manifestation of "arts-in-everyday-life" is the proposition that the arts funding agencies should promote the integration of "the arts into other pursuits"; to serve youth, the handicapped, and the aging; "build effective communities in neighborhoods and places of work"; rehabilitate criminals; and heal the sick.[15] All these purposes are worthy, but they call for amounts of money that are very large relative to the appropriations to the arts agencies. Real pursuit of these ends (not just lip service) would dilute the efforts of the agencies and make them substantial, not just marginal, supporters of amateur activities.

Relative to total public spending,[16] the government funds available for the arts are so small that heretofore the arts funding agencies generally have tried very hard to steer claimants for support of peripheral activities (like art as education or therapy) to other, much larger sources of public funds. But both NEA and, especially, the state arts councils have spent some money for activities that seem peripheral to the main mission. The most important case in point is architecture.

Architecture and the Scope of Government Support

Most state arts councils spend no money on architecture; NYSCA has a very small program in this field. In 1967, NEA initiated its Architecture + Environmental Arts Program,[17] and by the end of fiscal 1975, it had made grants totaling more than $11 million. Architects and urban designers do not produce art for art's sake, of course, nor is much of their everyday activity artistic in the traditional sense; it involves considerable engineering and other technical work. Thus, architecture poses some special problems for an arts funding agency.

One aspect of NEA's architecture program involves improving the quality of design in the buildings and operations of the federal government itself. In 1972, then-President Richard Nixon designated NEA as the lead agency in this effort. The assignment is logical and does not absorb much of NEA's funds. The program also has the task of bringing "the very best design into the experience of every citizen,"[18] a generally unexceptionable merit-goods goal that even an extremist cannot criticize with reference to captive audiences. Like it or not, we are exposed to the visible characteristics of the manmade environment; government may reasonably attempt to apply some qualitative standards to additions to that environment.

However, it is all too easy for a program with such an objective to become more concerned with city planning than with art, and most of the spending under the NEA architecture program recently seems to reflect such a shift. For example, in 1975, NEA moved vigorously into the field of neighborhood conservation. After a conference that discussed such arts issues as special zoning for preservation areas, "redlining" by financial institutions, and proposed federal subsidies for low-income homeowners in preservation areas, NEA made grants totaling $507,000 for thirty-nine projects, including a Trenton, New Jersey, plan to establish a park next to an abandoned canal. As the endowment itself recognizes:

> the concept of neighborhood conservation involves considerably more than preserving examples of fine architecture. Almost invariably it raises complex legal, sociological, economic, and even political questions seemingly far removed from the Arts Endowment's usual concerns.[19]

As a result of this involvement with city planning, NEA has diverted a significant portion of its limited funds to achieve trivial increases in total federal spending in a field within the jurisdiction of an agency of vast means (the Department of Housing and Urban Development). Moreover, NEA began making its categorical grants for design studies, zoning revisions, and the development of economic incentives to support urban development objectives just as HUD, after many years of making narrowly defined categorical grants for specific urban development projects, had abandoned that practice under new legislation providing for broad-purpose community development grants.

Equally important, the NEA program has strengthened the

hands of architects concerned with esthetics and the individual artist's inspiration, as opposed to public officials and social scientists (and some architects and urban designers) concerned with the city's functions as a complex social and economic organism, in determining the direction of American urban planning. During the previous decade, the literature of American urban planning had become heavily nonarchitectural, and academic urban planning programs had become largely independent of schools of architecture. The NEA program is, and has been seen to be, an announcement by the federal government that the older tradition was the right one–that urban plans should be shaped first and foremost by the esthetic perceptions of architects-as-artists and only secondarily by economic and social analysts.

The generally accepted arguments for federal government concern with the physical characteristics of American cities, including federal financial assistance for urban design activities (and the arguments against it) have little to do with NEA's announced objectives or with the theoretical case for public support of the arts. But NEA has defined architecture as being within the scope of the arts it will support financially; the program spawned by that definition has developed a life and logic of its own; and it is camouflaged from public and congressional scrutiny as urban planning by the other, more appropriate things the endowment is doing.[20]

Innovation and Subsidy

Although the fears expressed before the creation of NEA that government support would lead to bureaucratic interference with artistic creativity have proven unfounded, the by-now conventional wisdom that government support of the arts is unqualifiedly good for the arts still has a few critics. They complain not that legislators and bureaucrats interfere deliberately with the production of the new and the different but that government support inadvertently causes the small struggling groups that are said to be the fount of creativity to expand their operations and undertake financial commitments that introduce caution: when groups become preoccupied with institutional survival, the need to pay union wages, meet payrolls, and make interest payments on debt takes precedence over creativity; in contrast, the unsubsidized experimental group knows that its chances of institutional survival are slim, accepts the probability of financial failure, and, therefore, is free to do its own creative thing.

The line of dissent is most forcefully articulated by the "alternative theater" movement, a collection of eighty-odd groups (about half in New York and California), most of which receive no public support at all, and all of which operate under the most marginal of financial circumstances:

> The historically important thing about alternative theatre is not necessarily the quality of performance but its break with the commodity culture production pattern, that of the "rich" theatres in which operational and real estate costs have spiralled so disastrously that they can only be run by highly skilled manipulators of other financial and social systems and the performer must devote a separate career to obtaining entry.
>
> Performers' theatres discovered that scaled down commodity production, a la off-Broadway or regional theatre, is still a trap, with spiralling rent and promotion costs, and box office anxiety waiting for the miraculous hit. They learned to work in "spaces" rather than theatres; they learned that "poor" theatre emphasis on the performer leads to imaginative and inexpensive environmental design, that long, rigorous, exploratory rehearsal given to shaping performance material to the life of a community in which the theatre is rooted unearths audiences who don't want conventional theatre and ticket scales.
>
> They also discovered new economic facts. By settling for subsistence living, through scrounging, planning, and serendipity they found low level local funding, touring situations that can afford a short van hop company, "workshop" engagements in schools, community centers, rehabilitation projects.
>
> As a result, theatres with annual budgets of well under $100,000 are surviving with more vision, confidence and continuity than those with tenfold budgeting.[21]

In short, poverty is good for the arts and government support is bad simply because the large size attendant on government support transforms the artistic enterprise. Such dissenters are quick to note that innovation in the resident regional theater often consists of productions like *Raisin* or *Our Town* that are anything but avant-garde, despite the insistence on the part of people in the subsidized theater that fund-granting agencies stay at arm's length. Thus, Arena, for example, entirely eschews local private support.

This position contains more than a grain of truth, but it still does not destroy the case for government support of the arts, including government support directed at the new and different. Rather, it suggests that government support programs should not uniformly pressure small groups to expand and undertake substantially larger financial commitments but should provide small grants–even on a continuing basis–for groups that do not choose to grow. In addition, grant-making agencies should make an effort to dispel any impression that groups that do not meet the eligibility standards for public support programs–or do not choose to apply–are somehow inferior, nonprofessional, and not deserving of even private support. Given the individualism and predisposition toward anarchy that characterize the arts in this country, much artistic innovation can and will occur without public subsidy. And the ability of artists to innovate without recourse to public funds is a good thing, not a bad thing.

One area of innovation, administrative rather than artistic, has received little encouragement from the government arts agencies–pricing policies. The funding agencies have made grants to cover part of the costs of free and reduced-charge performances and presentations but they have made few grants explicitly to underwrite experiments in pricing. Like all experiments, those in price policy often fail, and few arts organizations can afford to take chances. The experiments that are in order involve both higher and lower prices.

Most arts organizations are reluctant, for a combination of ideological, public relations, and economic reasons, to charge very high prices for a small number of the best seats or, say, for queue-jumping admission to special exhibitions. The ideological objections amount to misplaced and distorted egalitarianism to the extent that they result in subsidy for the very richest members of the audience, in part from public funds. The public relations explanations also seem misguided; few ordinary members of an audience are likely to resent a policy of charging very high prices for tickets for a small number of seats in very desirable locations, and it is hard to believe that substantial donors would be bothered by higher ticket prices.[22]

The economic objection to experimental raising of ticket prices is that it might not work. When the Metropolitan Opera tried it, the extra-high-priced tickets did not sell, and the organization lost money. But by guaranteeing against loss, the public agencies could encourage experiments with both price raising and price cutting. Performing-arts organizations would do well to consider the example of major league baseball clubs, which for nearly forty years (dating from Larry McPhail's control of the Brooklyn Dodgers in the late 1930s) have engaged in aggressive and imaginative price cutting to maximize attendance and reach people of very modest means. Although most baseball clubs come out ahead financially from such experiments, they take risks that arts organizations dare not take unless public agencies underwrite them. Meanwhile, people who might pay more willingly are not being asked to do so, and seats that might be sold at some price are left empty. Until arts organizations conduct pricing experiments, they cannot demonstrate that they are maximizing potential earned income. And unless they are doing so, they have no legitimate claim on public subsidy to fill their earnings gaps.

The more or less permanent commitment of large portions of total appropriations to a more or less fixed list of arts institutions has just begun to emerge as a major unresolved problem of public arts support policy. The deceleration in the rate of increase in government arts appropriations created this problem, and, unless appropriations resume very rapid growth, the problem will worsen. It is already of major proportions in Britain (see Appendix A) and, to a slightly lesser extent, in continental Europe.

In the United States, since 1970, the larger institutions have begun receiving substantial amounts of public support, and although a few, such as the Philadelphia Orchestra, are not really dependent on that support, most take the $150,000 (or larger) NEA grants and, for New York institutions, the NYSCA grants to be part of their annually recurring income stream. They are "hooked" on public support and could go "cold turkey" only with considerable pain.

Moreover, these institutions have come to expect that the public grant amounts will rise, gradually if not rapidly, from year to year, and they plan their finances and activities accordingly. For their part, NEA and NYSCA, like the British Arts Council, are in the position of supporting numerous organizations more or less involuntarily for fear that withdrawal of public subsidy might precipitate insolvency. Thus, the funding agencies are as much locked into many of their existing grantees as the grantees are locked into the grantors.

As a result, the funding agencies are losing the capacity to undertake new programs, finance new initiatives, and support new applicants. Increasingly, like the British Arts Council and like most ordinary government agencies, NEA and NYSCA will be engaging in the opposite of zero-base budgeting. Heretofore, NEA and NYSCA have been able to operate in an entrepreneurial, not custodial, fashion. The energies of their staffs and their review panels and, indeed, the organizational ethos have been centered on exploring the new.

The first sign of NEA's recognition of the sea change came at a

Dance Program presentation before the National Council on the Arts in May 1976. The endowment's support for dance touring has grown from a $25,000 pilot project involving eight weeks of touring in 1968 to a program involving ninety-two companies touring for 432 weeks in fiscal 1975 and costing over $3 million of the Dance Program's $6 million budget. The Dance Panel concluded that NEA support for touring should level out near the present figure and that henceforth touring should be increasingly supported from state and local government funds, foundations, and earned income from television.[23] But recently, the two largest nonfederal government funding agencies, New York State and New York City, have been reducing their support of the arts, as have a number of other state and local governments. The Ford Foundation too has announced a policy of gradually reducing its support. If alternatives to NEA support are not forthcoming, NEA will have to choose between imposing a firm ceiling on the touring grants – even if such a policy causes companies like Paul Taylor that are largely dependent on touring to collapse – or accepting the lock-in and facing up to a shrinking ability to do other things.

The policy choices confronting the government arts funding agencies are more difficult by far than those that NEA and NYSCA have faced previously. In the best of all possible worlds, the agencies would be able to base their decision making on much more information about the state of the arts in the United States than they now have or can obtain. No policy analyst ever has enough information; yet decisions must be made and are made, continually. But in the arts, the extent to which decision making is shrouded in ignorance of even the most elementary kind of information is extraordinary by the current standards of almost any other field of public policy.

The size, composition, and trends of the arts industry as a whole are largely a matter of rough guessing. Information about major components of the parts of the overall industry that are the objects of subsidy is fragmentary at best. The Ford Foundation, ASOL, and similar surveys shed light on some of the larger nonprofit performing arts institutions and museums, but we have virtually no coherent and systematic information about the activities of smaller organizations and groups working in both conventional and novel art forms or about the art forms in which individual artists working on their own are predominant.

Even information on *government* activities in support of the arts is scarce, despite the fact that the inherent difficulties of securing such information are negligible[24] and that NEA is supposedly in partnership with state government agencies and should therefore know what they are doing.[25] There are no comprehensive data on local government arts activities or other state government spending outside the state arts councils; and the data on what the state arts councils other than NYSCA do are limited and sketchy. It is extremely difficult to make accurate and inclusive statements about the arts activities of federal agencies other than NEA, like the Humanities Endowment and the Corporation for Public Broadcasting, not to mention the line agencies like HEW.

Finally, the information that NYSCA and NEA tabulate and report on what they are spending money for and the results of their grants is far from adequate. NEA provides information in a number of forms: the annual report, which lists grant recipients and amounts organized by program but contains no description of the nature of the individual grants and no narrative discussion of the endowment's policies and problems; presentations to congressional committees that organize data in quite different forms and understandably are full of puffery and defensiveness; separate press releases on some but not all of the individual grants made, which do describe the nature of those grants; and *The Cultural Post,* a bimonthly journalistic report on selected NEA-supported activities.

In this respect, NEA differs significantly from most major national foundations and the British Arts Council, whose annual report opens with a frank narrative discussion of criticisms, quandaries, and policy choices made and includes full and intelligible lists of and data on the grants made. An hour or so of reading this document yields comprehension of the essentials of the Arts Council's activities and policy choices in the preceding year.[26]

Unless NEA places a high priority on rapid and substantial improvement of information on the arts and in its own reporting, it will continue to function in considerable ignorance of both the circumstances surrounding public subsidy and the consequences of its own activities. Fortunately, NEA at last has recognized many, if not all, of these deficiencies (it is unclear whether the endowment sees anything wrong with its own reporting), is devoting significant resources to an analytically minded research division, and is contracting for research on data-improvement, economic effects, and other matters on which knowledge is crucial for arts policy.[27]

7

The Direction of Public Policy:
Some Recommendations

Public policy toward the arts in the United States tends to be the sum total of many separate responses to narrowly defined questions rather than the result of a few decisions about broad issues. The fact is that government processes are not well designed to address such policy issues as the proper level of total public and private spending for the arts in the United States in 1980. The decisions that determine the shape of policy involve such issues as whether the standard size of the maximum NEA grant to the larger performing arts organizations should be increased next year by $10,000, $20,000, or not all all.

Yet it is essential to consider the optimum level of total direct support of the arts, which is the broadest of all issues on arts policy, if only because the commonly alleged pressing need for a vast increase in that level is a central theme of so much popular discussion. Specific policy decisions are, in fact, shaped by notions, explicit or implicit, of appropriate overall directions and limits. So I begin this chapter by grappling with the difficult question of how much subsidy there should be in the aggregate; later I make recommendations about more narrowly defined issues.

Given adequate data, a policy analyst could estimate, for example, not precisely but reliably enough, a schedule of the benefits from keeping a given museum open for more hours on a no-charge basis; such a schedule could be compared with a schedule of costs, presenting policymakers with a set of quantified options. Similarly, by comparing the costs of various proposed ways of dealing with income-distribution barriers to the arts with the income characteristics of those reached by new programs, the analyst could enable policymakers to arrive at reasoned and justifiable decisions on the extent of subsidy.

But if the decision to subsidize an activity is based not on market failure or on income distribution grounds but on the conviction that it confers benefits upon society beyond those realizable on the basis of income from private sources (earned and unearned), the optimal amount of such subsidy can never be determined precisely. No unique dollar value can be attached to a "merit-good."[1] Thus the inadequacy of the data base and the existence of merit-goods subsidies conspire to prevent the analyst from determining the economically optimal level of total public subsidy to the arts.

Many arts advocates do not concern themselves with analytical quibbles but instead seek some sort of simple formula that sets total subsidy at a high and increasing level, more or less automatically. One suggested approach is to link the subsidy to a specific variable outside the control of the legislature. But proposals to link the subsidy to, say, gross national product (GNP) or the size of the overall budget have no basis in logic. One advocacy group has recommended that

> each state should provide an average of no less than 10 percent
> of the operating costs of its arts organizations and that federal
> aid should provide an average of no less than 10 percent of the
> total costs of arts organizations throughout the country.[2]

The only conceivable rationale for this 10 percent-10 percent standard amounts to the fact that it is double the 1974–75 level for the arts organizations under study by its proponents.

Another approach to subsidy involves the earmarking of some set portion of the receipts from either existing taxes or new taxes on some aspect of commercial entertainment or leisure activities. In the early years of the Corporation for Public Broadcasting, for example, a number of arts subsidy advocates recommended that federal financing of public broadcasting be tied to the receipts from a special federal tax on the sale of television sets.[3] A more recent proposal, of more direct application, is that

> a fixed percentage of the taxes levied on the entertainment
> industry (understood here in the widest sense, to include rac-
> ing, movies, liquor, cigarettes, etc.) should automatically be
> transferred to state and city cultural commissions for the sup-
> port of the arts.[4]

This proposal has a number of flaws. It fails to demonstrate that the level of support the tax would permit is the right one. It also fails to identify the benefit that consumers of commercial entertainment will derive from subsidizing the arts. If the benefits of subsidy of the arts are broad social ones, then broad-based general taxes rather than narrowly based specific ones (in this case, on consumers of things apparently considered unworthy) should be the source of the funds. In addition, the receipts from the types of taxes usually levied on admissions, gambling, liquor, and tobacco in the United States tend to increase rather slowly; they tend to be inelastic with respect to income. Thus, they are inappropriate as a determinant of the level of arts subsidies.[5]

There is no shortcut way of determining the optimal level of public support of the arts. Consequently, support must be determined – as it has been up until now – in an admittedly rough fashion, through decisions on the merits of the separate components of art subsidies that are provided in pursuit of distinct objectives.

Any individual or organization can always find ways to use more money.[6] Moreover, so many arts organizations confront serious financial problems at any given time that an agency that provides subsidies will find itself compelled by budgetary constraints to deny some seemingly worthy applications. These considerations may argue for selected and marginal increases in public support, but they hardly prove the case for a very substantial increase in the total amount of subsidy here and now.

The presence or absence of a rigorously logical case for dramatic change in public policy is seldom conclusive in determining short-term political decisions. The rate at which total public support for the arts increases in the near future will be influenced by the general climate of opinion, by economic conditions, and by the strength of competing claims on public revenues. On balance, these factors should lead to relatively slow growth in direct public support of the arts in the foreseeable future. First, there is widespread opposition to further increases in the ratio of public expenditure to GNP, aggravated by concern about the (historically untypical) high rate of inflation over the last decade. Moreover, such functions as defense, job creation, health insurance, transportation, and correction of regional imbalances are competing with the arts for public funds. Finally, large *percentage* increases in arts subsidies, which were relatively inexpensive in absolute terms a decade ago, now require large *dollar* increases.

Substantial increases in total public support also are unlikely because, despite cries of alarm about the financial conditions of the arts, there is a glaring lack of evidence to support the contention that without massive transfusions of public money "we are going to become a land without music, without theater, without dance."[7] True financial desperation in the arts is relatively rare and seems unlikely to become universal.

There are a number of reasons for optimism. Even though public support has grown, private support for the arts also has increased substantially, both relatively and absolutely. The Ford Foundation has reduced its support of the arts, but the potential for large-scale private philanthropic support is far from exhausted. Data from both the Internal Revenue Service and the American Association of Fund-Raising Counsel indicate that giving to the arts has increased as a share of total private giving during the past fifteen years, and a further increase is a reasonable expectation. The most potent rivals to the arts for private gifts are hospitals and higher education. But over the past twenty years, these two sectors have experienced extremely rapid physical expansion and, in the next few years, they are unlikely to grow (or at least to grow at the same rapid rate) and should therefore have less need for and ability to attract gifts for capital purposes. Government may well increase its role in financing health and education and in that role is certain to press for tighter control over operating costs. As an expanding, still largely private sector, the arts should be an effective competitor for large increases in private support.[8]

The potential for increased support at the box office (or through other forms of earned income) also is far from exhausted, except perhaps in rare cases like that of the Metropolitan Opera. Evidence from case studies and other sources indicates that the price elasticity of demand may be even lower than the figure suggested by the fragmentary statistical data (see Chapter 5). In the extremely adverse economic circumstances following the oil price rise of late 1973, the earned income of many arts organizations increased even more rapidly than their operating costs; it could not have done so if ticket price increases had significantly narrowed the markets for the arts.

Furthermore, over the next decade, operating costs for major arts organizations should not rise much more rapidly than the general price level. The big rise in operating costs in the arts over the past decade need not continue. That rise represented in large part a "catching up" in the earnings of artists, which came about as a result of the availability of Ford Foundation and government funds, particularly for high culture. Even if orchestral musicians were entitled to increase their earnings more than twice as fast as the entire American work force between 1965 and 1974, they are unlikely to continue to do so indefinitely.[9] Even without such "excess" earnings increases, arts organizations will face cost pressures, but those pressures should be less, not more, severe than those they have been experiencing recently.

With some abatement in cost pressures, with leeway for increased earned income, and with prospects for success in private fund raising, traditional high-culture arts organizations do not appear to be threatened uniformly with financial disaster. The outlook for less traditional art forms, especially those that are more popular and participatory, also is promising. Although the role of private philanthropy for such art forms is negligible and may continue to be so, the role of the market is very large. Moreover, the evidence indicates that popular culture and amateur participation in the arts are highly income-elastic, superior consumer goods that will go on flourishing, independently of subsidy.

Recommendations

If the total level of direct public support for the arts increases at only a moderate rate in the future, if most major arts organizations are not in desperate financial straits (unless they are very badly managed or attempt overly ambitious expansion), and if the more popular and participatory side of the arts enjoys robust financial health, then greater selectivity in grant-making will be both necessary and sensible. My specific policy recommendations are based on this proposition. They are:

> Minimize or eliminate subsidies for amateur activities in the arts
> Subsidize the major arts institutions more selectively
> Continue to foster geographic dispersion, but require more state and local government matching
> Increase support of individual artists and service organizations
> Make some "profit-seeking" arts activities eligible for government support
> Define the jurisdiction of government arts-funding agencies carefully and narrowly

Amateur Activities

In pursuit of efficiency, grant-making agencies should, first, minimize or eliminate subsidies for amateur activities in the arts. Amateur participation may well be meritorious on its own; it may also help to build audiences and develop prospective professional talent. But at a time when participation in the arts is flourishing, such subsidies are largely superfluous. It would be especially wasteful to use federal funds for the support of amateur and quasi-amateur activities. Support by local governments may, however, be appropriate in places that are not served by bona fide resident professional activity or where support for the arts is commingled with support for recreation.

Some advocates of grant support have argued that subsidy is needed to extend to low-income people the benefits of amateur participation in the arts. Subsidy for amateur participation is highly attractive politically in countries with populist traditions or ideology, such as Australia, Sweden – and the United States. The decision to require, by statute, disperson of arts funds to sparsely populated states (the NEA block grants) or counties (NYSCA) reflects this tradition. But so much inefficiency is inevitably attached to amateur activities that the pressure to support them should be resisted. The politics of art subsidies may make it appear that willingness to support amateur efforts and popular culture yields greater appropriations for professional activities and high culture, but state legislatures have not, in fact, proved all that accommodating to the latter. With smaller increases in the offing, policy makers must make hard choices and then try to persuade legislatures to endorse them.

Major Institutions

At the other end of the spectrum, museums and performing-arts organizations with budgets of $100,000 or more account for close to 30 percent of NEA grants and a similar proportion of subsidies from other levels of government. The nation's major art institutions clearly qualify for support as vehicles for wider availability; in recent years, they have been reaching and building new audiences via free or cheap performances (or admissions to museums), touring or other forms of dispersing artistic activities from centralized sites, and promotion of "infant industries," like modern dance or opera in smaller cities. The majors also play an important role in preserving and enhancing the cultural heritage for future generations, an external benefit justifying subsidy even on narrow calculations of economic efficiency.

Government, especially at the federal level, is justified in providing the marginal funds necessary to preserve the national cultural heritage, but only if it is determined to be financially imperiled. A considerable portion of NEA grants provided on this ground appear not to have been truly essential for survival. Some NEA grants have substituted for private fund raising or have enabled state and local governments to escape responsibilities for their own institutions. Moreover, the availability of these funds has allowed arts organizations to neglect opportunities to maximize earned income and hold their production costs down. Many arts institutions are apparently conditioned to cry wolf, but NEA must be able to distinguish between such cries and real, specific financial problems. If a major institution really does need help, NEA should insist on matching support by state and local governments. The absence of a matching requirement makes it easy for localities or states to cut back on support of major institutions in the face of fiscal adversity.

Among institutionalized art forms, the most obvious candidates for reduced emphasis in NEA's budget are museums and symphony orchestras. These institutions now take the present level of support for granted as an integral part of their expected flow of income and would really suffer from an actual reduction in grant dollars. But NEA could freeze its grants at present levels. Even Philip Hart, who calls for increased government support, urges symphony orchestras to avoid calling upon government to solve all the financial problems caused by rapidly rising budgets and urges them to work hard at controlling their costs:

> I do not believe that [the] problem can be solved by increased government funding alone; the rapid rise in expenditures, of which musicians' pay is a major element, must be brought under control. . . . The time has come for the economic study of our orchestras to proceed beyond a definition and projection of financial needs (important as these are) to an analysis of what the orchestras *should* do, rather than merely what they are doing. The objective should be to arrive at some reasonable and just level of operations – of rate of annual increase in expenditures – that the orchestras can live with in accordance with the prospective funding of the income gap from private philanthropy and government aid. . . . [t]he orchestras must seek realistic balance between what their communities need and can support and what they can afford to pay their musicians. . . . [f]uture determination of compensation must balance [musicians'] needs against potential financial resources more equitably than in recent years.[10]

With effective cost controls, an increase in private contributions, and an ending of the evasion of responsibility on the part of state and local governments, there will be no real need for a *general* increase in NEA support of *all* symphonies and art museums during the next few years. In the event that these objectives are achieved but prove insufficient to assure financial survival, then the case can be reopened.

These strictures apply at least equally to some of the larger resident theater companies.[11] The lock-in problem can have especially serious consequences in theater. Art museums and symphony orchestras already are numerous and widely distributed, and few new ones are likely to be created. But fostering innovation in the theater requires opportunities for the creation of numerous new small theater groups (many of which will be short-lived). If the total budget for the NEA's theater program increases at a modest rate and the grants to the larger resident theater companies expand continuously, NEA will have little left with which to support new ventures.

Public support has been very successful in expanding audiences and artistic output for opera companies and the dance. NEA support of regional opera has not only brought this art form to large new audiences but also has assisted in raising artistic standards and fostering creativity; NEA and NYSCA support of dance companies directly and through touring has had similar results; and support from both NYSCA and NEA has rescued the Metropolitan Opera. But even though public money has, on the whole, been put to good use in these areas, more public money spent in the same way by the same institutions will not necessarily be put to even better use by them. Here, too, selectivity and more choice among organizations are in order.

The strategy of freezing grant levels for a good many recipients will lead to relatively slow growth rates in total NEA support for major institutions. Ideally, fewer established arts institutions should receive endowment support; this support should take the form of relatively large annual grants to institutions that still are confronted by financial problems despite their demonstrated aggressiveness in nonfederal fund-raising campaigns, sensible pricing policies, and careful control of costs.[12]

Geographic Dispersion

In the American political system, the pursuit of wider availability by means of dispersion of the arts and artistic experiences gives individual legislators something to show their constituents in return for their support of appropriations that otherwise go largely to subsidize upper-class institions and activities located in the large cities.

But significant amounts of the money spent for this objective are ineffectually or inappropriately spent. Mistakes and failures are inevitable in programs to bring the arts to new audiences and unserved populations. Such programs deserve to be tried, but government agencies should not persist in supporting unsuccessful efforts (such as a fair number of the programs in schools) or activities that cannot possibly further the objective of wider availability, such as bringing touring companies to Saratoga, to be viewed by vacationing New Yorkers. The level of government that should provide the subsidy is an especially important problem of efforts to widen availability. The federal government's job is to support activities that serve the national interest, not to substitute for state and local governments. At times, this responsibility calls for some force-feeding, in the form of federal support for artistic activities with only a very local impact. But the federal government ought not to provide indefinitely continued support for a highly localized program that receives – well after its birth – no support from local governments and little from state government funds.

These issues are of particular concern in connection with the spending for two NEA programs that cut across artistic "disciplines": the education program and the Federal/State Partnership. The education program is a principal means of furthering the objective of wider availability and providing income for individual artists. But many of the specific activities funded by this program are very local, and a fair proportion of those local activities receive little or no non-NEA public support. Although, for the most part, the Artists-in-Schools activities receive matching support from local school boards (but, usually, little state government money), the effectiveness of many school programs has been seriously questioned.

Under the Federal/State Partnership Program, NEA block grants to state arts councils now absorb more than one-eighth of the endowment's total appropriation. Although NEA counts them all as being fully matched, it does so by crediting all local public money and private gifts as matching funds. State governments by and large have not been generous with their own funds. The block grants finance the most local of activities and virtually nothing that can be said to have an impact beyond the boundaries of a state. Therefore, the federal government should attach a specific requirement of state government (or a combination of state and local government) matching funds for its block grants. The matching requirement should be a stiff one – at least two state/local dollars for every federal dollar. The past performance of the states suggests that some states (including a few that are by no means poor) will not meet the matching requirements and will forfeit NEA money. If representatives of those closest to such projects have so little regard for the projects on which some block grant funds have been expended, NEA can find other, more appropriate and useful ways in which to spend these funds. The prospect that some states will refuse to match, and thereby lose, the NEA funds does not argue against a stiff matching requirement, but in favor of it.[13]

Individual Artists and Art Service Organizations

The future financial prospects of the major art institutions and of amateur activities are somewhat brighter than those of the art forms in which professional activities are characterized mainly by individual artists working on their own, occasionally assisted by service organizations. The amounts, current and potential, of private support for the visual and literary arts, particularly the branches of those art forms for which market demand is small or, for all practical purposes, nonexistent, are negligible.

When the market does not work, government subsidy is necessary if creativity is to be fostered and creative work made accessible to a relatively large part of the population. In these art forms and in others in which regular employment for individual artists is infrequent (for example, young opera singers), artistic earnings are so low as to rationalize a subsidy that results mainly in an increase in earnings (by enabling more artists to work full-time).

Apparently, literature and the visual arts have been slighted in the allocation of public subsidy, not because they are considered less worthy, or because supporting them is perceived to be inconsistent with the broad objectives of public subsidy – not, in fact, because of deliberate policy at all, but because the applicants for funds are not large institutions.

It is incumbent upon NEA and other fund-granting agencies to take the initiative in overcoming the institutional differences among the art forms. Although NEA and especially NYSCA have sought to resolve this problem, at least in part, by heavy use of service organizations, the opportunities have not been exhausted. In fields where major institutions do not exist, the agencies should expand their fellowship and individual stipend programs and their use of service organizations as a means of breaking bottlenecks and generally assisting in the achievement of policy objectives.

The Arts and Profit

The agencies also should reconsider the profit/nonprofit dividing line in arts projects. The major live performing-arts organizations and museums obtain a large share of public support in part because subsidies are available only for activities organized on a not-for-profit basis. Certainly, neither arts subsidies nor any other government ment subsidies to promote worthy purposes ought to be drained away in the form of additional profits for commercial enterprises. Public agencies often ensure against this possibility by proscribing completely grants to organizations that do not satisfy the criteria set forth in the Internal Revenue Code and in other federal and state laws and regulations for nonprofit status. But much high-quality, professional artistic work is done for profit. Most literature is produced under profit-oriented auspices; the commercial galleries and the private market dominate the visual arts; music has its commercial impresarios; and, of course, in the theater, Broadway, the road, most Off-Broadway productions, most summer theater, and dinner theater are commercial enterprises.

Other large countries, notably Britain and France, do not absolutely proscribe public subsidy of artistic ventures under commercial auspices. Small amounts of public funds could be used to serve the public interest in connection with profit-oriented artistic enterprises. For example, NEA could provide publishers with minimum sales guarantees for poetry and other "serious" literary works that are likely to confront exceptionally small markets; underwrite exhibitions by younger visual artists in commercial galleries; use profit-oriented impresarios as presenters of touring performances; and use guarantees, other forms of underwriting, or ticket-price subsidies, on occasion, for commercial theater presentations.[14] Obviously, any relaxation of this proscription would be fraught with administrative problems and the potential for unjust enrichment. But profit/nonprofit combinations are common in other sectors of American life and have proved successful. Arts administrators and decision makers should be able to devise ways to avoid the pitfalls and realize the advantages of a more flexible position on involvement of the commercial sectors of the arts world.

Jurisdiction

Especially if the rate of increase in appropriations to arts granting agencies is slow, the granting agencies should strive to confine their support to the arts qua arts and not wander into territories such as art in education and art as therapy that are served by other government agencies with far greater amounts of money at their disposal. The NEA architecture program should be cut back drastically or even eliminated unless the endowment can define a set of activities that are clearly in the sphere of the arts and neither duplicate nor conflict with the activities of other federal agencies. If the endowment's architecture program is eliminated, the promotion of excellence in federal design should be specifically assigned to a different federal agency – one that supervises, advises, and/or services other parts of the federal government, rather than one like NEA, whose main function is to give money to nonfederal grantees.

Artists, as imaginative people probing the frontiers of their disciplines, will often wander, and so they should, into activities that are not art qua art. Inevitably, some public subsidy from the arts granting agencies will support pioneering ventures beyond the proper jurisdictional lines. The appropriate response is to support such pioneering but not to follow it with continued, expanding support of projects in the new field. The arts agencies should seek new funding for such ventures within government agencies that have both financial resources and missions that are consistent with such projects. Sometimes, arts agencies may be tempted to territorial imperialism as a means of building a new political constituency, but such constituencies can divert limited funds from the main artistic chance or, worse, arouse the hostility of far more powerful interest groups and their associated legislative committees and agency bureaucracies. A contest between the mighty education or housing establishments and the puny public sector arts establishment would be no contest at all.

The Mechanics of Grant Programs

Most agencies that disburse public funds provoke complaints about the bureaucratic difficulties of applying for, receiving, and reporting on grants, but the nonbureaucratic types who run the arts organizations discussed earlier expressed relatively little anguish about arts agency red tape. The ratio of compliments to complaints about their procedures was very high, with most of the complaints concerning: the emphasis by NEA and NYSCA, in varying degrees, on short-term rather than continuing grants; the NEA position that grants should be for specific projects and not for general institutional support; or the requirement that grants be matched by funds raised from other sources.

The agencies have operated under these rules for excellent reasons. In combination, they enhance the freedom of action of the granting agencies – their ability to shift funds among activities, undertake new initiatives, and gain the most impact for each dollar of public money expended. The rules also tend to foster self-reliance on the part of recipients and militate against the substitution of public money for private money.

But the extremely varied and changing fortunes of the recipient organizations also provide excellent reasons for departing from these rules. On occasion, NEA and NYSCA have shown a commendable willingness to bend their rules – for example, in NEA's general support grant to the Metropolitan Opera and in NYSCA's shift to general support grants after 1970. Often, however, they have resorted to subterfuge and pretense, which are in general bad public policy, even for worthy purposes. The appropriate public policy is to develop new rules that provide explicitly for the variations from general practice.

Neither NEA or NYSCA pretends that most of its grants to the larger arts institutions are one-time, fixed-term grants that may or may not be renewed. The agencies admit to a strong presumption that the grants will be renewed, upon annual application, at a level that differs only marginally (and is higher in most years) from the current grant level. Although they also maintain a similar presumption regarding many smaller institutions and many of the art-service organizations as well, most of the service organizations interviewed for this study, including some that are almost totally dependent upon public support, do not share the assumption that renewal can be expected more or less automatically. They believe that their organizational lives are newly at stake each year. More often than not, this uncertainty has adverse effects on their program planning and administration. It also impedes fund raising from alternative sources.

Because NEA and NYSCA are subject to the vagaries of the annual appropriations process, they cannot formally commit large chunks of their funds for several years at a time, but they can commit some part of their money in this way. The major federal research granting agencies (like the National Science Foundation and the National Institutes of Health), which function under similar conditions, make multiyear grants with annual renegotiation of the specific amounts and an escape clause to cover drastic cuts in appropriations.

This arrangement gives the recipient a reasonable degree of security and should be standard practice for service organizations that clearly serve on a continuing basis as the instruments of NEA and NYSCA.

For specific projects as opposed to institutional support, fixed-term, nonrenewed grants are both sensible and feasible to administer. Most special projects should not have indefinite lifetimes; within a few years they should come to an end or be transformed into something quite different. But in order to obtain NEA and NYSCA funds restricted to special projects, directors of resident theaters, opera companies, and museums have resorted to identifying sets of already planned activities that their organizations desperately want to do as "special projects." Thus, NEA and NYSCA have been making general support grants, in fact if not in name.

Organizations that already work on a close-to-year-round basis, like the larger symphonies, the Metropolitan Opera, and the Arena Stage, can undertake entirely new projects only by hiring additional artistic staff, perhaps eventually becoming an artistic "conglomerate" like the New York Shakespeare Festival. Few arts institutions wish to follow or are capable of following that route. Most want no more than to keep one full company intact and fully employed. As more large performing arts organizations achieve full programs, the special project requirement will become increasingly unrealistic.

Most NEA support for the larger dance groups is for the special project called touring. Income from touring (a substantial part of which is public subsidy to sponsors) serves as general support, but in order to obtain this support the organization must do something it considers harmful, that is, excessive touring. A more honest and even-handed policy would not require the dance companies to do more touring than orchestras, opera companies, and theaters in order to qualify for support.

The virtue of grants for special projects is that the size of each grant is relatively easy to determine. The costs of the project can be plausibly estimated, and the NEA and the grantee can negotiate about the size and scope of the effort and the appropriate budget. The appropriate size of a general support grant is more difficult to determine. Ideally, such a grant should reflect the complex differences in financial condition and scope of activity among organizations. But NEA's solution has been to offer each institution of a given type the same amount as a maximum basic grant. Aside from the "major" symphony orchestras, few actually receive identical amounts. Still, some kind of explicit formula seems called for. In their review of grant applications, NEA panels may be weighting the appropriate factors implicitly, but now that general support is the rule rather than the exception, the weighting needs to be explicit and public.

Although NEA and NYSCA continue to apply matching fund requirements, they have often interpreted this rule flexibly. For example, they use generous estimates of the dollar value of the in-kind contributions of local school boards to satisfy Artists-in-Schools matching requirements. The main problem with this requirement is that uniformity simply makes no sense. Some organizations engaging in highly worthwhile activities that serve national interests find it much easier than others to raise the matching funds. For example, in 1974–75, the twenty-nine ASOL major orchestras had income from private contributions, foundations, and non-NEA government sources that was more than seven times as much as their NEA grants. Their matching of the NEA grants was an exercise in bookkeeping, not fund raising.

Apart from ease or difficulty in matching, the rationale for a uniform 50-50 matching requirement is far from self-evident. A more logical matching rule might be one that deals with the nature of the benefits generated by the grantee's activities. If the benefits of an activity are national, diffused over the entire society, then perhaps it should be exempt from any matching requirement. In fact, the agencies do not require matching funds for fellowships to individual artists, and this exemption can be justified on just these grounds of general benefit. If the benefits are highly localized, then a very low NEA percentage is in order. And because much of the benefit from many artistic activities is realized by arts consumers – the audiences – who pay for those benefits, NEA should accept earned income as satisfying the matching requirements, especially in cases where the nonfederal share, under this approach, is very high.

Calculating the matching requirements individually for each grant would be unfair to grantees and would unduly burden NEA. But a formula that provides for a number of categories in addition to 50-50 (and 100-0) should be devised, with guidelines indicating which types of grants fall under which requirements. In the absence of such a formula, the matching requirement, like other grant practices, will increasingly be bent by subterfuge and pretense, for the best of reasons.

Conflicts of Interest

The adoption of formulas and guidelines for matching and assessment of needs for general support, the use of multiyear grant commitments, and in fact any steps to systematize decision making on the arts to a greater extent than is now the case will reduce the discretionary power of the staffs and councils of the fund-granting agencies, but only by a small amount. Arts activities and organizations in the United States are so varied that as long as Congress and the state legislatures appropriate blocks of funds to the grant-making agencies (as contrasted with line-item appropriations to named recipients), the agencies will have substantial freedom of action in choosing among applicants and in increasing or reducing, at least at the margin, the total amounts devoted to any one art form or program. This freedom of action in the grant review process carries with it the potential for conflicts of interest.

When public support was very modest, reached only a very small number of recipients and types of artistic activities, and came to negligible portions of recipients' income, the allocation of grant funds made little difference to the state of the arts. The small probability that any given organization could actually get significant support made the decision making process something of a lottery for the recipients. Today, the grant decision does make a difference and may be distorted by two kinds of conflicts of interest.

The obvious one – the stuff of newspaper headlines when it involves the military-industrial complex and Pentagon officials – arises from a personal (whether professional, monetary, or both) interest on the part of decision making officials in the fates of applicants for grants. For example, in a number of reported instances, NEA and NYSCA senior staff members have simultaneously served as directors of or consultants (sometimes paid, sometimes not) to recipient organizations. Numerous individuals have moved back and forth between jobs with the government funding agencies and service as principals in recipient organizations. Whatever the reality, when the director of a recipient group takes a year's leave to serve as chief of the program covering his or her art form at a granting agency and then returns to the former post, there is an appearance of impropriety.

Such things have taken place in part because of the need to build up the staffs of the funding agencies rapidly as their appropriations and responsibilities increased. By and large, knowledgeable people were already active in the arts organizations – and their services continued to be in demand. But in the arts as in public life generally it is necessary that justice be both done and be seen to be done. There is no reason to assume that a higher morality pervades the world of the arts or that the problem is trivial because the amounts of money are so small (compared to defense or construction contracts, for example). A passionate believer in what his or her own arts organization is doing is more likely to act in a highly prejudicial manner as a grant agency official than a mere mercenary. The mercenary acts for money, but the true believer acts in the name of the right and the good, the most powerful of all motivations.

Nor can obvious conflicts of interest be ignored on the ground that NEA and NYSCA rely heavily on peer review, by panels of nonofficials, in making grant awards. Officials have a lot of influence on panel decisions because they determine the agenda and the ways in which matters are presented to panels for decision. Moreover, the peer-review process itself contains inherent conflicts of interest. Almost inevitably, panels tend to look with favor upon activities that make sense to the panel members because they do such things themselves. Consciously or not, some panels amount to "old-boy" networks that respond favorably to applicants who are part of that network. As the competition for grants increases – and I believe it will – it will tempt advisory panelists to judge in ways that effectively keep outsiders out.

Most panel members have some awareness of these temptations, and some lean over backward to combat them. Peer review of federal grants for scientific research has similar problems that have not been entirely resolved in more than twenty-five years of experience with such grant programs. But those involved in scientific-research grant making explicitly recognize these problems and employ a variety of procedures to make peer review work better. Moreover, the scientific world is larger than the art world and has more widely accepted standards for evaluation of proposals. Arts grant-making agencies need to pay more attention to this issue rather than turning away criticism with the refrain, "But we have panels and peer review." One step in the right direction would be the designation, on occasion, of outside panels to review the panels.[15]

Advocates for the arts may feel that this study is both negative and Philistine. They will perhaps find it negative in concluding that the record of public support for the arts is a mixed one and Philistine in its refusal to grant that the case for more public support of the arts is self-evident. Yet to count a major new government undertaking as a partial success is anything but negative: most of the new non-arts-related government programs initiated in the 1960s have been commonly evaluated as failures, completely or mainly so.

In a democratic society in which policy decisions are expected to reflect the consent, if not the active wishes, of majorities and their representatives, the policy analyst is necessarily Philistine in the dictionary sense of being prosaic and critical of things outside "the realm of ordinary and conventional ideas." To be sure, recent surveys have shown that a large majority of Americans have a benign attitude toward the arts and that rather large minorities, in the 40–49 percent range, have some direct exposure to or experience with the various arts in the course of a year.[16] But only very small minorities have even enough commitment to attend a performance or museum more than once a year, and even smaller minorities are committed enough actually to pay money to enjoy the arts. It has been estimated that the audience for paid performances of serious music, opera, dance, and live theater was no more than 5 percent of the adult population in the mid-1960s.[17]

Today, affection for and experience of the arts in the United States is clearly widespread but shallow. This shallowness suggests the need for care in the nurture of what is a rather new thing, public support of the arts, lest the majority without a strong commitment to the arts decide this use of tax money is not such a splendid notion after all. My hope is in fact that this study will bolster the case for continuing public support. The arts are *not* on the verge of general collapse; instead, they are flourishing. Limited amounts of public funds should be deployed to forestall the occasional true financial crises in worthy undertakings and, generally, to foster arts activities whenever marginal infusions of subsidy are not merely desirable but really essential for the preservation, enhancement, and diffusion of our cultural heritage.

Appendix A

Public Support for the Arts in Britain

Geraldine L. Katz

Aside from the centuries-old practice of favoring a few individual artists with government sinecures, public support for the arts in Great Britain dates from the eighteenth and nineteenth centuries, when the government established a number of national museums. The British Museum was first in 1753, followed by the National Gallery in 1823, the Victoria and Albert Museum in 1852, the National Portrait Gallery in 1856, and the Tate Gallery in 1892 (open to the public in 1897). Toward the end of World War I, the government employed a number of artists "to record with brush and pen the course of the war and the men who fought it."[1] But prior to the 1920s, British government support focused on the visual arts and on art, history, and science museums.

In 1927, the British Broadcasting Corporation (BBC) was formed. Since its inception, the BBC has done extensive arts programming and maintained its own orchestras. The BBC's financing has come primarily from the annual license fees charged owners of television and radio sets. The Post Office collects these fees and transfers them to the BBC, minus the government's expense for collection.

In 1933, the British Film Institute was created to promote the production and exhibition of quality British films. It receives its financing from the Department of Education and Science and administers the National Film Theatre in London as well as the National Film Archive.[2] This institute served as the model for the American Film Institute, which receives the bulk of its support (over $1 million annually) from the National Endowment for the Arts.

During World War II, the government became for the first time an active patron of live performing arts. In 1938, a voluntary society, the Entertainment National Service Association (ENSA) was established. Calling on the talents of performers from the commercial theater, this organization was formed to bring live music and dramatic presentations to those in the military. It received funds for this purpose from the Exchequer and the Navy, Army, and Air Force Institute (a nonprofit organization that provided benefits for British servicemen). It also charged token admission fees. Within a few months, ENSA also began presenting programs in British factories and similar establishments in attempts to heighten the morale of all citizens involved in war activities.

In 1939, the Arts Advisory Committee and the Committee for the Employment of Artists in Wartime were established under the Ministries of Information and Labor, respectively. Both groups were heavily oriented toward the visual arts; the Arts Advisory Committee inaugurated the government's program of direct purchases of contemporary art works, a practice that has continued to the present.

In 1939, the Pilgrim Trust[3] took the first step toward the creation of the modern-day Arts Council of Great Britain (ACGB) by establishing the Committee for the Encouragement of Music and the Arts (CEMA) "to prevent cultural deprivation on the home front."[4] This organization offered assistance for both the visual and performing arts. Early in 1942, the British government became involved in CEMA's activities. ("Committee" was now changed to "Council".) With John Maynard Keynes as its first director, CEMA established full-time directorships in the areas of music, drama, and the visual arts. Although headquartered in London, CEMA set up offices in the provinces in order to reach as much of the British populace as possible.

In 1945, Parliament created the Arts Council of Great Britain to continue in peacetime the wartime programs begun by CEMA. Unlike the advocates of a national arts council in the United States during the 1960s, those in Britain encountered no opposition to the council's establishment, probably because the CEMA and BBC programs had been so successful. Keynes noted that the council's birth attracted little attention from the British public. He commented: "I do not believe it is yet realized what an important thing has happened. State patronage of the arts has crept in. It has happened in a very English, informal unostentatious way – half-baked if you like."[5] Parliament gave the council the status of a permanent government body; it was to be funded by a grant from the Treasury and accountable to Parliament. In 1946, the council received a royal charter, which described the council's objectives:

> To develop and improve the knowledge, understanding and
> practice of the fine arts; to increase the accessibility of the arts
> to the public throughout Great Britain; and to advise and coop-
> erate with Government Departments, local authorities and
> other bodies on any matters concerned whether directly or
> indirectly with the foregoing objects.[6]

In 1967, a new royal charter placed the council under the Department of Education and Science instead of the Treasury; the council's
objectives remained the same, except that the term "fine arts" was
changed to "the arts."

Under the terms of the charter, the council consists of a chairman
and not more than nineteen other members. The Paymaster General
appoints the members and chairman after consultation with the
Secretaries of State for Scotland and Wales, for terms not to exceed
five years. The council elects its own vice-chairman and, again in
consultation with the Scottish and Welsh Secretaries of State, appoints two committees known as the Scottish Arts Council and the
Welsh Arts Council. These two groups receive most of their public
support through a direct grant from the ACGB.

Advisory panels, composed of individuals who are active in the
arts, assist the council in the fields of drama, music (including opera
and ballet), literature, visual arts, and young people's theater. The
members of these panels are appointed for three-year terms.

The ACGB offers subsidies to arts organizations in the form of
general revenue (that is, general support) grants, supplemental
grants and guarantees (against loss), touring grants and guarantees,
capital-expenditure grants, grants to encourage presentation of new
and neglected plays, festival grants, training grants, and transport
grants. The council also makes grants to individuals. Organizations
applying for assistance must provide proof of their nonprofit status,
hold board meetings not less frequently than every three months,
and adhere to union guidelines. Once they obtain council support,
recipients must submit all financial information requested by the
council, receive council approval before allowing any of their members to acquire subsidiary-rights in any work they produce, and
receive council consent for overseas engagements or performances
for charitable purposes. If a grantee fails to fulfill its obligations or if
the organization is dissolved, it must return a portion of its grant to
the ACGB. If an organization receives a smaller amount of funding
than it has requested, it must submit a revised operating budget for
that year illustrating the effect of the shortfall on its activities.

The council determines the amounts of the grant and guarantee

Table A-1. *Finances of the British Arts Council, Selected Years, 1945–46 to 1975–76 (in Thousands of Pounds)*

Financial year	Total government grant to Arts Council	Allocation to	
		Scotland	Wales
1945–46	235	—	—
1950–51	675	82	—
1955–56	820	82	34
1960–61	1,500	110	61
1965–66	3,910	270	210
1966–67	5,700	468	305
1967–68	7,200	708	448
1968–69	7,750	795	528
1969–70	8,200	898	568
1970–71	9,300	1,067	585
1971–72	11,900	1,335	963
1972–73	13,725	1,426	994
1973–74	17,388	2,179	1,558
1974–75	21,335	2,415	1,852
1975–76	26,150	3,000	2,050

Source: Eric W. White, *The Arts Council of Great Britain* (London: Davis-Poynter, 1975), Appendix C.

components of the subsidy for each organization on a case-by-case basis. For example:

> If the amount the Council can provide is considerably less than what the organization needs, a fixed grant helps to stabilize the receiving body's financial position. . . . [I]f an organization possesses strong reserves, it is advantageous to include a guarantee element in the subsidy. . . . [T]he strength of the aided body's governing board, the trend in its box office takings, and the type of artistic programs undertaken all are important considerations. If the concert income or box office returns vary greatly, the inclusion of a guarantee in the total subsidy is advantageous. . . . Ordinary annual grants tend to be viewed by the recipient as fixed income, whereas a guarantee constitutes a constant reminder throughout the year that all expenditures must be justified.[7]

Table A-1 shows the trend in Arts Council expenditures since 1945. Outlays were very modest in the first twenty years and began to climb rapidly only in the mid-1960s. They rose especially sharply in the 1970s, in part because of the severe inflation in Britain in recent years. The figures in the table are not adjusted for inflation. But in his 1974–75 annual report, the council's secretary-general asserts that, although the total government grant tripled from 1967–68 to 1974–75, the real value of the grant adjusted for inflation rose by less than 70 percent in this period.[8]

From its earliest days, the British Arts Council has explicitly given a high priority to the preservation and further development of the major established organizations in the performing arts, including both the London-based "national companies" and the larger resident companies in other cities. As the retiring secretary-general put it, in the context of inflationary pressures, "If an inadequate grant is likely to cause the insolvency of an enterprise built up over many years, something which means a great deal to the community, and which receives subsidy from other sources, the obligation to prevent this happening will always seem overriding."[9] Thus, in most years in the past three decades, music (including opera and ballet) has absorbed between one-half and three-fourths of Arts Council funds; music and drama combined have absorbed, in most years, more than 80 percent of the funds. That proportion has declined slightly in the latest years because the arts councils for Scotland and Wales have received disproportionately large increases in their funds (they "retail" ACGB funds) and, in 1974–75, spent "only" 60 to 70 percent of their funds for music and drama.

Although ACGB has placed progressively less emphasis on the major institutions recently, they still loom large in council grants. In 1967–68, the five national companies (the Royal Opera, English National Opera, Royal Ballet, National Theatre, and Royal Shakespeare Theatre) received grants equal to 38 percent of total council expenditure; in 1974–75, they received 27 percent. In 1967–68, the national companies plus five major orchestra groups and five major regional repertory theater companies accounted for just under one-half of total expenditure; in 1974–75, they accounted for 36 percent of total expenditure.[10] Even at this level, though, British public support benefits the "majors" far more than U.S. public support programs do. (Table A-2 shows the distribution of Arts Council spending by program in 1974–75.)

Eric W. White, former director of the Arts Council's literature program, contends:

> Most of the beneficiaries are regular customers who renew their applications year after year; and it is easier to cater for these than for new applicants who are trying to make a case for subsidy for the first time. The demands on the Council's funds

Table A-2. *Arts Council of Great Britain Expenditures, 1974–75 (in Thousands of Pounds)*

| Program | ACGB Programs | | | |
	England	Scotland	Wales	Total
National companies	5,773	—	—	5,773
Music*a*	2,654	1,038	758	4,450
Drama*a*	3,290	583	375	4,248
Touring*b*	862	45	—	907
Visual arts	994	226	87	1,306
Literature	199	69	116	384
Regional art associations	1,747	—	167	1,914
Arts centers and regional projects	309	101	183	592
Festivals	76	152	41	269
Housing the Arts	497	7	47	550
Other*c*	234	—	42	276
Total	16,636	2,220	1,814	20,670

Note: Because of rounding, detail may not add to totals.
*a*Excluding national companies. *b*Nearly all for music and drama touring.
*c*Mostly "Education in the Arts."
Source: From Arts Council of Great Britain, *Thirtieth Annual Report and Accounts, 1974–75.* Excludes capital expenditure from capital account and council operating costs; thus totals disagree with those in Table A-1.

> are so absorbing that it has never been able to build up any reserves, and newcomers can only be taken on in any one year if the increase in the Council's grant-in-aid is sufficient to warrant a measure of expansion as well as consolidation.[11]

The concern for decentralization that has reduced the relative importance of the major arts organizations in Britain as recipients of public support has also increased the importance of regional arts associations. In 1964–65, these organizations represented only a little over 1 percent of the council's total expenditures; by 1974–75, their share amounted to close to one-tenth of the total expenditure of the council. White explains that "not all of this increase, however, represents 'new money'. Already there has been a handover from the council of responsibility for some existing activities, including arts centres and arts clubs, music societies, small-scale festivals, and various literary activities; and, with responsibility, cash is handed over too."[12] By 1973, there were thirteen regional art associations in England, with many, but not all, receiving support from local authorities, local educational institutions, and the private sector in addition to council funds. During this same year, the council created a new post of director for regional development, with responsibilities for research as well as development and coordination of the activities of the council's Committee on Regional Policy.

Unlike the National Endowment for the Arts (NEA) in the United States, the British Arts Council, through its Housing the Arts program (shown in Table A-2), makes grants for capital expenditures. In addition, the council has been the conduit for government capital assistance to the new National Theatre complex, erected on the South Bank of the Thames, at an estimated cost of £16 million.[13] Ordinarily, Housing the Arts funds must be matched pound-for-pound with those from the private sector or municipal and regional authorities so that the council is responsible for no more than 50 percent of the project's costs. From 1965 to 1971, the ACGB supported 123 such projects at a cost of nearly £3 million.[14]

Like its American counterparts, the British council utilizes a number of art service organizations, some created for the purpose of servicing the council. For example, the council is responsible for the establishment of the Theatre Investment Fund, which makes public funds available to the commercial theater for the production of new plays and high-quality revivals. The fund also administers a touring program for ACGB.

The council itself runs an organization called Opera for All, which plans and arranges for opera touring. In addition, ACGB is leaseholder of Wigmore Hall, a recital hall, but does not arrange its concerts. The council produces a small number of films and dispatches mobile units throughout Britain to exhibit its own and other films. The Scottish and Welsh councils, unlike the English Council, directly provide a number of musical concerts. The Welsh Arts Council holds a music competition for young Welsh singers every three years.

Another independent organization, created in 1954 at the council's request, is the Poetry Book Society, which supplies its members with a fixed number of new poetry volumes annually. Membership varies between 700 and 1,000 people each year. By 1973, the society had distributed over 60,000 poetry volumes. The purpose of the society is to encourage British publishers to undertake the production of poetry books by assuring them of sales of at least 1,000 volumes annually. Recently, a New Fiction Society has been established on this pattern. In addition to indirect aid through support for literary magazines and small independent presses, the council offers direct grants to British writers. During 1974–75, literature grants amounted to about 2 percent of the council's total budget.

Since its inception, the council has sought to aid individual creative artists (although it spends only small amounts of money for such purposes). In 1945, Keynes commented in a radio broadcast on the role of public policy with regard to the individual artist:

> The artist walks where the breath of the spirit blows him. He cannot be told his direction; he does not know it himself, but leads the rest of us into fresh pastures and teaches us to love and enjoy what we often begin by rejecting, thus enlarging our sensibility and purifying our instincts. The task of an official body is not to teach or to censor but to give courage, confidence, and opportunity.[15]

The 1965 white paper on the arts that led to the large increase in government support in the ensuing years also strongly endorsed government support for individual artists.

In its visual arts programming, the council functions as art collector and curator; it directly operates the Hayward Gallery and the Serpentine Gallery in London. From 1946 through 1970, it mounted nearly 1,000 exhibitions, and although many of these were held at the Hayward and Serpentine Galleries, scores of exhibitions also were sent out on tour each year. In addition to purchasing a permanent collection of contemporary British paintings and sculpture, the ACGB pays a hiring fee to artists when it borrows their works for exhibition. The council also commissions prominent British art critics and curators to write catalogues for these exhibits. The Scottish and Welsh councils operate art galleries in Edinburgh, Glasgow, and Cardiff. In 1974–75, the visual arts program accounted for about 6 percent of total council expenditure. Interestingly, the Scottish Arts Council gave the visual arts considerably more emphasis than did its English or Welsh counterparts.

Although the council is part of the Department of Education and Science, it has not, unlike the (NEA), instituted major arts-education programs. Its educational activity consists of support for such programs as Work in Schools (visual arts), Writers in Schools, Young People's Theatre, the transport subsidy program, which brings the public to the art form (the opposite of touring), and visual art exhibition touring. In addition, such council grant recipients as Covent Garden, the Sadler's Wells, symphony orchestras, and repertory theaters have their own programs to encourage youth attendance at regular professional performances.[16]

The Arts Council of Great Britain is characteristically British in its respect for established institutions, its tolerance of the eccentrically different, and its ability to articulate its policies with assurance and elegance of expression.[17] Like its counterparts in North America, the council has some serious problems; for example, its efforts to encourage decentralized arts activities and to assist, if only in a small way, individual creative artists are developing a constituency whose interests conflict with those of the more traditional arts council constituency, the people associated with the major established organizations, in the performing arts especially.[18] Such conflict is somewhat newer in Britain than in the United States, and Britain's economic position is very difficult. In a comment on the Arts Council's 1975–76 annual report, *The Economist* pointed out that because of mounting financial pressures, the council "is obliged to make judgments that could be avoided, or at least mitigated, during the decade in which Britain's investment in the arts grew steadily. By making these judgments the council will in practice be formulating policy more specifically than in the past."[19]

Moreover, the other sources of public subsidy to the arts in Britain, which provide a larger share of total direct public support than the Arts Council itself, also are vulnerable to economic adversity. The BBC's spending for arts programming is roughly equal to total Arts Council expenditure. The BBC relies for its finance on a highly inelastic revenue source, radio and television license fees, and British governments generally oppose increasing these fees, even in more bouyant economic periods. Total local government support of the arts (excluding support of nonarts museums) amounts to perhaps one-half of Arts Council expenditure. But rigid ceilings have been placed on local government spending.

Foundation support for arts activities in Britain is modest at best. The Carnegie U.K. Trust has helped establish a national public library scheme and has offered support to amateur groups in music and drama. The Pilgrim Trust (which supported CEMA in the early days of World War II) has cooperated with the Arts Council in establishing the poetry program's grant to the British Museum and university libraries, enabling them to acquire the working manuscripts of contemporary British writers. The Calouste Gulbenkian Foundation offers assistance for arts projects located primarily outside of London and for projects concerned with new and experimental art forms. The Phoenix Trust supports literary and artistic endeavors as well as research. But total private support is quite small and perhaps even more exposed to economic adversity than any of the forms of public support.

Appendix B

Some Highlights of Government Support for the Arts in the United States

1846   The Smithsonian Institution is created by Congress.
1859   President James Buchanan appoints a National Art Commission; it collapsed in 1861 for lack of congressional appropriations.
1893   Municipal Art Society of New York City is founded.
1897   Congressional proposals introduced for a National Office of the Arts.
1899   Utah·Art Institute established—the first state-created arts council.
1909   President Theodore Roosevelt appoints a thirty-member Council of Fine Arts.
1910   President Taft signs a bill establishing the National Commission on Fine Arts.
1933   The Civil Works Administration grants Treasury funds to the Public Works of Art Project. A little over $1 million in funds was allocated to thirty-six hundred artists through this program, which ended in March 1934. Assistance was also available for theater and music projects.
1934   In April, the Federal Emergency Relief Administration's Emergency Work Program assists about one thousand artists by disbursing funds directly to the states. This program ended in June 1935 and was replaced by Federal Project Number One.
1934   President Franklin D. Roosevelt establishes Treasury Department's Relief Art Project (TRAP), which assigned artists to decorate federal buildings.
1935   Works Progress Administration establishes Federal Project Number One and the Federal Art Project, Federal Music Project, Federal Writers Project, Federal Theater Project, and Federal History Project.
1937   Government accepts the Mellon Collection as a gift forming the core of the National Gallery of Art collection.

1939   Emergency Relief Act of 1939 abolishes the Federal Theater Project and transfers other Federal One programs to the states.

1951   President Truman asks for a report on the state of the arts with respect to government. Report was submitted in 1953 to President Eisenhower.

1954   President Eisenhower initiates a Program for Cultural Presentations Abroad. Congressional appropriations for this touring activity totalled $16.2 million during 1955–61.

1955   President Eisenhower in his State of the Union message advocates the establishment of a Federal Advisory Commission on the Arts.

1958   President Eisenhower signs a law creating a National Center for the Performing Arts to be located in Washington, D.C.

1961   Legislation is introduced to establish a Federal Advisory Council on the Arts. The bill was defeated.

1961   New York State establishes a Council on the Arts (NYSCA).

1962   President Kennedy appoints August Heckscher as his Special Consultant on the Arts.

1963   Heckscher's report to the President, "The Arts and the National Government," is published. It recommends the establishment of an Advisory Council on the Arts and a National Arts Foundation to administer grants-in-aid. In June 1963, President Kennedy established by executive order a President's Advisory Council on the Arts. The council was never activated.

1963   In December, the Senate approves, by a voice vote, a bill requested by President Kennedy to establish a National Arts Foundation. The House took no action on this bill which would have empowered the National Arts Foundation to make matching grants to states and nonprofit professional groups.

1964   President Johnson appoints Roger L. Stevens as Special Assistant to the President. Later in the year, the President signed a bill establishing the National Council on the Arts, an advisory body of citizens prominent in the arts.

1965   The President appoints Roger L. Stevens as Chairman of the National Council on the Arts. Later in the year, Congress passed and the President signed a bill establishing the National Foundation on the Arts and Humanities. Roger L. Stevens was named Chairman of the National

Endowment for the Arts (NEA) and Henry Allen Moe Chairman of the National Endowment for the Humanities (NEH), shortly succeeded by Barnaby Keeney.

1965   The Elementary and Secondary Education Act is passed by Congress authorizing schools, under Titles I and III, to develop innovative projects that can utilize the services of art groups and cultural resources.

1966   NEA begins with an appropriation of $2.5 million. 1,834 applications were received.

NEA programs begun in 1966:

Music:	aid to composers and musical groups to prepare and perform new works.
Dance:	support for several touring efforts and choreographers' fellowships.
Literature:	poetry in schools.
Theater:	institutional support.
Education:	grants to recent graduate artists, musicians, and creative writers, and sabbatical grants for teaching artists.

1967   Architecture + Environmental Arts Program begun.
Federal/State Partnership Program begun.
Public Media: Assistance for production and distribution of arts programming on television. American Film Institute established.
Visual Arts: Works of Art in Public Places Program begun.

1968   Dance Touring Program initiated.
Museum Purchase Plan initiated.

1969   President Nixon proposes extending the National Foundation on the Arts and Humanities for three more years and doubling the budgets of NEA and NEH to $20 million each.

1970   Artists-in-Schools Program initiated.
Jazz Program begun.
Orchestra Program begun.
Visual Arts: museum scholarship program begun.

1971   Museum Program initiated.

1972   Federal Design Improvement Program initiated.
Expansion Arts: Tour Events Program established.
Public Media Program expands – film preservation.
Museum Program expands – conservation of collections.
Dance Program expands – regional development of dance companies.

1973   Congress passes a three-year re-authorization bill for $72.5
        million in 1974; $100 million in 1975 and $126 million in
        1976.
        Craftsmen's fellowships are offered by Visual Arts Pro-
        gram.
        Theater Program expands—theater for youth, theater train-
        ing, and touring.
        Visual Arts Program expands—visual arts in performing
        arts.
        Architecture—National Theme Program begun.
1974   Special Projects receives program status. Folk Arts Program
        is begun under Special Projects.

Appendix C

Detailed Breakdown of Grants Made by the National Endowment for the Arts, Fiscal 1971–74

The *Annual Reports* of the NEA for the fiscal years 1971–74 provide the basic data for this Appendix. However, the characterizations of grants by purpose and other aspects of the classification scheme used here are original with this study. Because NEA reports and releases are anything but clear in describing the purpose of specific Endowment grants, some grants may have been misclassified.

Table C-1. *Institutional Aid (in Thousands of Dollars)*[a]

Program	1974	1973	1972	1971
Architecture				
Cultural facilities design	90	183	128	—
Excellence in Federal design				
Dance				
Management and administration	162	88	—	—
Resident professional dance companies	292	450	217	—
Services to the field	183	164	115	165
Museums				
Special exhibitions	3,329	806	939	348
Catalogs	436	—	—	—
Conservation laboratories	172	42	147	—
Conservation of collections	347	368	145	100
Renovation, climate control	1,534	724	648	—
Utilization of museum collections	700	698	548	—
Music				
Music festivals	—	312	—	—
Opera program	5,344	3,471	2,591	598
Orchestra program	7,172	4,760	5,307	3,761
Services to the field	210	153	59	—
Public Media				
American Film Institute	1,100	1,100	1,038	1,087
Regional development	276	157	146	—
Special Projects				
Crafts	—	15	49	—
Community arts council development	—	80	—	—
Theater				
Professional theater companies/short season	2,834	2,021	1,590	1,444
Theater for youth	200	100	—	—
Services to the field	398	83	—	60
Total institutional aid	25,158	16,017	13,667	7,563

Note: Because of rounding, detail may not add to totals.

[a]Grants to institutions for general or specific programmatic purposes considered to be so central to the main missions of the organization that, one way or another, the organization would have to raise these funds to assure its continuation, in the long run if not in the short run.

Table C-2. *Aid to Individuals Channeled through Institutions (in Thousands of Dollars)*

Program[a]	1974	1973	1972	1971
Dance				
Visiting choreographers	44	22	27	—
Literature				
Services to the field	279	151	99	90
Poets and writers in developing colleges	43	42	49	21
Museums				
Purchase plan	835	405	500	90
Museum training	290	174	119	98
Training in conservation	300	375	151	—
Visiting specialists	151	92	182	98
Music				
Jazz/folk presentations	215	153	198	32
Choral program	70	72	48	—
Independent schools of music	797	787	555	—
Public Media				
Cable TV interns	101	—	—	—
Media studies	245	210	174	—
Short film showcasing	99	—	—	—
Special Projects				
NEA interns	33	12	—	—
Theater				
Professional training	115	76	—	—
Visual Arts				
Services to the field	100	148	72	—
Exhibition aid	139	116	—	3
Total aid to individuals (indirect)	3,856	2,833	2,171	441

Note: Because of rounding, detail may not add to totals.

[a]Grants to institutions for programs that directly involve artists or arts professionals, including training activities, purchase of works or services, and organizations providing supporting services to individual artists (organizations providing supporting services to institutions, such as the American Symphony Orchestra League, are included in the "institutional aid" section of the Appendix).

Table C-3. *Direct Aid to Individuals (in Thousands of Dollars)*

Program	1974	1973	1972	1971
Architecture				
Design fellowships	—	—	29	2
Dance				
Choreography fellowships	225	150	124	146
Education				
Arts administration fellowships	80	50	50	9
Literature				
Creative writers fellowships	470	300	195	6
Museum				
Museum professionals fellowships	107	141	163	—
Music				
Composer/librettist/translator				
fellowships	357	72	47	—
Jazz/folk/ethnic fellowships	205	74	47	18
Public Media				
Filmmakers (through American Film				
Institute)	260	260	—	—
Graduate fellowships	67	—	—	—
Visual Arts				
Fellowships	920	853	30	197
Total aid to individuals (direct)	2,691	1,900	685	378

Note: Because of rounding, detail may not add to totals.

Table C-4. *Commissioning, Production, and Research Awards (in Thousands of Dollars)*

Program[a]	1974	1973	1972	1971
Architecture				
Academic and professional research	269	237	436	111
Dance				
Dance criticism	22	—	—	—
Production grants	453	136	123	247
Workshops (commissioning)	2	96	35	—
Film/video documentation	162	—	—	—
Education				
Film documentation	54	24	45	—
Literature				
American authors films	103	—	—	—
Literary magazines	300	250	170	50
Small/independent presses	—	5	5	25
Music				
Contemporary music projects	145	48	123	49
Audiovisual experiments	—	—	32	—
Public Media				
American Film Institute preservation	390	390	300	—
Programming in arts	1,456	367	183	—
American film series for TV	250	—	—	—
Research and development	15	40	—	—
Joint projects with Corporation for Public Broadcasting	139	163	52	104
Theater				
New plays, developing theaters	436	408	463	312
Visual Arts				
Visual arts in performing arts	27	83	—	—
Works of art in public places	679	307	450	119
Workshops, short-term activities	270	190	277	63
Photography publications	—	30	—	—
Total commissioning, etc.	5,171	2,773	2,695	1,078

Note: Because of rounding, detail may not add to totals.

[a]Grants supportive of the production of art, either by direct commissioning or by research, experimentation, and documentation.

Table C-5. *Grants for Public Education, Awareness, and Outreach (in Thousands of Dollars)*

Program[a]	1974	1973	1972	1971
Architecture				
National theme	2,899	666	—	—
American architectural heritage	—	133	—	—
Public education and awareness	531	92	193	—
Dance				
Touring	2,016	1,474	1,347	693
Education				
Alternative educational forms	334	240	142	—
Expansion Arts				
Arts exposure	901	441	183	308
Community cultural centers	393	298	225	—
Instruction and training	1,863	1,384	527	—
Neighborhood art services	203	148	50	—
Special summer projects	470	242	151	—
Touring events	150	—	—	—
Museums				
Wider availability of museums	759	702	481	182
Music				
Audience development	450	440	530	—
Theater				
Regional touring	292	209	—	—
Visual Arts				
Residencies	174	252	108	27
Artists-in-Schools				
Architecture	62	62	—	—
Crafts	356	—	—	—
Dance	474	375	191	93
Film	412	383	320	93
Music	64	46	85	26
Poetry	538	510	464	270
Special	417	158	42	7
Theater	189	150	50	25
Visual arts	571	529	374	183
Subtotal, Artists-in-Schools	3,082	2,211	1,536	697
Total public education	14,527	8,930	5,475	1,906

Note: Because of rounding, detail may not add to totals.

[a]Includes all grants whose purpose seems mainly to educate the general public, to make more people aware of the arts or to reach audiences not reached by more conventional means. In other words, the audience or general public appears the direct beneficiary of the grant, and the artist only incidentally, the reverse of the situation in connection with the earlier sections of this Appendix.

Table C-6. *Grants for General Programs (in Thousands of Dollars)*

Program[a]	1974	1973	1972	1971
Architecture				
General programs	12	—	—	66
Miscellaneous	22	—	—	—
Dance				
General programs	380	178	281	—
Education				
General programs	26	5	96	145
Expansion Arts				
General programs	104	13	—	—
State arts agencies	15	—	—	—
Literature				
General programs	198	28	—	—
Museums				
General programs	61	2	—	—
Special projects	31	66	125	11
Music				
General programs	288	50	209	730
Special projects	863	—	—	—
Public Media				
General programs	285	80	87	74
Special Projects				
General programs	219	430	238	479
Interrelated programs	426	—	—	—
State arts agencies	—	478	370	50
Services to the field	217	—	—	—
Theater				
General programs	526	439	644	205
State arts agencies	157	—	—	—
Visual Arts				
General programs	27	2	4	144
Total general programs	3,857	1,792	2,052	1,905
Federal/State Partnership	10,558	6,871	5,500	4,125

Note: Because of rounding, detail may not add to totals.

[a]Grants that are made in areas for which there are no specific NEA guidelines but are consistent with the general goals of the Endowment. Includes bloc grants to the state arts councils under the Federal/State Partnership Program.

Appendix D

Cross-tabulations by Purpose and Program of Grants Made by the National Endowment for the Arts, Fiscal 1971–74

The Annual Reports of the NEA for the fiscal years 1971–74 provide the basic data for this Appendix. However, the characterizations of grants by purpose and other aspects of the classification scheme used here are original with this study. Because NEA reports and releases are anything but clear in describing the purpose of specific Endowment grants, some grants may have been misclassified. For detail, see Appendix C. The notes to Appendix C also apply to this Appendix.

Table D-1. *Purposes of Grants by NEA, by Program*

	Grants in thousands of dollars			
Purpose and program	1974	1973	1972	1971
Institutional aid				
Architecture	469	437	127	—
Dance	637	702	332	165
Museum	6,517	2,638	2,428	448
Music	12,727	8,687	7,957	4,359
Public Media	1,376	1,257	1,184	1,087
Special Projects	—	95	49	—
Theater	3,431	2,204	1,590	1,504
Total	25,158	16,017	13,667	7,563
Aid to individuals channeled through institutions				
Dance	45	22	26	—
Literature	323	192	148	120
Museum	1,576	1,045	952	286

Table D-1 (*cont.*)

Purpose and program	Grants in thousands of dollars			
	1974	1973	1972	1971
Music	1,081	1,012	800	32
Public Media	444	210	174	—
Special Projects	33	12	—	—
Theater	115	76	—	—
Visual Arts	239	263	72	3
Total	3,856	2,833	2,171	441
Direct aid to individuals				
Architecture	—	—	29	2
Dance	225	150	124	146
Education	80	50	50	9
Literature	470	300	195	6
Museum	107	141	163	—
Music	561	146	95	18
Public Media	327	260	—	—
Visual Arts	920	853	30	197
Total	2,691	1,900	684	378
Commissioning, production, and research awards				
Architecture	269	237	436	111
Dance	639	232	158	247
Education	54	24	45	—
Literature	403	255	175	75
Music	145	48	155	49
Public Media	2,249	960	535	104
Theater	436	408	463	312
Visual Arts	977	610	727	182
Total	5,171	2,773	2,695	1,078
Grants for public education, awareness, and outreach				
Architecture	3,431	890	193	—
Dance	2,016	1,474	1,347	693
Education	334	240	142	—
Artists-in-Schools	3,082	2,211	1,536	697
Expansion Arts	3,980	2,512	1,137	308
Museum	759	702	481	182
Music	450	440	530	—
Theater	292	209	—	—

Table D-1 (*cont.*)

Purpose and program	Grants in thousands of dollars			
	1974	1973	1972	1971
Visual Arts	174	252	108	27
Total	14,517	8,930	5,475	1,906
Grants for general programs				
Architecture	34	—	—	66
Dance	380	178	281	—
Education	26	5	96	145
Expansion Arts	119	13	—	—
Literature	198	28	—	—
Museum	92	90	125	11
Music	1,152	50	209	730
Public Media	285	80	87	74
Special Projects	862	908	607	530
Theater	683	439	644	205
Visual Arts	27	2	4	144
Subtotal	3,857	1,792	2,052	1,905
Federal/State Partnership	10,558	6,871	5,500	4,125
Total	14,415	8,664	7,552	6,030

Note: Because of rounding, detail may not add to totals.

Table D-2. *Program, by Purpose*

Program and purpose	Grants in thousands of dollars			
	1974	1973	1972	1971
Architecture				
Institutional aid	469	437	128	—
Direct aid to individuals	—	—	29	2
Commissioning, etc.	269	237	436	111
Public education, etc.	3,431	890	193	—
General programs	34	—	—	67
Total	4,202	1,564	785	179
Dance				
Institutional aid	637	702	332	165
Aid to individuals (indirect)	44	22	27	—
Direct aid to individuals	225	150	124	146
Commissioning, etc.	639	232	158	247
Public education, etc.	2,016	1,474	1,347	694
General programs	380	178	281	—
Total	3,942	2,759	2,268	1,251
Education [a]				
Direct aid to individuals	80	50	50	9
Commissioning, etc.	54	24	45	—
Public education, etc. [a]	3,416	2,451	1,679	697
General programs	26	5	96	145
Total	3,576	2,530	1,869	851
Expansion Arts				
Public education, etc.	3,980	2,512	1,137	308
General prgrams	119	13	—	—
Total	4,099	2,525	1,137	308
Literature				
Aid to individuals (indirect)	323	192	148	120
Direct aid to individuals	470	300	195	6
Commissioning, etc.	403	255	175	75
General programs	198	28	—	—
Total	1,394	775	518	201
Museums				
Institutional aid	6,517	2,638	2,428	448
Aid to individuals (indirect)	1,576	1,045	952	286
Direct aid to individuals	107	141	163	—
Public education, etc.	759	702	481	182
General programs	92	90	125	11
Total	9,051	4,615	4,149	927

Table D-2 (*cont.*)

Program and purpose	Grants in thousands of dollars			
	1974	1973	1972	1971
Music				
Institutional aid	12,727	8,687	7,957	4,359
Aid to individuals (indirect)	1,081	1,012	800	32
Direct aid to individuals	561	146	95	18
Commissioning, etc.	145	48	155	49
Public education, etc.	450	440	530	—
General programs	1,152	50	209	730
Total	16,116	10,382	9,746	5,188
Public Media				
Institutional aid	1,376	1,257	1,184	1,087
Aid to individuals (indirect)	444	210	174	—
Direct aid to individuals	327	260	—	—
Commissioning, etc.	2,249	961	535	104
General programs	285	80	87	74
Total	4,682	2,767	1,980	1,264
Special Projects				
Institutional aid	—	95	49	—
Aid to individuals (indirect)	32	12	—	—
General programs	862	908	607	530
Total	894	1,015	656	530
Theater				
Institutional aid	3,431	2,204	1,590	1,504
Aid to individuals (indirect)	115	76	—	—
Commissioning, etc.	436	408	463	312
Public education, etc.	292	209	—	—
General programs	683	439	644	205
Total	4,957	3,335	2,696	2,021
Visual Arts				
Aid to individuals (indirect)	239	264	72	3
Direct aid to individuals	920	853	30	197
Commissioning, etc.	977	610	727	182
Public education, etc.	174	252	108	27
General programs	27	2	4	144
Total	2,336	1,981	941	552
Federal/State Partnership				
General programs	10,558	6,871	5,500	4,125
Total	10,558	6,871	5,500	4,125

Note: Because of rounding, detail may not add to totals.
[a] Includes Artists-in-Schools.

Appendix E

State Arts Agencies:
Programs and Funds

In the course of this study, all the state arts agencies were asked to supply their most recent annual reports and whatever supplementary information on programs and funding they could offer. Ten of the fifty state agencies (and the District of Columbia) did not respond. Most of the reports received were for 1973–74; a few were for 1972–73. The reports differ considerably in the extent of program and financial detail, and their program classifications also differ. What follows is a precis of the annual reports for thirty-nine of the forty states responding (New York, which is discussed in the text of Chapter 4 at length, is excluded), listing their arts programs, with financial information where supplied.

The thirty-nine states accounted for 85 percent of total state government appropriations to arts agencies in the forty-nine states other than New York in 1973–74; they include thirteen of the fifteen states (again, excluding New York) that appropriated more than $250,000 for the state arts agency that year.

Alabama 1972–73: Total expended $354,847

Architecture and Environmental	$ 3,000
Arts Education	103,024
Dance	3,805
Humanities	2,223
Literature	4,147
Multi Arts	45,797
Music	36,954
Museums	10,693
Theater	26,492
Visual Arts	5,255

Alaska 1974: Total expended $210,989

Community Arts Council Grants	$49,500
Cultural Heritage Grants	6,050
Dance Grants	8,629
Literature Grants	350
Music Grants	20,992
Program Service Grants	43,095
Resident Performing Arts Routing	16,270
Theater Grants	19,428
Visual Arts Grants	15,325
Other Grants	31,350

Arizona 1973–74: Total expended $599,378

Development Program	$248,825
Educational Enrichment	24,758
Festival Program	158,634
Touring Program	77,476
Visual Arts	85,796
Administrative Costs	3,889

Arkansas 1973–74: Total expended $480,006

Music and Other Performing Arts
Visual Arts
Special Projects
Artists-in-Schools

California 1974: Total expended $1,013,748

Performing Arts (grants to dance companies, symphonies, theater groups, chamber orchestras, performing-arts workshops, opera troups, and other groups concerned with the performing arts)	$476,533
Arts Councils and Special Programs (groups concerned with community-level programs)	170,107
Communications and Environmental Arts (architecture, television)	134,627
Visual Arts Organizations (art galleries, artists-in-residence, art museums)	169,497
Touring Program Grant (NEA coordinated)	62,984

Connecticut 1974: Total expended $897,203

Community Development Program (urban neighborhood arts programming)	$200,000
Education Program	104,024
Direct Aid Program (supports overall operational costs of organizations, no strings attached)	80,000
Grants to Professional Arts Organizations (includes program development, aid to individual artists, minigrants, and exemplary projects)	403,264
Information Center	59,915
Special Projects (Regional Arts Programming Study, tristate Music Touring Program, Dance Tour, Arts Administration Internships)	50,000

Delaware 1973: Total expended $146,215

Architecture and Environmental Arts (sculpture, art in public places)	$ 2,663
County and Community Arts Development (technical assistance, arts letters, etc.)	7,638
Dance (Dance-in-Schools)	13,000
Education (residencies, arts-related courses, student tickets)	21,427
Expansion Arts	8,716
Literature (Poets-in-Schools, printing)	10,340
Music (symphonies, singers, chamber groups, concerts)	43,067
Public Media (television, film)	3,260
Theater	15,590
Visual Arts (art galleries, lectures, painters-in-residence)	32,214

Florida 1973–74: Total expended $1,858,924

Federal and State Funds	$ 378,924
Private Funds	1,480,000
Education and Special Programs (Artists-in-Schools, Community Development, Art Festivals)	
Performing Arts (Dance, Literature, Music, Theater)	

Florida (*cont.*)

Visual Arts (Architecture and Environmental
Design, Museums, Arts Centers and
Touring Exhibitions, Film and Public
Media)

Georgia 1974: Total expended $313,662

Performing Arts	
Dance	$16,400
Drama	20,634
Music	
Crafts	13,675
Education	
Artists-in-Schools and Residencies	161,915
Special Projects	
Community Arts	40,265
Technical Assistance	23,567
Art Training	14,000

Hawaii 1972–73: Total expended $396,714

Performing and Visual Arts Events (Arts Festivals, Dance, Literature, Music, Theater, Crafts, Fine Arts, Graphic and Design)	$198,517
Ethnic Group Presentations	48,200
Artists-in-Schools, Artists in the Community, and Artists in Neighborhoods	64,200
Audience Building, Art in State Buildings, General Operations	85,747

Idaho 1974: Total expended $358,250

Poetry (Poetry-in-Schools, workshops)
Opera
Theater
Dance
Visual Arts
Music
Historical Societies
Special Projects

Illinois 1971–72: Total expended $693,256
(creative artists awards, museum ticket plan, visual arts touring exhibitions)

Education/Special Programs	$138,738
Free Street Program	222,370
Performing Arts	234,450
Visual Arts	97,698

Indiana 1973–74: Total expended $201,020

Programming Grants	
Music	$62,298
Multi–Arts	51,125
Visual Arts	32,653
Dance	23,384
Theater	21,225
Film/TV	10,185
Writing	150

Iowa 1973–74: Total expended $443,217

Dance (ballet companies, Dancers–in–Schools)
Literature (writer's tour, poetry readings)
Music (organizations, performances, touring)
Theater (touring, summer festivals)
Visual Arts (workshops, residencies, tours)
Special Programs

Kansas 1973–74: Total expended $230,149

Touring Assistance	$35,120
Artistic Resource Development	87,720
Artists–in–Residence	14,915
Community Arts Agency Development	30,595
Special Projects	8,533
NEA Dance Touring	17,566
NEA Special Projects	10,000
NEA Artists–in–Schools	25,700

Kentucky 1973–74: Total expended $348,352

Professional Touring	$95,395
Visual Arts	26,968
Resource Development	118,188.55
Literary	4,995
Artists-in-Schools	46,525
Program Development	9,960
Dance Residency	2,000
Governor's Contingency Fund Grants	44,317

Louisiana 1973–74: No breakdown of funding available

Grants for Theater, Literature, Music, Youth
and Art, Dance, Film and Photography,
Art, Environment and the Arts, and Special
Projects

Maine 1973–74: No breakdown of funding available

General Grants Program (matching grants to
arts organizations)
Commission Sponsored Programs
Artists-in-Schools Programs
Performing Arts Program (listing of Maine
performing artists willing to tour
throughout the state, Dance Touring
Program)
Community Arts Development (grants for
technical assistance to local arts councils)
Information Program
Visual Arts (touring art shows and
photographic exhibitions)
Preservation Grants (awarded to historical
societies, museums, libraries, towns to
assist them with restoration)

Maryland 1973–74: No breakdown of funding available

Grants to Major Institutions (performing or
exhibiting institutions of statewide
significance in need of funds for
undertaking new projects or to continue
existing activities)

Development Grants (performing and
exhibiting organizations concerned with
upgrading artistic standards, improving
management, developing new audiences, or
providing new services)
Art Series (chiefly for arts councils,
universities, schools to sponsor concerts or
exhibits)
Individual Events (same as above, except for
one performance or exhibit)

Massachusetts 1974: Total expended $480,457

Financial Assistance (provides funding for nonprofit, professionally directed arts and humanities organizations)	$437,447.85
Historic Conservation (matching funds for professional restoration of objects of artistic or historical significance)	17,924.55
State/Local Partnership Services (community arts councils, arts centers, etc.) (in 1975, jumped to $122,616)	11,084
Technical Assistance (offers services of a specialist for up to three days; pilot in 1974, no listing of funds)	
Artists-in-Residence (no listing of funds)	
Artists-in-Schools (no listing of funds)	
Creative Artist Services (aid to individual artists pilot projects) (up to $75,000 for 1975)	14,000
Touring (no funds listed)	

Michigan 1974–75: Total expended $1,234,439

Community Special Projects	$291,100
Community Assistance Program	115,720
Michigan Artrain	
Partnership Activities	
Major Arts Organizations	
Expanding Arts Resources	537,929
Bicentennial Arts Activities	165,025
Artists-in-Schools	99,300
Community Arts Council Administration Grants	25,365

Minnesota 1973–74: Total expended $389,969
(no detailed description for each category available;
fellowships to individuals in all areas;
Artists–in–Residence, Artists–in–Schools)

Architecture	$40,000
Dance	36,616
Music	87,182
Opera	14,313
Literature	13,063
Theater	67,325
Visual Arts	52,677
Research and Development	28,793
Regional Development	50,000

Missouri 1973–74: No breakdown of funding available

Touring Programs
Community and Regional Program
Special and Recurring Programs (Dance
    Touring, Artists–in–Schools,
    Artists–in–Residence, Education Project,
    Visual Arts Touring, and Technical
    Assistance)

Nebraska 1975: Total expended $778,020
(No breakdown of funding available)

Special Project Grants
Community Arts Assistance Grants
Artists–in–Schools
Dance Touring

Nevada 1975: Total expended $173,387

Major Organizations	$42,896
Performing Arts Organizations	58,132
Visual Arts Organizations	22,975
Education	30,986
Expansion Arts	18,398

New Mexico 1973–74: Total expended $396,900

Architecture	$ 300
Crafts	26,000
Dance	700
Drama	20,800
Education	11,200
Historic Preservation	11,600
Literature	3,000
Music	44,300
Painting and Sculpture	6,900
Special Aid to Children	7,600
Special Projects	2,800
TV/Film	1,700
Private Funds	260,000

New Jersey 1974: Total expended $250,000
(fellowships to individual artists also available)

Grants made for Audience Development,
　Technical Assistance, Festivals, Special
　Projects, Educational Programs,
　Community Services and Ticket Subsidy in
　the following areas:
　　Music
　　Dance
　　Visual Arts
　　Theater
　　Film
　　Environment and Design
　　Writing and Expansion Arts

North Carolina 1973–74: No breakdown of funding
available

Artists-in-Schools Program
Community Development Program (aid to
　community and county arts councils)
Conferences
Consultant Service (technical assistance)
Dance Residencies
Intern Program (train future arts
　administrators)
Poetry Readings

North Carolina (*cont.*)

Television/Radio Commercials (public service
announcements to promote fund drives for
the arts)
Visiting Artists (residencies for artists at
community colleges)
Grants
    Grants to Nonprofit Organizations
    General Grants
    Literary Grants
    Local Government Grants (pilot program
    for local government to program for the
    arts)
    Salary Assistance Grants

North Dakota 1973–74: No breakdown of funding available

Grants are made to arts organizations, but
specific programs are not listed with
funding.

Ohio 1974: Total expended $1,085,904

Touring
Workshop Residencies
In-School Programs
Festivals
Architecture and Environmental
New Arts Organizations
Existing Arts Organizations
Aid to Individual Arts
Mini-Grants and Special Programs

Oklahoma: No breakdown of funding available

Touring Programs
Organizational Assistance
Technical Assistance
Ticket Endowment Program
Humanities Projects
Education Programs
Special Projects

Oregon 1973–75: Total expended $1,511,619
($682,275 public; $829,344 private)

Mental-Correctional/Ethnic, Education/Aging Programs (special programs)	$ 10,000
Community/Organizational Grants	320,000
Artists-in-Schools	122,440
Volunteer Lawyers for the Arts	7,450
Dance Touring	10,000
Internship	9,500
Manpower Development and Training	6,000
Emergency School Aid Act, Jefferson High School, Portland	67,759

Rhode Island 1973–74: Total expended $434,968
($126,228 state; $247,575 federal; $61,165 other)

Artists-in-Residence
Restoration
Crafts
Arts and the Aging Program
Arts in Corrections Program
Ticket Endowment Program
Happenings (neighborhood program)
Touring
Special Projects
Grants-in-Aid to Individuals

South Carolina 1973–74: Total expended $491,912

Arts-in-Education (Affiliate Artist, Artist-in-Residence, Filmmakers-in-Schools, In-School Concerts, Poets-in-Schools)	$199,311
Contemporary Arts (Film Festivals, Arts-in-Prison, Youth Film Production Grants, Film Equipment Loan Program)	86,446
Professional Arts (Dance Touring, Ticket Subsidy, Ensemble Residency Program)	98,956
Grants-in-Aid (Architecture, Dance, Film/Photo, Literary Arts, Music, Theater, Visual Arts, Multi-Media Individuals)	107,179

Tennessee 1973–74: Lists artists/fees available for touring
and artists/fees offering services

Community Arts Assistance
Cultural Resources
Community Grant-in-Aid
Special Programs
Artists-in-Schools
Ticket Endowment Program
Touring Program

Texas 1974: Total expended $395,000

General Assistance	$ 49,762
Major Institutions	40,000
Community Assistance	17,112
Touring Program	98,126
Artists-in-Schools	220,800

Utah 1974–75: Total expended $502,621

Community Art Programs	$ 84,225
General State Organization Program Support	107,096
Touring or Statewide Impact	191,500
NEA Programs	31,300
Administration and Miscellaneous	88,483

Vermont 1973–74: Total expended $200,000

Community Arts Councils	$25,000
Arts Organizations	45,000
Individual Artists	15,000
Special Projects	25,000
Touring Aid	50,000
Council Projects (Artists-in-Schools, Music in the Parks, Children's Festivals, etc.)	40,000

Washington 1973–74: Total expended $119,750

Touring Performing Arts	$ 5,700
Major Performing Arts Organizations	26,750
Dance Development	13,481
Circulating Visual Arts Exhibits	7,120
Community Partnership	17,224
Direct Support of Artists	14,100
Special Projects	35,375

Appendix F

Persons Interviewed for the Case Studies

The sources for information about the sixteen arts organizations discussed by name in Chapter 5 include, in addition to annual reports and other documents, interviews with principals in those organizations conducted during 1975 and interviews with several people in other organizations – foundations, government funding agencies, and service organizations – conducted during 1975 and early 1976. The latter group of interviews were conducted mainly to secure more general information and views about the arts and government policy, but they also shed some light, directly or indirectly, on the sixteen named organizations. The conclusions, appraisals, and opinions expressed in the body of Chapter 5 cannot be ascribed to *any* of these people; they are the views of the interviewers, not the interviewees. Indeed, some of them have views about arts policy or about specific organizations that sharply diverge from those expressed here.

Anania, Michael. Chairman, Coordinating Council of Literary Magazines, July 28, 1975.

Bliss, Anthony A. Executive Director, Metropolitan Opera Association, August 19, 1975.

Clark, Richard. President, Affiliate Artists, Inc., July 29, 1975.

Collinge, Robert. General Manager, Baltimore Opera Company, August 26, 1975.

Crouch, Ned. General Manager, Charlotte Symphony Orchestra, August 20, 1975.

Fichandler, Thomas. Executive Director, Arena Stage, August 12, 1975.

Fleckman, Neil. Administrator, Paul Taylor Dance Company, August 22, 1975.

Gingrich, John. Executive Director, American Association of Dance Companies, January 22, 1976.

Grace, Trudie. Executive Director, Committee for the Visual Arts, September 4, 1975.

Guthrie, Ann. Program Information Office, National Endowment for the Arts, April 16, 1975; September 24, 1975; and November 13, 1975.

Hofer, Lynne, and Roger Larson. Young Filmakers, September 4, 1975.

Kaufman, Nancy. Visual Arts Office, Creative Artists Public Service, Inc., December 15, 1975.

Kummel, Herb. Executive Director, Dance Notation Bureau, January 22, 1976.

Lockwood, William. Festival Director, Mostly Mozart Festival, Lincoln Center, August 11, 1975.

Marron, Vincent and Janet Gracey. Theatre Development Fund, January 23, 1976.

Martin, Gerry. Executive Director, Young Audiences, Inc., July 28, 1975.

Michalski, Kirsten. Executive Secretary, P.E.N. American Center, July 25, 1975.

Phillips, William. Honorary Chairman, Coordinating Council of Literary Magazines, September 8, 1975.

Sheldon, Richard. Program Officer, Division of the Humanities and the Arts, the Ford Foundation, January 23, 1976.

Sokoloff, Boris. Manager, Philadelphia Orchestra, August 14, 1975.

Sydeman, Hope. Financial Administrator, New York City Ballet, September 11, 1975.

Thurston, Ellen. Program Information Director, New York State Council on the Arts, November 25, 1975.

Williams, Galen. Executive Director, Poets and Writers, Inc., August 13, 1975.

Wyckoff, Robert. President, American Crafts Council, August 26, 1975.

Notes

Chapter 1. The Open Questions

1   These data and Table 1-1 include all the identifiable government spending in support of the arts qua art. They exclude spending for art within the educational system (although that spending employs artists and supports artistic production in schools and colleges), aside from grants from the National Endowments and state arts councils to educational institutions. No doubt there is some spending by public agencies, other than explicitly arts agencies (especially at the federal level), that supports art qua art (rather than art as education, therapy, or the like), but it is almost impossible to identify such amounts. For derivation of the estimates in Table 1-1, see Chapter 4. The definition of "direct public support of the arts" used in Table 1-1 is employed throughout this book.

2   Indirect subsidies are discussed in more detail in Chapter 3.

3   Of course, tax deductibility and other forms of indirect government support of the arts also pose important policy questions, but the issues are different. It *is* important that the magnitude of indirect support be measured more precisely and its effects on the recipient organizations studied. Michael O'Hare of the Massachusetts Institute of Technology is now engaged in such a study for the Twentieth Century Fund. It is to be completed in 1978.

4   This figure includes most, but not all, of the 210,000 people classified in the first two industry groups in part II of Table 1-2 and small numbers classified in the other industry groups.

5   Nonfarm wages, salaries, and proprietors' income of $678.0 billion divided by 78,560,000 persons engaged in nonfarm production. (Source: *Survey of Current Business,* July 1974.)

6   For the performing arts as a whole, Table 1-4 shows total expenditures of $6.9 billion. According to the 1972 *Census of Business,* total expenditures of nonprofit theater companies, symphony orchestras, and other classical or serious music and dance groups amounted to only $258 million. Allowing for the incomplete coverage of the census and for more popular programming that is eligible for governmental subsidy (for example, jazz, folk, and ethnic music), the total expenditures of nonprofit live performing-arts organizations were probably only a little over $300 million. All the estimated expenditures for the visual arts in Table 1-4 – another $300 million – were in

forms eligible for subsidy. All other arts expenditures of the types eligible for subsidy – in the literary arts, for arts programming on noncommercial broadcasting stations, in filmmaking, by nonprofit service organizations, by arts festivals and community arts centers and groups – probably did not exceed another $300 million. In all, $900 million seems a generous estimate of the total size (in 1972) of the arts sector that is the likely target for direct public support.

Chapter 2. The Case for Support

1   "The Presidency and the Arts," *The New York Times,* October 31, 1976.

2   Richard A. Posner, "The Probable Effects of Pay Cable Television on Culture and the Arts," in Richard Adler and Walter S. Baer, eds., *The Electronic Box Office: Humanities and Arts on the Cable* (New York: Praeger, 1974), p. 82.

3   The Endowment's stated objectives are discussed more fully in Chapter 4.

4   Until recently, the individual's rate of return, in the form of higher lifetime earnings, from higher education was so large that it would have paid most people to attend even if they had had to pay full costs.

5   William J. Baumol and William G. Bowen, *Performing Arts – The Economic Dilemma* (New York: The Twentieth Century Fund, 1966), Ch. 4.

6   National Research Center of the Arts, Inc., *A Study of the Non-Profit Arts and Cultural Industry of New York State* (New York, 1972).

7   The Ford Foundation, *The Finances of the Performing Arts,* Vol. 1 (New York, 1974).

8   Associated Councils of the Arts, *Americans and the Arts: A Survey of Public Opinion* (New York, 1975).

9   In the Ford Foundation study, the average price realized on tickets sold in 1970–71 was $3.47, a price that obviously precludes frequent attendance by people with modest incomes. The performing arts do not differ in this respect from other live spectator events, like major league sports, which the poor also do not attend in large numbers. However, I believe there is rather less societal concern about people going through life without seeing a live professional football or hockey game than there is about not having exposure to the performing arts.

10 A survey of New York audiences of the Joffrey Ballet conducted by the National Research Center of the Arts found that three of every ten people attending the performances for the first time had seen the company previously on the "Dance in America" television series and 59 percent of them said the television show led to their attendance.

(National Endowment for the Arts, *The Cultural Post,* No. 8, November/ December 1976, p. 15.)

11   The greater variety of program offerings found in radio, for which there are many more channels available than in television, is indicative of the result of making more outlets available.

12   The federal government has a long tradition of subsidizing experimentation in other fields on just these grounds. It does so on a massive scale in the support of scientific research, space exploration, and weapons development. Since the early 1960s, it has also subsidized experimentation in transportation, housing, law enforcement, income maintenance, education, and other social programs.

13   Another reason for "wasting money" on artistic efforts that fail has been advanced by British critic Bernard Levin: it is a "prophylaxis against timidity" on the part of the granting agencies; "the eventual alternative to wasting money on [rubbish] will not be to spend it on masterpieces but to spend it only on work admired by the *Daily Express.*" *The Times* (of London), October 22, 1976.

14   National Endowment for the Arts, *The Cultural Post,* No. 8, November/December 1976, p. 14.

15   See Michael Sterne, "Broadway Season Gives City a Reason to Applaud," *The New York Times,* June 2, 1977, p. B1.

16   Baumol and Bowen, *Performing Arts.* Professor Baumol has extended his analysis, updated some of the data, and examined specific performing-arts institutions in subsequent studies, for example, a study of the New York theater conducted under the auspices of the New York City Cultural Council and New York State Council on the Arts, published in January 1972. It is fair to say that the Baumol-Bowen argument is now the most frequently cited and insistently urged reason for public support of the performing arts, repeated in every congressional committee hearing; conference on the arts; and book, monograph, or article on the present and future financial prospects for the performing arts. The success of this idea is mainly a tribute to its internal logic, which is presented in an elegant and well-documented fashion. But it may be attractive to some arts advocates because it makes a case for open-ended public support for *all* forms of the performing arts, whereas most other arguments call for more limited and, in some cases, diminishing public support.

17   These calculations are based on a linking of the data in the Ford Foundation, *Finances,* vol. 1, for 1965–66 through 1970–71 and advance unpublished data provided by the foundation for the period 1970–71 through 1973–74. The estimates suffer from the obvious flaw that, properly speaking, price and income elasticity of demand should be estimated simultaneously. However, for a period as brief as nine years, this flaw should not be serious.

18   Baumol and Bowen, *Performing Arts,* Appendix, Table III-C, p. 429.

19   The data are personal consumption expenditures for "admissions to legitimate theaters and opera, and entertainments of nonprofit institutions (except athletic)" in the national income accounts. The revised estimates are substantially lower than the earlier ones.

20   It should be noted that other data suggest that the revised personal consumption expenditure series continues to overstate actual consumer spending in the earlier years of the 1960–75 period, and thus the "true" income elasticity figure could be significantly higher. However, the overstatement in the earlier years would have had to be at least 40 percent of the reported figure, relative to the data for the later years, for the "true" income elasticity to be as high as 1.25, and a 60 percent overstatement would be necessary to bring the income elasticity to 1.75.

21   In "The Probable Effects of Pay Cable Television on Culture and the Arts," Richard A. Posner argues that "pay cable television offers attractive opportunities for increasing the productivity of the arts, perhaps quite substantially, and thereby markedly enhancing the commercial revenue potential of the arts and of related cultural activities" (p. 89). Of course, live and television performances are quite different things; television is not a means of increasing the productivity of live performances. But it *is* a way to increase the productivity of the performing *organizations,* and spectacularly so. Its major drawback is that it might very well destroy financially many smaller performing organizations, much as the televising of major league baseball games wiped out many minor league teams. Thus, while greatly increasing access to the performing arts in the aggregate, pay cable television might reduce access to live performances per se. Conceivably, it also might reduce employment opportunities for artists.

22   Examples used by Baumol and Bowen, *Performing Arts,* p. 164.

23   The country house built by the Prince-Archbishop, which today houses the Salzburg Seminar in American Studies.

24   For additional examples of accepted changes in the presentation of classical music, see Donal Henahan, "How Did They Play Mozart 200 Years Ago?" *The New York Times,* July 11, 1976.

25   The numbers cited above clearly depend on the initial assumption that the arts will lag in productivity by 1.4 percentage points a year. There seems no good reason to assume that the arts should do much worse than the services as a group have done previously. Moreover, services now amount to a large share of the total economy; consequently, improvement in productivity for the economy as a whole must be lower than it was when agriculture, mining, manufacturing, and common-carrier transportation (all high-productivity-change sectors) were relatively more important.

26   Obviously, other grounds may justify increasing specific subsidies as

relative prices rise – for example, to provide cheap tickets for new audiences.

27 Martin Mayer, commenting on an earlier draft of this book, asserts that the best strategy for attracting and retaining the most talented people *is* the strategy of paying higher wages:

> Art is an inherently wasteful activity . . . at the key points when subsidy may be demanded, you really don't know who the most talented are. By the time this has been demonstrated, the most talented probably don't need subsidy any more. In arts education as in all education, you get diminishing returns: the larger the pool you send to college, the smaller the fraction that benefits significantly by the experience – but there are important individuals who would not show up in your final product if you had applied a finer screen at entry. I think it is true that budget-makers and planners forget the psychic satisfaction aspect of compensation for artists, and that income levels somewhat below those of comparably trained people in other fields will suffice to draw a large enough candidate pool to assure the flow of talent. But not too much below. And the best way to encourage participation in the lottery over time is to provide a lot of little prizes: i.e., living wages for orchestral musicians.

28 Philip Hart, in his study of the symphony orchestra, concludes that the large Ford Foundation program of grants to orchestras, launched in 1966, was responsible for major wage claims and militant action by major orchestra musicians in the late 1960s. Hart expresses fear that increased government funding may have a similar effect. See *Orpheus in the New World* (New York: Norton, 1973), pp. 342–3, 473–4. See also the discussion in Chapter 5.

29 Ford Foundation data for performing arts companies for the 1965–66 to 1973–74 period suggest that increased subsidy *did* tend to increase compensation levels for some art forms. See Chapter 5.

30 A 1973 report of a special committee set up by the British Arts Council to consider pricing policies of subsidized performing-arts organizations found that a good number of these organizations (especially the ones outside London) tended to keep top prices unduly low, often on the entirely unjustified ground that such a policy maximized attendance. The committee recommended more "tilting" of price schedules, that is, a bigger spread between the prices of the most expensive and the cheapest seats. Arts Council of Great Britain, *Report of the Committee of Enquiry into Seat Prices* (London, 1973).

31 Quoted in *Washington International Arts Letter,* Vol. 15, No. 7 (July/August 1976), p. 1082.

32 This account is based upon the report in the *Chronicle of Higher*

Education, October 11, 1976. Berman's nomination lapsed with the adjournment of Congress and the end of President Ford's term of office. President Carter did not renominate Berman.

33 Robert Brustein, "The Coming Crisis for the Arts: Who's Going to Foot the Bill?" *The New York Times,* September 15, 1974, Section 2; Zelda Fichandler, "Theaters or Institutions?" in International Theatre Institute of the United States, *The American Theatre, 1969–70* (New York: Scribner's, 1970), pp. 105–16.

34 "Arts Management and the Art of Music," Research Paper No. 26, Management in the Arts Research Program, Graduate School of Management, University of California at Los Angeles, (1975). Of course, some people in the arts celebrate the virtues of the market-place; as the writer Wallace Stegner put it, ". . . art must make its way with some reasonably representative audience if it is to be any-thing but a pleasant self-indulgence," *The Uneasy Chair* (New York: Doubleday, 1974), p. 126.

35 The Metropolitan Opera was not included in the projections because its finances did not exhibit consistent trends in the study period. In financial terms, the Met is so huge (it alone accounted for one-eighth of total expenditures of the group of 166 in 1970–71) that its inclu-sion would be highly distorting.

36 From November 1970 to November 1975, consumer prices increased by an annual average rate of 6.9 percent; we show 4.5 percent here because this set of projections more closely matches the 5.1 percent annual price inflation rate between the 1970–71 and 1973–74 seasons, and our data for the finances of the performing arts extend only to 1973–74.

37 In 1970–71, the $26 million remaining after local nongovernmental contributions was financed as follows:

Government grants	$7.8 million
National foundation grants	8.2 million
Endowment earnings used for operations	7.8 million
Endowment principal used for operations	2.7 million

38 In 1975 and 1976, the Council on Foundation Project in the Arts conducted four semiannual economic surveys of a sample of arts organizations throughout the country. These surveys have indicated that arts organizations are faring rather better than the Ford Founda-tion study's projections suggest, despite a severe rate of inflation and the worst recession since the 1930s (which was *not* anticipated in the Ford study). In the face of recession, the surveyed groups have been able to generate increases in individual and corporate giving and substantial increases in earned income. Deficits have *not* mounted alarmingly, as might have been expected, nor have programs been cut back on a widespread basis.

Chapter 3. Patterns of Public Support

1 In Britain, property taxes also are important as a source of public funds, but the British have made little use of property tax exemption to foster socially desirable activities. For example, in 1970–71, London local governments levied about £350,000 ($900,000) in property taxes ("rates") on museums, galleries, and similar institutions. In the same year, the Greater London Council and the London boroughs spent about ten times this amount to support local museums and galleries and to subsidize nongovernmental artistic and cultural activities and facilities. (Calculated from tables in Greater London Council, *1970 Annual Abstract of Greater London Statistics,* 1972.)

2 This figure is based on the assumptions that the market value of the property owned by tax-exempt artistic organizations would be taxed at an average rate of 2 percent (were such property taxable) and that the aggregate market value of the property is $7.5 billion. In the light of the national wealth (and other) statistics, which indicate that, as of 1968, the value of land and buildings owned by *all* nonprofit organizations other than colleges and hospitals was less than $30 billion, I regard these figures as upper limits.

3 The American Association of Fund-Raising Counsel, in its 1975 annual report, *Giving USA,* estimates that total gifts and bequests to the "arts and humanities" amounted to $1.28 billion in 1974. Data in that report suggest that roughly $900 million of this total came from individuals, $100 million from bequests, and $140 million each from corporation gifts and private foundation grants. On the basis of data from federal individual income and estate tax returns and the tax rate schedules, it is possible to estimate plausibly the marginal rate of tax to which the average donor was subject. These various estimates in combination suggest that the total federal tax liability avoided by making gifts to the arts and humanities in 1974 was roughly $550 million; state and local tax savings may have been another $95 million. If art museums are classified with the arts rather than with the humanities, it is probable that the arts' share of the $645 million was much the largest portion, perhaps in excess of $500 million.

Studies done for the Commission on Private Philanthropy and Public Needs (see *Giving in America: Toward a Stronger Voluntary Sector,* 1975, p. 55) suggest that individual giving may be far in excess of the AAFRC estimate. A highly accurate survey of corporate gifts to the arts in 1973, conducted by the accounting firm of Touche, Ross and Co., for the Business Committee for the Arts, estimates total corporate support of the arts at $144 million in that year (*Survey of Business Support of the Arts, 1973* [New York, August 1974]). This amount is about double the AAFRC estimate for a year later for the "arts and humanities" combined. In the light of this and the higher estimates of individual giving to the arts implied by *Giving in America,* it would not be unreasonable to estimate the subsidy from tax deductibility for all donors to the arts at $700 million in 1974.

In an unpublished paper entitled "Indirect Government Aid to the Arts: The Tax Expenditure in Charitable Contributions" (September 1976), Kerry D. Vandell and Michael O'Hare estimated the subsidy to the arts from the deductibility of contributions from federal individual income tax returns to be between $180 million and $240 million in 1972. That estimate is consistent with the 1974 estimate of more than $500 million noted above, the latter including subsidy associated with corporate income, estate, and gift taxes and with state and local taxes as well as federal individual income taxes.

4   Perhaps the most persuasive proponent of this view is Stanley S. Surrey. See his *Pathways to Tax Reform* (Cambridge: Harvard University Press, 1973). For a highly skeptical discussion of this argument and the allegation that property tax exemptions are terribly costly, see Dick Netzer, "Property Tax Exemptions and Their Effects: A Dissenting View," *Proceedings of the Sixty-Fifth Annual Conference on Taxation, October 1972* (Columbus, Ohio: National Tax Association, 1973).

5   For a spirited and cogent defense of this position, see the Arts Council of Great Britain, *Twenty-Ninth Annual Report and Accounts, 1973–74* (London: ACGB, 1975), pp. 11–12.

6   Broadcasters, public or commercial, seldom report their finances in formats that clearly indicate just how much they spend for the arts as distinct from news, public events, and "mere" entertainment. However, according to one estimate, in 1973–74, when its total budget was £141 million the BBC spent £25 million on "drama, serious music and arts features." (Lord Redcliffe-Maud, *Support for the Arts in England and Wales,* Calouste Gulbenkian Foundation [London: 1976], pp. 107–8). In that year, the Arts Council, the British counterpart of the U.S. National Endowment for the Arts, spent £17.5 million (Arts Council of Great Britain, op. cit.).

7   See the background paper by Martin Mayer in *Bricks, Mortar, and the Performing Arts, Report of the Twentieth Century Fund Task Force on Performing Arts Centers* (New York: The Twentieth Century Fund, 1970), pp. 15, 22–3.

8   Department of Cultural Affairs, Swedish Ministry of Education and Cultural Affairs, *The State and Culture in Sweden* (Stockholm: The Swedish Institute, 1970), pp. 63–4.

9   These estimates are derived from data in *The State and Culture in Sweden.* That report includes in its totals public support of libraries, museums other than art museums, archives, and arts education. I have excluded those categories to provide comparability with Table

1-1, and I have made 1970–71 estimates for local governments and some minor central government categories. Payments to individual artists were SKr 14.7 million (or just under $3 million at SKr 5 = $1) and estimated total direct public support SKr 295 million.

10 Spending for these awards was roughly £250,000 ($650,000); total expenditure was £17.5 million ($45 million). (Arts Council of Great Britain, *Twenty-ninth Annual Report,* various tables.)

11 Calculated from data in National Endowment for the Arts, *Annual Report 1974* (Washington, D.C., 1975).

12 Compiled from annual reports of the state arts councils.

13 Nancy Hanks, "The Creative Artist–Cornerstone of Culture," in Associated Councils of the Arts, *The Creative Artist: Chances for Change* (New York, 1975), p. 6.

14 Ibid., p. 8.

15 The models for the government arts foundation in the United States were the large private foundations as well as the National Science Foundation and the National Institutes of Health, both of which "retail" government research funds to nongovernmental organizations and individuals under vague legislative guidelines, extensively using nongovernmental advisory panels and referees.

16 See Appendix A for an extended discussion of the history and functioning of the British Arts Council.

17 Lord Redcliffe-Maud: *Support for the Arts* contains a mixture of hard data and rough estimates for various recent years, on the basis of which it appears that total direct public subsidy for the arts in the fiscal year 1975–76 was between £100 and 105 million, exclusive of support for nonarts museums. That year, the total government grant to the Arts Council was £28,450,000. The British Film Institute, with an appropriation of about £2 million in 1975–76, also operates as an arts foundation. Thus, the two arts foundations combined accounted for no more than 30 percent of total public subsidy.

18 This estimate is based on fragments of data contained in the following sources: Frank T. Pasquill, *Subsidy Patterns for the Performing Arts in Canada* (Ottawa: The Canada Council, February 1973); Mary C. Sullivan, *The Group of Twenty-Nine* (Ottawa: The Canada Council, October 1973); Sam Book, *Economic Aspects of the Arts in Ontario* (Toronto: Ontario Arts Council, 1973); and Ontario Arts Council, *Annual Report 1973–74.*

19 Both UNESCO and the Council of Europe have been encouraging social accounting for the arts that would provide such data. For an example of a comprehensive set of such accounts for Britain, with partial data for 1970–71, see Alan Peacock and Christine Godfrey, "Cultural Accounting," *Social Trends* (London: Her Majesty's Stationery Office, November 1973), pp. 61–5.

20 The Australia Council grant (from the central government) was

A\$20.0 million in 1974–75 and A\$23.7 million in 1975–76 (*The Economist,* March 27, 1976).

21   Based on data in Hans Jochen Freiherr von Uslar-Gleichen, "The Federal Republic of Germany: Culture, Economics and Politics," in *The Arts, Economics and Politics: Four National Perspectives,* Aspen Institute for Humanistic Studies, 1975 (hereafter cited as *The Arts, Economics and Politics*).

22   These data are derived from *The State and Culture in Sweden.* They do not include any estimates of the costs of arts programming by the Swedish Broadcasting Corporation. If such programming amounted to 10 percent of total broadcasting production costs (contrasted with the 18-percent figure for the BBC indicated by the data cited earlier in note 9 above), then total public support of the arts including broadcasting in 1970–71 can be set at the equivalent of \$66 million, or about \$8.20 per capita.

23   Gerard Bonnot, "French Cultural Policy: Evolution and Current Issues," and Claude G. Menard, "French Cultural Policy," in *The Arts, Economics and Politics.* These two papers are replete with factual information, but a number of apparent inconsistencies (perhaps a result of the translation) make it difficult to be completely confident about the global estimates.

24   In the United States, the limit for corporations is 5 percent and, for all practical purposes, there is no limit for individuals.

25   The receipts of nonprofit organizations in Britain are fully subject to the value-added tax; even the Arts Council itself must pay value-added tax on the exhibitions and performances it presents and the publications it sells.

26   It has been estimated that business support of the arts in Britain amounts to no more than £400,000 a year (*The Financial Times,* September 24, 1975), compared to more than \$100 million in the United States. In *Support for the Arts,* Lord Redcliffe-Maud estimates private foundation support at no more than £1 million annually (p. 110).

27   The finances of opera in the two countries are a case in point: in 1974–75, the Arts Council grant to the Royal Opera House was £2.6 million, one and a half times box office receipts of £1.8 million (Mark Blaug, *Why Are Covent Garden Seat Prices So High?* [London: Royal Opera House, 1976], p. 4). For the twenty-nine opera companies in the Ford Foundation survey, government grants of all kinds equaled only 13 percent of earned income in 1973–74.

Chapter 4. Direct Subsidy Programs

1   See Appendix B for a capsule history of the early, mostly abortive federal initiatives.

2   There is, by now, a considerable literature on the New Deal art programs, including William F. McDonald, *Federal Relief Administration and the Arts* (Columbus: Ohio State University Press, 1969); Richard D. McKinzie, *The New Deal for Artists* (Princeton: Princeton University Press, 1973); June deHart Mathews, *The Federal Theatre, 1935–39* (Princeton: Princeton University Press, 1967); and Claire S. Chow, "Looking Back on the Federal Theatre Project," in *The Cultural Post,* Issue 8, November/December 1976, pp. 6–7.

3   McDonald, *Federal Relief Administration*, p. 52.

4   Ibid., p. 371.

5   Chow, "Looking Back," p. 6.

6   McDonald, *Federal Relief Administration,* McKinzie, *The New Deal,* and Chow, "Looking Back," passim.

7   McKinzie, *The New Deal,* p. 39.

8   Ibid., p. 42.

9   Chow, "Looking Back," p. 7.

10   McKinzie, *The New Deal,* p. 151.

11   Ibid., p. 179.

12   These events during the 1950s and early 1960s are summarized in John S. Harris, "The Politics of Government Patronage of the Arts in the United States," *Parliamentary Affairs,* Vol. 20 (1967), pp. 315–28.

13   From a letter of President Kennedy to August Heckscher on June 10, 1963, in response to August Heckscher's report. By 1963, the National Science Foundation and the National Institutes of Health were well-established federal mechanisms for encouraging "science and learning."

14   "The Politics of Government Patronage," p. 325.

15   Alvin Toffler, *The Culture Consumers* (Baltimore: Penguin Books, 1965), p. 208.

16   The authorizing legislation permits the Arts Endowment to use up to 20 percent of the funds allocated for grants to nonprofit organizations without matching by the recipient organization.

17   The authorizations for NEH and NEA have been exactly the same for most of the past eleven years. The appropriations for the two endowments usually differ marginally, occasionally because of the different appropriations from the Treasury Fund (presumably reflecting estimates of what private donations will be). In the ten-year period 1966–75, total appropriations to NEA were $252 million and total appropriations to NEH were $226 million.

18   The reauthorization bill enacted in 1976 applies to four (not three) fiscal years, 1977 through 1980, and provides dollar spending ceilings well above the appropriations for fiscal 1977 and 1978; for 1979 and 1980, it calls for "necessary expenditures" without specifying any dollar amount. The *appropriation* for fiscal 1977 is $85 million; supple-

mental funds are to be provided in fiscal 1977 for a newly enacted "challenge grant" program ($12 million for fiscal 1977).

19　However, NEA grants to the larger performing arts organizations, especially the major symphony orchestras, are in effect general support grants that are described as project grants. The 1976 reauthorization statute provides for a new type of grant, a "challenge grant," which is a one-time multiple-year grant to an institution to strengthen its financial base by securing new and increased sources of continuing income. Without specific authorization, NEA made a challenge grant of this type to the Metropolitan Opera in 1974.

20　This is even more evident when one examines the detailed data in Appendix C.

21　Excluding the Federal/State Partnership Program, which consists largely of block grants to state arts councils and is not a program of grants to arts-producing entities but a way of "wholesaling" federal arts money that assures wider geographic dispersion among the producers of the arts.

22　Most of the urban design activities supported by NEA's Architecture Program are strikingly similar to those supported by the Department of Housing and Urban Development.

23　Without listing and analyzing every single NEA grant (and examining in detail the outlays of the state arts councils from NEA block grants), it is impossible to characterize by art form grants made under the other four major programs – Education, Expansion Arts, Special Projects, and the Federal/State Partnership. The Education program, via Artists-in-Schools, undoubtedly provides significant assistance to the visual and literary arts, but the other programs probably share the general bias in the direction of the performing arts.

24　This appraisal is based on National Foundation on the Arts and Humanities, *Estimates of Appropriatoins for the Fiscal Year 1976,* submitted to the Congress, February 1975. It provides estimates by program for fiscal 1975 (exclusive of expenditures from the Treasury Fund that are activated by private donor decisions) and plans for fiscal 1976. The narrative permits estimates by program for 1976, although such estimates are not explicitly shown.

25　NEA, to its credit, has never claimed that there is some national purpose to be achieved by favoring one art form over another, simply as art form; it is not clear how NEA decides upon priorities among art forms.

26　Unfortunately, NEA annual reports do not provide enough detail to distinguish precisely among purposes. Unquestionably, some expansion arts grants result in the production of new works, but the program is explicitly designed not to produce new art but to reach new audiences.

27 There is no solid evidence on state expenditures of the NEA grants per se, only on the total outlays of funds, regardless of source, by the state agencies. But one bit of evidence is this: In fiscal 1974, the state arts councils financed largely with NEA money (twenty-nine of the fifty state arts agencies received over half their funds from NEA) spent relatively low percentages of their budgets on institutional support and high percentages on touring and educational activities. (See National Endowment for the Arts, *Study of State Arts Agencies: A Comprehensive Report,* prepared for NEA by the National Research Center of the Arts, Inc., 1976, Tables 6 and 76.)

28 *Estimates of Appropriations for the Fiscal Year 1976,* op. cit.

29 This criticism ignores the issue of differences among regions in direct state or local commitment to support of the arts. Until fiscal 1976, New York State's and New York City's direct financial support of the arts exceeded the *total* NEA appropriation; it continues to amount to a large *multiple* of NEA grants to New York activities. In most of the rest of the country, state and local government support of local artistic activities is a small *fraction* of NEA support for those activities. This issue is discussed further below.

30 This criticism is less applicable to the theater than to other art forms. Over the last decade, NEA has supported a large fraction of the highly innovative yet fully professional efforts in theater.

31 The Office of Education of the U.S. Department of Health, Education, and Welfare operates a few readily identifiable programs in support of arts education, including an "Alliance for Arts Education" program, "Special Arts Projects" grants under the Emergency School Aid Program (these grants closely resemble NEA's Artists-in-Schools Program), and grants for equipment purchases and minor remodeling. In fiscal 1974, these art education activities involved total expenditures of less than $5 million, according to information in Associated Councils of the Arts, *Cultural Directory* (New York, 1975). The National Park Service spends more than $2 million annually, minus reimbursements, for maintenance and housekeeping operations at the John F. Kennedy Center for the Performing Arts in Washington (*Washington International Arts Letter,* Vol. XV, No. 7, July–August 1976, p. 1083).

32 National Endowment for the Humanities, *Program Announcement: 1974–75,* p. 2.

33 In the reauthorization hearings in late 1975, leading congressional supporters of the two endowments complained about the low visibility and lack of public awareness of NEH programs, compared to NEA activities.

34 The source of these figures is a CPB brochure, "Public Broadcasting and Financing – Where the Money Comes From," 1975. Total income in 1974 was roughly $290 million. In contrast, in 1973, net

broadcast revenue of the commercial broadcasting stations and networks was $5 billion (*Statistical Abstract of the United States, 1975*).

35   Like the two endowments, CPB seems to believe that an annual report naming the recipients of grants without indicating the nature or purpose of the grant is adequately informative. Even in congressional hearings before friendly committees, officials are typically unable (or unwilling) to provide much more coherent and comprehensive information, despite requests year after year.

36   National Endowment for the Arts, *The Cultural Post,* Issue 13, September/October 1977, p. 8; *The New York Times,* October 22, 1977.

37   The commercial sports analogy is a deliberate illustration of this point. The arguments commonly used in favor of local subsidies to commercial sports are rather similar to those used in support of local subsidies to local arts organizations. See, for example, N.J. Sports & Exposition Authority *v.* McCrane, 119 N.J. 427 (1971).

38   Utah and Virginia formally established arts councils before New York, but New York's was the first to become operational in a grant-making sense.

39   NYSCA, *Annual Report, 1969–70,* p. 29. In the four years beginning in 1961–62, NYSCA subsidized 656 performances at a cost (to the Council) of $906,000, or $1,380 per performance.

40   Ibid. By 1968–69, NYSCA support provided only one-third of total artists' fees for touring performances.

41   In early 1971, the New York Legislature staged a celebrated "revolt" against the governor's budget, which provided for very large tax increases, and most state agencies suffered in the appropriations process.

42   New York State Commission on Cultural Resources, *Cultural Resource Development: Planning Survey and Analysis, Preliminary Report* (Albany, March 1973).

43   Concerned Citizens was essentially one of the various aliases used by Associated Councils of the Arts (ACA); ACA was and is the most prominent advocate for the major arts organizations throughout the country.

44   Amyas Ames, "For the Life of the Arts in New York State." Testimony before the public hearing held jointly by the New York State Assembly Ways and Means Committee and the Senate Finance Committee, February 13, 1974, published as a brochure by Concerned Citizens.

45   NYSCA press release, October 24, 1975.

46   This is not to deny that there is a case for encouraging amateur artistic activity. See Chapter 6.

47   In March 1973, Manhattan accounted for 73 percent of total statewide employment in the performing arts and museums; the other four boroughs accounted for 11 percent (U.S. Department of Com-

merce, *County Business Patterns, 1973: New York,* CBP–73–34, 1974). If anything, these data understate the degree of concentration of artistic activities in Manhattan because they do not include the visual arts, literature, or films and television.

48 The council, quite sensibly, considers that the value of services provided in a given county by a statewide organization should be credited against the seventy-five cents per capita requirement; it does not interpret the requirement to mean that only direct grants to organizations and individuals located within a county should be taken into account.

49 Interview with Lynne Hofer and Roger Larson of Young Filmakers, September 4, 1975.

50 Amyas Ames, "For the Life of the Arts."

51 The list included twenty-one museums, ten of them art museums.

52 Report to the New York State Council on the Arts by a Special Ad Hoc Committee chaired by Edward M. Kresky, NYSCA, January 17, 1975.

53 As in New York, the arts in Puerto Rico significantly contribute to its attractiveness to visitors and, of course, tourism is the island's most important industry. Public support of the arts in Puerto Rico also appears to be an expression of national and cultural identity. In any event, the effort is substantial: Commonwealth government appropriations in 1975 relative to personal income were more than twice as high as New York State government appropriations.

54 To put this effort in some perspective, it should be noted that only fifteen state governments spend less than $1 billion for all purposes annually.

55 However, a few states do make line-item appropriations for the direct support of selected institutions, notably art museums and symphony orchestras.

56 NEA's 1976 *Study of State Arts Agencies,* prepared by the National Research Center of the Arts, contains tables that seem, superficially at least, to contradict this characterization. Table 76 in that report indicates that 57 percent of total fiscal 1974 project expenditures for all state arts agencies other than NYSCA was devoted to "program support of institution or organization," "staff salary support," or "basic (or general operating) support of institution or organization." But the annual reports summarized in Appendix 5 make it clear that many of the institutions so supported are community arts agencies, sponsors of touring engagements, and operators of summer festivals, not major or "primary" institutions. Similarly, Table 73 in the NEA study indicates that about 40 percent of project expenditures in fiscal 1974 were in support of the more traditional "serious" art forms, like orchestral music, opera, modern dance and ballet, and poetry (with the rest for combinations of art forms, public media, and less tradi-

tional forms within the performing and visual arts). The evidence suggests that the support of these traditional art forms by state arts agencies was for artists in schools, school performances, touring, and other education and outreach activities.

57   The simple correlation coefficient between personal income per capita in calendar 1973 and the NEA allocation as a percentage of combined state and NEA funds in each of the fifty states is −0.409, implying a weak tendency for state matching to rise with personal income per capita. That correlation coefficient suggests that only one-sixth of the variation among the states in the mix of NEA and state funds can be attributed to income differentials per se (that is, R^2 =0.1669).

58   The U.S. Census Bureau, in its reports on state and local finances, has a rather fine breakdown, but as of 1973–74, there was no function separately identified for which expenditures by all local governments combined were less than $200 million; local government support of the arts is clearly well below that amount.

59   Including a number of cities not shown in Table 4-17, such as Chicago, Detroit, St. Louis, and Los Angeles, that provide in excess of $1 million annually from tax funds for the art museum.

60   According to data supplied by the American Symphony Orchestra League – the results of its annual survey of twenty-nine "major" and seventy-six "metropolitan" U.S. symphony orchestras – orchestra associations received $5 million from local governments in 1974–75. This excludes any amounts spent directly by the local government in supporting services, such as building maintenance, which do not show in the accounts of the orchestra association. In the same year, state governments made payments, other than through the arts councils, of $1.8 million to symphony orchestras.

61   As throughout this study, I exclude public spending on the arts within educational institutions as part of regular educational programs.

Chapter 5. Effects of Public Support

1   From $21 million in calendar 1965 to $282 million in calendar 1975, according to the estimates in Table 1-1.

2   An untapped source for case-study analysis is the grant applications submitted in successive years to NEA and state arts councils. But because the applications are not in the public domain, this kind of analysis can be done only by the staffs of the granting agencies.

3   Another high-quality data series is the annual survey done by the American Symphony Orchestra League (ASOL). The ASOL data cover a longer span of years than do the Ford Foundation data and provide somewhat greater detail. However, because the Ford sym-

phony-orchestra panel heavily overlaps the ASOL "major" and "metropolitan" orchestra categories (in dollars, the Ford panel is roughly 90 percent of the two ASOL categories), I do not separately analyze the ASOL data here. In his superb study of the symphony orchestra as an American cultural institution, *Orpheus in the New World,* Philip Hart makes extensive and detailed use of ASOL (and other) data. Hart's views regarding public subsidy of symphony orchestras differ strikingly from mine. Still, the Hart book is a model of a serious study of the arts.

4   The Ford Foundation, *Finances,* Vol. 1.

5   Ibid., pp. 28–9.

6   The new sample is not simply the old 166 organizations less 13 dropouts; it contains both additions and deletions. It includes more theater companies and significantly fewer orchestras and modern dance companies. In dollar terms, the significant differences are confined mainly to orchestras and modern dance.

7   As Table 5-1 indicates, the average income of the Ford sample organizations was just over $1 million in 1971–72, while the average income for the *Census of Business* group was only slightly over $300,000.

8   In this analysis, I often explicitly exclude the Metropolitan Opera from the aggregates for the sample because of the Met's huge relative size. In 1965–66, the Met alone accounted for one-sixth of the total income of the 166 organizations and in 1973–74, for one-eighth of the total for the 153 organizations.

9   A significant share of the income shown as nongovernment services income in the accounts of dance companies may actually be financed from government grants to sponsoring organizations.

10 If government grants were the source of much nongovernment services income for dance, then dance also experienced such a decline.

11 If all the performing arts organizations in the Ford sample received *all* their earned income from private sources from ticketed performances and made expenditures *only* for ticketed performances and government-subsidized free performances, the Ford data would readily support a reliable multiple-regression analysis. Difficulties in measuring prices, output, and unit costs arise because the arts organizations in the sample do so many things in addition to presenting ticketed performances of their own companies.

12 *Statistical Abstract of the United States, 1975,* p. 366.

13 That is, 1.595 divided by 1.408.

14 That is, $1.958 [1 - 0.25(0.133)] = 1.893$.

15 Ignoring, for the moment, the obvious facts that the organizations in the survey have other sources of income than ticket sales and public subsidy and that ticketed performances are not their sole artistic activity.

16 Hart, *Orpheus* has a good account of the Ford Foundation project and

its effects (pp. 339–45). His book is the source of most of the follow-ing information.

17   In 1970–71, ASOL changed the format for tabulating its survey results so that 1969–70 is the latest year for which Ford endowment income is shown separately in the published tabulation.

18   It is, perhaps, somewhat confusing to jump back and forth among data for the sixty-one orchestras covered by the Ford grant program, data for the larger group covered by the Ford statistical surveys, and data for the still larger groups covered by the ASOL surveys. How-ever, these groups overlap substantially; the overlap between ASOL and Ford surveys was noted earlier. Only three orchestras in the grant program were not in either of the two Ford surveys (1965–66 to 1970–71 and 1970–71 to 1973–74), and they accounted for less than 2 percent of the total trust fund. Another three orchestras (in-cluding one very large one, the Chicago Symphony) in the grant program were not among the respondents in the second Ford survey panel; they accounted for nearly 6 percent of the trust fund. All of the orchestras in the surveys but not in the grant program were small ones, with budgets of $500,000 or less in 1970–71. We estimate that the twenty-three nongrant recipients included in the second Ford survey group accounted for less than 8 percent of total 1970–71 operating expenditures of the seventy-eight orchestras in that group. In dollar terms, the Ford surveys and the Ford grant program had close to an 85 percent overlap (that is, total operating expenditures of orchestras covered by both the surveys and the grant program were close to 85 percent of the combined operating expenditures of all orchestras included in one or the other, or both, of the groupings). Thus, it seems valid to treat these groups of orchestras as virtually identical.

19   Hart, *Orpheus,* pp. 109–19; 156–64.

20   Ibid., pp. 314–23.

21   Ibid., p. 328. Cf. also pp. 342–3.

22   A few orchestras received small expendable grants after 1970–71, however.

23   Another "spill-over" possibility (although a remote one): if con-sumers have fixed budgets for admissions to the live performing arts, a reduction in ticket prices made possible by subsidy for one artistic organization would leave those consumers with more money to spend on admissions to other performances.

24   *The Wall Street Journal,* May 15, 1974.

25   Directors, managers, or other officers of all sixteen were interviewed; the names of those interviewed appear in Appendix F. In most cases, the subjects provided substantial documentary material. In addition, the Philadelphia Orchestra is the subject of one chapter in Philip Hart's *Orpheus in the New World,* and of more than one book, nota-

bly Herbert Kupferberg, *Those Fabulous Philadelphians* (New York: Scribner's, 1969.)

26 Hart, *Orpheus,* pp. 147–148, 154.

27 In 1974–75, the Philadelphia Orchestra alone accounted for 22 percent of the income from recordings, television, etc., of all twenty-nine ASOL majors.

28 The city of Philadelphia also subsidizes the orchestra in a way that is significant but does not appear on the orchestra's books: the Parks Department handles ticket requests and supplies facilities and supporting services for the Robin Hood Dell concerts, without charge. The Dell concerts provide employment and income for the musicians but are financed outside the orchestra's regular budget (for the most part) by the Friends of the Dell, Inc. See Kupferberg, *Philadelphians,* p. 164.

29 In 1973–74, the seventy-eight orchestras in the Ford survey raised 4.5 percent of their total operating income from corporate gifts.

30 However, the Pennwalt Corporation sponsored a European tour in 1974–75.

31 National Committee for Symphony Orchestra Support, "Funding the Arts: An Economic, Educational and Cultural Priority," March 1975.

32 Edward Arian's book on the Philadelphia Orchestra. *Bach, Beethoven and Bureaucracy* (University of Alabama Press, 1971) discusses this at some length; see also Hart, *Orpheus,* pp. 143–4, and Kupferberg, *Philadelphians,* passim.

33 For example, if the Philadelphia Orchestra were as effective in corporate fund raising as other orchestras in the Ford survey, it could come close to replacing all public funding.

34 Hart, *Orpheus,* p. 164, argues that the Ford grant did so in 1966.

35 According to the Revised Prospectus for 1975–76, the top ticket price for any performance (including the non-tax-deductible portion of the price for the gala opening concert) is $9, which does not seem at all high for the nation's number-one orchestra, which fills 92 percent of its seats over the season and regularly sells out nearly all its best seats on a subscription basis *before* its prospectus for the new season is printed.

36 For income data through 1973, see U.S. Department of Commerce, *Survey of Current Business,* April 1975.

37 A 24 percent increase in ticket prices for the 1975–76 season was accompanied by a substantial *increase* in the subscription audience.

38 Another comparative statistic is that the Met's operating expenditures in 1972 were nearly one-tenth of total operating expenditures for all 747 nonprofit performing-arts organizations covered by the *Census of Business* and shown in Table 5-1.

39 Contributions from individuals that had been less than $1.5 million

in 1964–65 increased to $2.5 million in 1965–66, $5.8 million in 1966–67, and $3.1 million in 1967–68.

40 For data on historical tends in capacity sold, see Metropolitan Opera Association, *Annual Report 1974–75,* p. 11.

41 This calculation assumes that the additional attendance would have increased expenses by negligible amounts. It should be noted that few major opera companies in the world come close to selling even 90 percent of capacity over a season.

42 *Madame Butterfly,* in Central Park, on July 1, 1975, appears to be the record-holder, to date, according to Met officials.

43 In 1973–74 and again in 1974–75, individual contributions were more than $2 million higher than in 1972–73.

44 The difference is more than made up by the Met's guarantee of supplemental unemployment benefits, up to 50 percent of salary, for musicians for the remaining eight weeks of the year.

45 In January 1977, the Met announced the formation of a partnership with the Kennedy Center in Washington to present major international performing companies in both houses and sponsor their U.S. tours, beginning with a two-month tour of the Stuttgart Ballet in the spring and summer of 1977. At the same time, the Met and the American Ballet Theatre (ABT) announced plans to make the Met ABT's permanent home in New York, starting with an eight-week season beginning in April 1977, under arrangements providing for an equal division of income and expenses.

46 William H. Hadley, quoted in Stephen E. Rubin, *The New Met in Profile* (New York: Macmillan, 1974), p. 32.

47 Of course, the competition among a small number of first-rank opera companies for superstar soloists bids up their fees and probably harms the finances of the top half-dozen international-class opera companies. As a group, they would be better off if they were to collude to keep down soloists' fees, but they are unlikely to do so.

48 In 1974–75, to replace federal and state support, overcome the bottom-line deficit, and preclude additional depletion of capital, the Met would have required least $3 million more in income. The Met's main season box office income was about $9 million. If the elasticity of demand for Met attendance with respect to ticket prices were the 0.25 figure used earlier in this chapter, ticket prices would have had to be increased by close to 55 percent to generate an additional $3 million. However, the price elasticity of demand for Met admissions suggested by the 1970–71 experience is 0.36. If the true elasticity figure were 0.33, the indicated ticket price increase would be roughly 90 percent, and if the true elasticity figure were any higher, *no* price increase could have yielded one-third more box office income. The fact that total ticket income of the Met has been virtually constant for the past five years suggests that these crude calculations are correct

and that the Met has little if any capacity for covering a larger fraction of its costs from ticket income.

49 Fewer than 850,000 seats were available for all performances during the thirty-one-week New York season that prevailed prior to 1975–76.

50 Presumably a good share, but not all, of the subsidy from NYSCA is granted on the grounds that New Yorkers do benefit more than anyone else from the existence of the Met.

51 Covent Garden aside, all the first-rank European opera companies exceed the Met in all these respects, which are not in themselves measures of quality.

52 The Met's long history of financial crisis, associated with specific management decisions or blunders, not inexorable long-term cost trends, provides little support for the Baumol-Bowen thesis. However, in the light of the apparent high price elasticity of demand, the Met may very well present a Baumol-Bowen case for steadily increasing levels of public support over time in future years.

53 Opera America is the subject of an adulatory article by Shirley Fleming, "When 43 Opera Companies Get Together," *The New York Times,* July 11, 1976.

54 In 1973–74, thirty-five theater companies responded to the annual fiscal survey conducted by the Theatre Communications Group (TCG); the Ford Foundation 1973–74 data cover two other theater companies not in the TCG survey. Aside from the largest of all the nonprofit companies, Joseph Papp's New York Shakespeare Festival, which was not included in either survey, the thirty-seven companies comprise virtually all nonprofit professional theater companies with budgets of more than $100,000 operating in 1973–74. Of the thirty-seven, only five are located in New York City.

55 This amount includes the "cash reserve grant," which provides for four annual advances until June 30, 1977, to be used as working capital to cover financing needs within a given fiscal year. If specified conditions are met, the funds will form a permanent reserve fund beginning July 1977.

56 In 1975, the District of Columbia arts council made a grant to Arena for the first time, in the amount of $10,000. Arena has not sought assistance from the state arts councils in neighboring Maryland and Virginia – although much, if not most of its audience, is comprised of residents of those states – because these arts councils have very limited appropriations.

57 For both Arena and the group as a whole, national foundation support provided 8 percent of total income.

58 Zelda Fichandler, "Theatres or Institutions?" International Theatre Institute of the United States, *The American Theatre, 1969–1970* (New York: Scribner's 1970), pp. 110–11. Washington is reputed to

be a bad town for private fund raising; sometimes this stinginess is ascribed to a sense of impermanence on the part of many of its better-off residents, sometimes to the overpowering presence of an exceedingly rich and extravagant federal government.

59   In the summer of 1975, Thomas Fichandler, Arena's Executive Director, reported some signs of increasing difficulty in foundation fund raising, however.

60   Hall and Eugene Lee, Trinity's set designer, are advocates of "environmental theater" productions, in which actors appear behind and alongside the audience during the course of the play's action.

61   High ticket prices have not been the cause of this difficulty, apparently. The *top* ticket price in 1974–75 ($7) was below the *average* ticket price that had been estimated necessary a year earlier, if the company were to be fully self-supporting on the basis of box office income and sold 80 percent of capacity. In such a situation, even the richest and most dedicated theatergoer is being subsidized from public and private funds.

62   Budgets for the years after 1973–74 project NEA support at up to 20 percent of total income.

63   The payment was made through City Center, which allocated portions to each of the constituent organizations.

64   In addition, Ford made a separate $100,000 grant to the company that year.

65   An appropriate analogy might be the failure of a well-established professional sports team, say in basketball, to draw full houses during the weeks when there is the maximum overlap in the basketball, football, and hockey seasons.

66   The Rockefeller Foundation supported a tour of London, Paris, Madrid, and Barcelona in late 1975.

67   The fifteen ballet and modern dance groups included in the Ford surveys received just under $1 million in direct grants from NEA in 1973–74. But touring performances by these companies probably accounted for a major share of the $747,000 in NEA sponsor grants under its Large Company Touring Program and a significant share of NEA's $824,000 in grants to state arts councils for the Coordinated Residency Touring Program. It is likely that, in 1973–74, total *indirect* public support of the Ford dance groups, through grants to sponsors, amounted to at least half of total direct support, and an even higher proportion of direct support for the Paul Taylor Company.

68   *The New York Times,* October 4, 1976; National Endowment for the Arts, *The Cultural Post,* Issue 9, January/February 1977, pp. 14–15.

69   All eight of the organizations described in this section are located in New York City. Many art service organizations are located elsewhere, but New York provides a wide range of types from which to select a varied sample for study.

70   Hart, *Orpheus,* in the chapter on "Education and the Musical Experience" (pp. 427–40), points out that self-evaluation efforts in music education programs are rare and that the very ambitious Lincoln Center Student Program, addressed to junior and senior high school students, also was evaluated (by a New York University School of Education group) and judged to have "a relatively slight impact" (p. 439). It is not clear that the evaluation techniques used in either the Taft study of Young Audiences or the study of the Lincoln Center program support strong conclusions as to the merits of these programs.

71   Schools are required to pay 50 percent of the costs of the intensity programs; most schools have not been willing to adopt the new system and prefer the less costly one-time recital.

72   Young Audiences estimates that its average performer receives about 15 percent of his annual earnings from Young Audiences, which makes financial support from the Trust Fund an appropriate activity for that fund.

73   Affiliate Artists, Inc., *Annual Report, Fiscal 1974.*

74   Ibid.

75   An evaluation done by J. R. Taft Corporation in 1971 (financed as was the similar evaluation of Young Audiences) had recommended this shift, but Affiliate Artists had been trying to enlist arts councils as presenters at that time.

76   Of course, subsidy may be just as efficient in cases in which its effects are not readily quantifiable, but in this case, the efficiency of the subsidy can be quantitatively demonstrated.

77   In 1975, a typical printing job with a commercial cost of $500 to $600 was billed by the Print Center for $150.

78   Martin Mayer, who reviewed a draft version of this book, considered these conflicts not all that hard to resolve and asserted that the Arts Council in Britain does so essentially by using some of its funds to make grants in a fixed proportion to the recipients' box office (or other commercial) receipts and the remainder for awards that are an expression of judgment independent of the organizations' own ability to generate operating income. The difficulty of using that approach in this country is that it would provide substantial public support for large, well-financed organizations not in clear need of such support (for example, the Philadelphia Orchestra). It would act as an incentive for some economically inefficient increases in charges, such as museum admissions. And it would have little applicability to art forms and types of organizations that have little or no capacity to generate operating income. Thus, it is not a general solution; it might work for selected art forms, like opera or theater, although even then only to a very limited extent.

79   If the artists who have been exhibited in Artists Space sold numerous

works, received commissions, or gained commercial gallery affilia-
tions on the basis of their CVA exhibitions, the duplication could
easily be rationalized. But the experience to date of Artists Space
exhibitors in these regards has not been a spectacular success.

80   Baumol and Bowen surveyed audiences at free performances and
found that such audiences, like those at paid performances, have high
median incomes, are very well educated, and are largely professionals. (Baumol and Bowen, *Performing Arts,* pp. 96–7.)

81   With the possible exception of the New York City Ballet's
difficulties with the musicians in the 1976–77 season. But an alternative explanation is available, namely, that the musicians were unusually recalcitrant because they realized that the New York City Ballet,
with its Ford Foundation grants, was no longer on the edge of
insolvency. Their recalcitrance was also understandable because the
underlying problem was a reduction in the length of their employment for reasons that had nothing to do with the ballet.

Chapter 6. Support and Public Interest

1   See Chapter 4.

2   This pricing policy works because the entire costs of the Central Park
season are underwritten, in advance, by government and private
contributions.

3   The writing of novels and plays, production of feature-length films,
and the Broadway stage are all fields in which the risk of failure is
extremely high, but the financial rewards from the rare success can
be enormous. Thus, there is no shortage of workers and support in
these areas, and while most efforts are not very innovative, many
are.

4   *The New York Times,* March 24, 1976.

5   New York State Council on the Arts press release, January 13, 1977.
This study also showed that while operating expenditures rose by 17
percent during the three years, earned income rose by 27 percent and
contributions from private and federal government sources by 26
percent. Aggregate deficits increased but almost entirely because of
the lack of growth in state and local government support.

6   Philip Hart, *Orpheus,* Ch. 17.

7   National Endowment for the Arts, *The Cultural Post,* Issue 9, Janu-
ary/February 1977, p. 14.

8   Over the past quarter-century, recordings have become increasingly
close substitutes as the quality of home audio equipment has increased sharply and the relative price of that equipment declined
equally sharply. Records themselves have had similar quality and
price trends. Of course, a live symphony orchestra performance is
very different from recordings or ensemble concerts. But some part
of the potential audience for the symphony performance surely sees

the alternatives as second-best substitutes to be resorted to (perhaps with regret) if symphony ticket prices rise rapidly relative to the alternatives.

9   Philip Hart, *Orpheus,* especially Ch. 19.
10   Ibid., pp. 467–9.
11   In this respect, as in others, New York is a special case. Because so many of the arts are concentrated in New York, New York State and New York City properly devote more money to this form of support of the arts than other states and localities.
12   In order to avoid penalizing the states, cities, and countries that now provide support of their institutions, NEA might count *current* levels of state-local public support as matching the NEA *increases.*
13   In Canada, where support of amateur activities has been fairly important, the emphasis has moved toward the professional in recent years. In Australia, in contrast, the very large recent increases in the level of public support involve substantial expenditures in support of amateur participation. In Sweden, there appears to be little criticism of the heavy expenditure for amateur activities.
14   National Endowment for the Arts, July/August 1976.
15   This language is taken from a "transition memo" sent to the White House after the November 1976 election by NEA Chairman Nancy Hanks and excerpted in *The Cultural Post,* Issue 9, January/February 1977, p. 3.
16   In calendar 1975, the arts subsidies tallied in Chapter 4 amounted to only 0.05 percent of total public spending as recorded in the national income accounts.
17   The use of the plus sign rather than the word "and" in the title of the program is not a typographical error; it may say rather more than was intended by its authors about their clarity of purpose.
18   NEA, *Guide to Programs,* 1975–76, p. 11.
19   *The Cultural Post,* May/June 1976, p. 7.
20   No doubt because of the endowment's ventures into historic preservation under the Architecture Program, the Rail Transportation Improvement Act signed into law in October 1976 authorizes an appropriation of $5 million in fiscal 1977 to NEA to help preserve old and architecturally important railway stations. Half of the money is to be granted to communities for planning activities, and half is to be used for actual maintenance of stations in serious disrepair. If the provision is actually funded, it will pull the endowment still further into the city planning business and will compel NEA to develop an entirely new set of grantee relationships, not with the nonprofit arts organizations it knows but with local governments. This congressional assignment seems singularly inept – another example of what happens when noble intentions get in the way of hard thinking.
21   *Alternative Theatre,* Vol. 1, No. 1, September 1975, p. 7.
22   Of course, high-income people may prefer to support arts organiza-

tions through tax deductible gifts rather than higher ticket prices. However, arts organizations may be able to accommodate the tax provisions by making more general use of the distribution of the best seats on a "benefit" basis, and counting part of the cost of the tickets as a contribution.

23 *The Cultural Post,* July/August 1976, p. 14. An additional problem is that the demand for NEA support from dance touring sponsors is far in excess of the 430-odd weeks funded, leading to suggestions that the NEA pick up less than one-third of the touring companies' costs, as at present. If that step reduced the gross income of the companies that rely heavily on touring, such as the Paul Taylor Dance Company, it could result in their demise.

24 The Governments Division of the Census Bureau has collected information on the finances and employment of state and local governments in great detail for decades, and in recent years has expanded its surveys in cooperation with specialized federal agencies that require even more detail for their grant programs.

25 Moreover, the congressional committees NEA deals with repeatedly ask, with little success, for more data on state and local government expenditures for the arts.

26 To be sure, as critics have pointed out (see Appendix A), the council's annual reports are often inconsistent and contradictory from one year to the next; the point here is not the quality of the logic but the fullness and explicitness of the discussion.

27 A sharply dissenting note on the value of data and research on the arts is sounded in *Art Letter,* Vol. 6, no. 1, January 1977, under the title "The Arts Study: A Useful Tool or Waste of Money?" The article attacks NEA's $500,000 research budget and its contracts with the National Research Center of the Arts as essentially wasteful. But the attack focuses heavily on research of the audience-survey type, which it sees (rightly) as conducted largely for lobbying purposes, yielding results that are unpersuasive and contradictory, with a role essentially similar to the political polls.

Chapter 7. Direction of Public Policy

1 Professor Kenneth Arrow won the Nobel Prize in Economics for theoretical work that demonstrated (to oversimplify) the impossibility of finding optimal solutions to resource-allocation problems when "merit-goods" and similar factors must be considered in decision making.

2 National Committee for Cultural Resources, "The National Report on the Arts," October 1975, p. 5. This committee's membership included chairmen, trustees, directors, and other officers of state arts councils, major arts institutions, universities, and labor unions.

3 This proposal was formally recommended by the Carnegie Commis-

sion on Educational Television in 1966. For a review a number of alternative earmarked taxes as revenue sources for public broadcasting, see Dick Netzer, *Long-Range Financing of Public Broadcasting* (New York: National Citizens Committee for Public Broadcasting, 1969).

4 Ichak Adizes, "The Cost of Being an Artist," Research Paper No. 25, Management in the Arts Research Program, Graduate School of Management, University of California at Los Angeles (Los Angeles, September 1974), p. 13.

5 The Twentieth Century Fund Task Force on Performing Arts Centers in 1970 recommended a more limited form of earmarked taxation, the allocation to arts centers of part of the real estate tax receipts generated by increased land values in the surrounding area (*Bricks, Mortar,* p. 4). To the extent that the new performing-arts center actually generates a net increase in land values – rather than a transfer in land values from other parts of the city or surrounding area (which is often the case for improvements that do not lower transport costs) – this proposal has some attraction. But it is important to avoid double-counting the increased tax receipts, that is, using them as an argument for a public subsidy for the capital costs of the arts center and then using them to provide operating cost subsidies.

6 To cite a recent, somewhat absurd, example, Clive Barnes in *The New York Times* of February 6, 1977, gives as an illustration of the dire need of the dance world for additional public subsidy the Eliot Feld Ballet's risking a season (in March 1977) at the enormous City Center 55th Street Theater:

> The Feld company has every right in the world to appear in a large Broadway house, in addition to its home on Lafayette Street in Joseph Papp's Public Theater. Why should the company have to incur such an enormous financial risk?

But why, in view of the evidence of empty seats for dance in New York, should the taxpayer pay for the Feld company's "right" to appear in a large Broadway house?

7 Ibid.

8 This reasoning rests upon the assumption that there will be no radical reforms in the provisions of the federal income and estate tax laws concerned with deductions for charitable contributions and that there will not be drastic reductions in the rates of those taxes (above the bottom brackets, in which contributors to the arts are few).

9 The Baumol-Bowen thesis predicts a *proportionate* rise in artists' earnings, not a rise that is two or more times as great as earnings in general.

10 Hart, *Orpheus,* pp. 472–3.

11 In particular, it is quite wrong to increase federal grants to an institution in order to substitute for local private fund raising that the

institution avoids, on ideological grounds (the Arena case), especially when its counterparts elsewhere find that they can do such fund raising without destroying artistic integrity.

12   This prescription does not apply to use of the Treasury Fund, which has proven its worth as a means of encouraging private contributions. It would be appropriate to maintain easy access to the Treasury Fund for arts institutions that do not meet the needs and performance tests indicated above as requirements for grants from regular NEA funds.

13   It has been asserted that this view contradicts the objective of wider availability. That assertion is valid only if one agrees that the federal government should be completely indifferent about how money for the arts is spent in pursuit of the objective of wider availability – that *any* expenditure of federal money for local arts projects is a good thing, deserving priority. This seems an unacceptable proposition. Moreover, it is surely a recipe for substitution of federal money for other sources of support.

14   Occasionally, even now public funds subsidize enterprises for profit, for example, when a subsidized performing arts center presents a commercial theater production. The proscription appears to apply to the more venturesome and avant-garde profit/nonprofit combinations, but not to the more crassly commercial ones, like presentation of middle-brow stage productions.

15   An illustration from the world of science is the designation by the National Academy of Sciences of a special committee to review the social science research activities of the National Science Foundation. This committee reported in late 1975.

16   National Research Center of the Arts, *Americans and the Arts: A Survey of Public Opinion* (New York: Associated Councils of the Arts, 1975), Ch. 1, 3, and 4.

17   Baumol and Bowen, *Performing Arts,* p. 96; Hart, *Orpheus,* pp. 386–7. No doubt the percentage has increased since then, but the gross attendance data suggest that it doubled at best. In the National Research Center survey cited above, 46.6 million adult Americans reported attending an average of 3.5 live theater performances in 1973, for a total attendance of 163 million. Yet the estimated combined *paid* attendance of all forms of professional theater, nonprofit and commercial, in 1973–74 was well *under* 25 million.

Appendix A. Public Support for the Arts in Britain

1   John S. Harris, *Government Patronage of the Arts in Great Britain* (Chicago: University of Chicago Press, 1970), p. 19.

2   Michael Green and Michael Wilding, *Cultural Policy in Great Britain,* UNESCO Studies and Documents on Cultural Policies (Paris, 1970), p. 49.

3   This philanthropic organization was established in 1930 with the object of conserving the British heritage in all its aspects. Its founder was the American millionaire Edward Harkness.

4   Harris, *Government Patronage,* p. 25.

5   Ibid., p. 39.

6   The Arts Council of Great Britain, "What It Is and What It Does," August 1972, p. 5.

7   Harris, *Government Patronage,* pp. 81–2.

8   The Arts Council of Great Britain, *Thirtieth Annual Report and Accounts, 1974–75,* p. 24.

9   Sir Hugh Willatt, "The Economic Situation and the Arts in Great Britain," *The Arts, Economics and Politics: Four National Perspectives* (Aspen Institute for Humanistic Studies, 1975), p. 61.

10 Arts Council of Great Britain, *Thirtieth Annual Report,* p. 16.

11 Eric W. White, *The Arts Council of Great Britain* (London: Davis-Poynter, 1975), pp. 82–3.

12 White, *The Arts Council,* p. 246.

13 *The Economist,* March 6, 1976.

14 White, *The Arts Council,* p. 235.

15 Quoted by White, ibid., p. 60.

16 Harris, *Government Patronage,* p. 322.

17 However, some critics of the Arts Council argue that this graceful style masks an underlying vagueness and obscures contradictions in the council's statements of policy. In an article written after reading the council's first twenty-six annual reports, Karen King and Mark Blaug conclude that, "The Arts Council certainly has *objectives* – but most of them are too ill defined to make evaluation possible. . . . It is not too much to say that in 26 years of official reportage they have failed to produce a single coherent and operational statement of their aims." ("Does the Arts Council Know What It Is Doing?" *Encounter,* September 1973, p. 16.)

18 One observer, comparing public support of music in Britain and the United States, argues that despite the rhetoric the Arts Council is not doing an effective job of audience development for music and that, at the same time, its support of the major orchestras does not result in a high level of orchestral accomplishment, by international standards, even in London. If the tasks of a government arts foundation are summarized as "raising and spreading" – raising standards in the arts and spreading accessibility in geographic, social, and other terms – this observer concludes that "the major subsidizing body in Britain is busy instead with the more depressing activity of spreading and lowering." (Bernard Jacobson, "Paying the Piper: Music Subsidy in the United States and Great Britain," *Musical Newsletter,* Vol. 6, No. 2, Spring 1976, p. 18.)

19 *The Economist,* October 30, 1976.

Bibliography

Arts Administration, Cultural Policy, Art, and the Individual

Abercrombie, Nigel. *Artists and Their Public*. Paris: U.N.E.S.C.O. Press, 1975.

Adizes, Ichack. "Administering for the Arts: Problems in Practice, An Explorative Study." Research Paper No. 15, Management in the Arts Research Program, Graduate School of Management, U.C.L.A., March 1972.

"The Cost of Being an Artist: An Argument for the Support of the Arts." Research Paper No. 25, Management in the Arts Research Program, Graduate School of Management, U.C.L.A., September 1974.

Cwi, David, and Albert Diehl. *In Search of a Regional Policy for the Arts: Phase I Report Prepared for the Joint Committee on Cultural Resources*. Baltimore, Maryland: Johns Hopkins Center for Metropolitan Planning and Research, 1975.

Eddy, Junius. "Government, the Arts and Ghetto Youth." *Public Administration Review*, Vol. 3, No. 4, July/August 1970.

Faine, Hyman R. "Unions and the Arts." *The American Economic Review*, Vol. 62, No. 2, May 1972, pp. 70–7.

Gans, Herbert J. *Popular Culture and High Culture: An Analysis of Taste*. New York: Basic Books, 1975.

Georgi, Charlotte. *The Arts and the World of Business: A Selected Bibliography*. Metuchen, N.J.: The Scarecrow Press, 1973.

Greyser, Stephen A., ed. *Cultural Policy and Arts Administration*. Cambridge, Mass.: Harvard University Press, 1973.

Hall, James, and Barry Ubanov. *Modern Culture and the Arts*. New York: McGraw-Hill, 1972.

Hanks, Nancy. "The Creative Artist – Cornerstone of Culture," in *The Creative Artist: Chances for Change*. New York: Associated Councils of the Arts, 1975.

Hapgood, Karen. "Planning and the Arts." Report No. 313 of the American Society of Planning Officials, Planning Advisory Service Reports. Chicago, October 1975.

Harris, John S. "Arts Councils: A Survey and Analysis." *Public Administration Review*, Vol. 30, No. 4, July/August 1970.

Kando, Thomas. *Leisure and Popular Culture in Transition*. St. Louis: C.V. Mosby, 1975.

McMullen, Roy. *Art, Affluence and Alienation: The Fine Arts Today.* New York: New American Library (Mentor Books), 1968.

Mayer, Martin. *Bricks, Mortar and the Performing Arts.* New York: The Twentieth Century Fund, 1970.

The National Committee for Cultural Resources. *National Report on the Arts.* New York, 1975.

The National Research Center of the Arts, Inc. "Americans and the Arts: Highlights from a Survey of Public Opinion." New York, 1974.

Americans and the Arts: A Survey of Public Opinion. New York: Associated Councils of the Arts, 1975.

Pfeffer, Irving. "Fine Arts: A Problem in Risk Management." Research Paper no. 7, Management in the Arts Research Program, Graduate School of Management, U.C.L.A., September 1971.

Prieve, E. Arthur, and Ira W. Allen. *Administration in the Arts: An annotated bibliography of selected references.* Madison, Wisconsin: Center for Arts Administration, University of Wisconsin, 1973.

Reiss, Alvin H. *The Arts Management Handbook.* New York: Law-Arts Publishers, Inc., 1974.

Culture and Company: A Critical Study of An Improbable Alliance. New York: Bobbs-Merrill, 1972.

Scitovsky, Tibor. "Arts in the Affluent Society: What's Wrong with the Arts is What's Wrong with Society." *The American Economic Review,* vol. 62, No. 2, May 1972, pp. 62–9.

Scott, Mel. "Federal/State Partnership in the Arts." *Public Administration Review,* Vol. 30, No. 4, July/August 1970.

Scott, Mel, ed. "Symposium: Government and the Arts." *Public Administration Review,* Vol. 30, No. 4, July/August 1970.

Stegner, Wallace. *The Uneasy Chair.* New York: Doubleday, 1974.

Taper, Bernard. *The Arts in Boston.* Cambridge, Mass.: Harvard University Press, 1970.

Toffler, Alvin. *The Culture Consumers: Art and Affluence in America.* Baltimore: Penguin Books, 1965.

United Nations Educational, Scientific and Cultural Organization. *Cultural Policy: A Preliminary Study.* Paris: U.N.E.S.C.O. Press, 1969.

Cultural Rights as Human Rights. Paris: U.N.E.S.C.O. Press, 1970.

Voegeli, Thomas J. *Handbook for Tour Management.* Madison, Wisconsin: Management Center for Arts Administration, Graduate School of Business, University of Wisconsin, April 1975.

Wertheimer, Barbara M. *Exploring the Arts: Handbook for Trade Union Program Planners.* New York: New York State School of Industrial and Labor Relations, Cornell University, 1968.

Winter, William O. "The University, the City and the Arts." *Public Administration Review,* Vol. 30, No. 4, July/August 1970.

Art and Education

Association of College, University and Community Arts Administrators, Inc. "College and University Support of the Professional Touring Performing Arts." Madison, Wisconsin: 1974.
"1975–76 Concert Season: A Prediction." Researched and analyzed by Robert Moon, Fall 1975.
Brustein, Robert. "Theater and the University." *The New Republic,* November 16, 1974, pp. 13–6.
Eddy, Junius. "The Upsidedown Curriculum." *Cultural Affairs,* Summer 1970.
Gould, Samuel B., et al. *The Arts and Education: A New Beginning in Higher Education.* New York: Special Studies of Rockefeller Brothers Fund Project, 1968.
Lowry, W. McNeil. "The University and the Creative Arts." *Educational Theatre Journal,* Vol. 14, No. 2, May 1962.
Schubart, Mark. *Performing Arts Institutions and Young People: Lincoln Center's Study, "The Hunting of the Squiggle."* New York: Praeger, 1972.
Staples, Donald, and Winston Sharples. "A Proposal on Educational Activities to the American Film Institute from the University Film Association." Presented at A.F.I. Board Meeting, October 16, 1975.
Union of Independent Colleges of Art. *Annual Report: 1973–74.*
U.S. Office of Education. "Support for the Arts and Humanities." Washington, D.C.: U.S. Department of Health, Education, and Welfare, 1972.

Foreign Government Support of the Arts

The Arts Council of Great Britain. "Survey of Visual Artists – Their Incomes and Expenditures and Attitudes to Arts Council Support." Research Report no. 4, 1974.
Thirtieth Annual Report and Accounts: 1974–75. London, 1975.
Twenty-Ninth Annual Report and Accounts: 1973–74. London, 1974.
"What it is and What it does," 1972.
Aspen Institute for Humanistic Studies, Program in Pluralism and the Commonweal. *The Arts, Economics and Politics: Four National Perspectives.* Seminar proceedings, March 22–26, 1975. Foreword by Waldemar A. Nielsen. Papers presented: Anthony Phillips, "The Arts, Economics and Politics: Four National Perspectives" (pp. 1–24); Gerald Bonnot, "French Cultural Policy: Evolution and Current Issues" (pp. 25–40); Claude G. Menard, "French Cultural Policy" (pp. 41–50); Hans Jochen Freiherr von Uslar-Gleichen, "The Federal Republic of Germany: Culture, Economics and Politics" (pp. 51–8); Sir Hugh Willatt, "The Economic Situation and the Arts in Great Britain" (pp. 59–64); Sara P. Garretson and Carol B. Grossman, "The Arts in the United States: Inflation, Recession and Public Policy" (pp. 65–80).

Book, S. H., S. G. Loberman, and the National Research Centre of the Arts. "The Audience for the Performing Arts: Highlights of a Study of Attendance Patterns in Ontario." Ontario Arts Council, 1974.

Book, Sam. "Economic Aspects of the Arts in Ontario." Ontario Arts Council, 1973.

Dace, William. *Subsidies for the Theater: A Study of the Central European System of Financing Drama, Opera and Ballet: 1968–70.* Manhattan, Kansas: AG Press, 1972.

Dorian, Frederick. *Commitment to Culture.* Pittsburgh: University of Pittsburgh Press, 1964.

The Economist, August 3, 1974; March 8, 1975; August 30, 1975; and March 6, 1976.

The Financial Times, September 24, 1975.

Fortier, Andre. "Is There a Future for the Symphony Orchestra in Canada?" The Canada Council, April 28, 1974.

Girard, Augustin. *Cultural Development: Experience and Politics.* Paris: U.N.E.S.C.O. Press, 1972.

The Greater London Council. *1970 Annual Abstract of Greater London Statistics.* 1972.

Green, Michael, and Michael Wilding. *Cultural Policy in Great Britain.* Paris: U.N.E.S.C.O. Press, 1970.

Harris, John S. *Government Patronage of the Arts in Great Britain.* Chicago: University of Chicago Press, 1970.

McKinsey and Company, Inc. "Directions for the Dance in Canada." The Canada Council, April 1973.

The Observer, May 25, 1975.

Ontario Arts Council. *Annual Report: 1973–74.*

"On Tour Kit." Reports included: "Attractions on Tour"; "The Artist for Schools"; "Music on Tour"; and "Resources Franco-Ontariennes on Tour," 1974.

Panasuk, Christine. "An Analysis of Selected Performing Arts Occupations." The Canada Council, July 1974.

Pasquill, Frank T. "Subsidy Patterns for the Performing Arts in Canada." The Canada Council, February 1973.

Schonberg, Harold C. "A Critic's Notebook." A series of articles on European opera companies for *The New York Times,* February 10, 12, 14, 16, 17, 23, and 26, 1975; and March 2, 9, 16, 19, and 21, 1975.

Sullivan, Mary C. "The Group of Twenty-Nine." The Canada Council, October 1973.

Urwick, Currie and Partners. "An Assessment of the Impact of Selected Large Performing Companies Upon the Canadian Economy." The Canada Council, September 1974.

White, Eric W. *The Arts Council of Great Britain.* London: Davis Poynter, 1975.

Foundation, Corporate, and Private Support

American Association of Fund-Raising Counsel, Inc. *Giving U.S.A.: 1975 Annual Report.*

Business Committee for the Arts. "516 Ways BCA Companies Supported the Arts in 1973–74."

Carnegie Corporation of New York. "List of Grants: 1974." Reprinted from the *Annual Report 1974.*

Chagy, Gideon. *The New Patrons of the Arts.* New York: Abrams, 1972.

Chagy, Gideon, ed. *Business in the Arts, 1970.* New York: Eriksson, 1970.

The State of the Arts and Corporate Support. New York: Eriksson, 1971.

Commission on Foundations and Private Philanthropy. *Foundations: Private Giving and Public Policy.* Chicago: University of Chicago Press, 1970.

Commission on Private Philantropy and Public Needs. *Giving in America: Toward a Stronger Voluntary Sector.* 1975.

Fenn, Dolores. "Money to Art: A Special Supplement." *The Print Collector's Newsletter,* Vol. 5, No. 5, November/December 1974, pp. 117–24.

The Ford Foundation. "Current Interests." March 1974.

Annual Report 1973.

Gingrich, Arnold. *Business and the Arts: An Answer to Tomorrow.* New York: Eriksson, 1969.

Klein, Howard. "Feeling the Pinch: Private Philanthropy." *The New Republic,* November 16, 1974, pp. 19–21.

Lowry, W. McNeil. "Art and Intensity." 1965. Reprinted by the Ford Foundation.

"The Arts and Philanthropy." 1962. Reprinted by the Ford Foundation.

Lynden, Patricia. "The Modern Medicis." *Cue Magazine,* February 28, 1976, pp. 17–8.

Pifer, Alan. "Foundations and Public Policy Formation." Reprinted from Carnegie Corporation of New York, *Annual Report 1974.*

Rockefeller Brothers Fund. *Annual Report: 1973.*

Soper, Susan. "The Arts Are Learning to Mean Business." *Newsday,* March 21, 1976.

Literature

Chute, Marchette. *P.E.N. American Center: A History of the First 50 Years.* New York: P.E.N. 1972.

CODA: Poets and Writers Newsletter. Vol. 2., No. 3, January 1975; Vol. 3, No. 1, October/November 1975; Vol. 3, No. 2 December 1975/ January 1976; and "The Supplement," Winter 1976.

Congrat-Butlar, Stefan, ed. "Copyright in the USSR." New York. P.E.N., 1973.

"Copyright–U.S. and International." New York: P.E.N., 1973.

"The USSR Accession to the Universal Copyright Convention." New York: P.E.N. 1973.

Coordinating Council of Literary Magazines. *Biennial Report: 1972–73.*

Hentoff, Nat. "U.S. Writers Draft 'Enemies List.' " *The Village Voice,* September 22, 1975.

P.E.N. American Center. *Grants and Awards Available to American Writers.* New York, 1975.

Grants and Awards Available to Foreign Writers. New York, 1975.

The World of Translation: Papers Delivered at the Conference on Literary Translation. New York City, 1970.

The Writer as Independent Spirit: Proceedings of the XXXIV International PEN Congress. New York, 1967.

Poets and Writers, Inc. "Financial Statements, June 30, 1974." New York, 1974.

Performing Arts

Adizes, Ichak. "The Unique Character of Performing Arts Organizations and the Functioning of Their Boards of Directors: A Managerial Analysis." Research Paper No. 4, Management in the Arts Research Program, Graduate School of Management, U.C.L.A., June 1971.

Affiliate Artists, Inc. "Annual Report Fiscal 1974"; and "Facts About Affiliate Artists."

Ames, Amyas. "Toward Human Priorities." *Playbill,* February 1976, pp. 27–30.

Baumol, William J., and William G. Bowen. *Performing Arts: The Economic Dilemma.* New York: The Twentieth Century Fund, 1966.

Brown, Les. "Lincoln Center is Ready to Televise Its Events" *The New York Times,* December 1, 1975.

The City Center of Music and Drama, Inc. "Financial Statements with Supplementary Information." June 30, 1974.

The Ford Foundation. *The Finances of the Performing Arts.* Vol. 1, *A Survey of 166 Professional Resident Theaters, Opera, Symphonies, Ballets and Modern Dance Companies.* New York, 1974.

The Finances of the Performing Arts. Vol. 2, *A Survey of the Characteristics and Attitudes of Audiences for Theater, Opera, Symphony and Ballet in Twelve U.S. Cities.* New York, 1974.

Unpublished statistics updating *The Finances of the Performing Arts,* Vol. 1. Covers 153 organizations from 1970–71 through 1973–74.

Granfield, Michael. "The Live Performing Arts: Financial Catastrophe or Economic Catharsis." Research Paper No. 8, Management in the Arts Research Program, Graduate School of Management, U.C.L.A., October 1971.

Hutchinson, William. "Arts Management and the Art of Music." Research Paper No. 26, Management in the Arts Research Program, Graduate School of Management, U.C.L.A., 1975.

National Endowment for the Arts. *Economic Aspects of the Performing Arts: A Portrait in Figures.* May 1971.

Rockefeller Panel Report. *The Performing Arts: Problems and Prospects.* New York: McGraw-Hill, 1965.

J. R. Taft Corporation/Comlab, Inc. "An Evaluation of the Impact and Effectiveness of Affiliate Artists, Inc." Prepared for the NEA and the Sears Roebuck Foundation, October 1971.

"Summary: An Evaluation of the Impact and Effectiveness of Young Audiences, Inc." Prepared for NEA and the Sears Roebuck Foundation, October 1971.

Tucker, Carll. "How Classical Record Companies Differ from Their Big Brothers." *The Village Voice,* September 8, 1975.

Young Audiences, Inc. "Corporate Contributors. 1973–74"; *Newsletter,* Vol. VI, No. 2, July 1974; and Vol. VII, No. 1, March 1975; "Guidelines for Intensity Programming"; and "Directions in Intensity Programming."

Dance

Association of American Dance Companies. "The State of Dance in the United States: Parts I and II." New York, 1972.

Mazo, Joseph H. *Dance is a Contact Sport.* New York: Saturday Review Press, 1974.

National Association of Regional Ballet. "Profile '74."

National Endowment for the Arts. *Directory of Dance Companies: Fiscal Year 1976.*

Paul Taylor Dance Foundation, Inc. "Budget: Fiscal year May 1, 1974–April 30, 1975"; "Projected Budget May 1, 1975–April 30, 1976"; and "Auditor's Report as of April 30, 1975."

Terry, Walter. *The Dance in America.* New York: Harper and Row, 1971.

Young, Henry, Jr. "A Report to the Midrange New York Dance Companies on the Feasibility of a Combined Broadway Season." New York Dance Alliance, January 1976.

Opera

Adizes, Ichak. "Seattle Opera Association: A Policy-Making Case for Management in the Arts." Boston: Intercollegiate Case Clearing House, 1971.

Bing, Rudolf. *5,000 Nights at the Opera.* New York: Doubleday, 1972.

Central Opera Service. "Opera Companies and Workshops in the United States and Canada." 1975.

The Economist, March 29, 1975.

Henahan, Donal. "An Elite Still Calls the Tune of the Met Board." *The New York Times,* March 28, 1975.

The Metropolitan Opera Association. "White Paper on the Metropolitan Opera." 1971.

Annual Report 1972–73; Annual Report 1973–74; and *Annual Report 1974–75.*

Opera America, Inc. "Annual Statistical Report." Unpublished material begun in 1973.

Rich, Alan. "Suicidio or Ritorna Vincitor–The Met's Choice." *New York Magazine,* March 24, 1975, pp. 70–1.

Rockwell, John. "Met: $35 Tickets and a Lingering Deficit." *The New York Times,* September 24, 1975.

Rubin, Stephen E. *The New Met in Profile.* New York: Macmillan, 1974.

Sargeant, Winthrop. "Profiles: A Miracle in the Desert, John Crosby of Santa Fe Opera." *The New Yorker,* August 4, 1975.

Teran, Jay R. S. "The New York Opera Audience: 1825–1974." Unpublished Ph.D. dissertation, Department of Drama, New York University, October 1974.

Orchestras

American Symphony Orchestra League. "Composite Financial Data Summary for Major and Metropolitan Orchestras, 1969–70 through 1974–75." Unpublished material.

Arian, Edward. *Bach, Beethoven and Bureaucracy: The Case of the Philadelphia Orchestra.* University, Alabama: University of Alabama Press, 1971.

Charlotte Symphony Orchestra. "Financial Statement. 1974–75."

Davies, John. "Orchestral Discord." *New Society,* January 8, 1976.

Field, Gladys S., ed. *The Musicians' Guide: Directory of the World of Music.* New York: Music Information Service, 1972.

Hart, Philip. *Orpheus in the New World.* New York: Norton, 1973.

Livingstone, William. "Mostly Mozart Wears Well." *Stagebill,* Vol. 2, No. 11, July 1975.

Mayer, William. "Live Composers, Dead Audiences." *The New York Times Magazine,* February 2, 1975, pp. 12–42.

The National Committee for Symphony Orchestra Support. "Funding the Arts: An Economic, Educational and Cultural Priority." March 1975.

The Philadelphia Orchestra Association and The Academy of Music. "Financial Statement 1973–74"; "Financial Statement 1974–75."

The Philharmonic-Symphony Society of New York, Inc. "Annual Report to the Members of the Board of Directors for the Fiscal Year Ending August 31, 1974."

Taubman, Howard. "The Symphony Orchestra Abroad: A Report of a Study." Vienna, Virginia: The American Symphony Orchestra League, Inc., 1970.

Thompson, Helen M. "Report of Study on Governing Boards of Symphony Orchestra." Vienna, Virginia: The American Symphony Orchestra League, Inc., 1958.

Theater

Actor's Equity Association. "Salaries of Membership," n.d.; "Dinner Theatre List 1975"; "Theatres Operating Under the LORT Contract," n.d.; "Summer Stock List 1975 Season"; and "Winter Stock List 1974–75 Season".

American Educational Theatre Association. *Humanities and the Theatre.* Washington, D.C., 1973.

Arena Stage. "The 1973–74 Season." September 1974.

Calta, Louis. "U.S. Offers Funds to British Troupe." *The New York Times,* January 14, 1975.

The Council of Stock Theatres. "Membership List," n.d.

Cumming, Richard. "A Short History of Project Discovery." Trinity Square Repertory Company, n.d.

Fichandler, Zelda. "Theatres or Institutions." In *The American Theatre 1969–70,* edited by the International Theatre Institute of the United States, pp. 105–16. New York: Scribner, 1971.

Goldman, William. *The Season: A Candid Look at Broadway* New York: Harcourt Brace Jovanovich, 1969.

Greenberger, Howard. *The Off-Broadway Experience.* Englewood Cliffs, N.J.: Prentice-Hall, 1971.

Guernsey, Otis L., Jr., ed. *The Best Plays of 1969–70; The Best Plays of 1970–71; The Best Plays of 1972–73; The Best Plays of 1973–74;* and *The Best Plays of 1974–75.* New York: Dodd, Mead, 1970 through 1975 respectively.

Hewitt, Alan. "Like It Is, Man: Professional Theater Employment. 1961–68." *Performing Arts Review,* Vol. 1, No. 4, 1970, pp. 623–67.

"Professional Theater Employment, 1970 Season." *Performing Arts Review,* Vol. 2, No. 4, 1971.

"Professional Theater Employment: 1972 Season." *Performing Arts Review,* Vol. 3, No. 4, 1972.

Lahr, John. "Mirror of the American Moment." In *Theatre 71,* edited by Sheridan Morley. London: Hutchinson, 1971.

Little, Stuart W. *After the Fact: Conflict and Consensus – A Report on the First American Congress of Theatre.* New York: Arno Press, 1975.

Moore, Thomas Gale. *The Economics of the American Theater.* Durham, North Carolina: Duke University Press, 1968.

Morley, Sheridan, ed. *Theatre 71.* London: Hutchinson, 1971.

The New York City Cultural Council and New York State Council of the Arts. "Study of the New York Theater: Summary and Recommendations." Basic report prepared by William J. Baumol, 1972.

The New York Times Directory of the Theater. New York: Arno Press, 1973.

Novick, Julius. *Beyond Broadway: The Quest for Permanent Theatres*. New York: Hill and Wang, 1968.

Poggi, Jack. *Theater in America: The Impact of Economic Forces, 1870–1967*. Ithaca, New York: Cornell University Press, 1968.

Schumach, Murray. "Papp Will Go Traditional: Cites Audience 'Hostility.'" *The New York Times,* March 8, 1975.

Taylor, Nora E. "Theatre in Providence: It is 'a one-to-one confrontation.'" *The Christian Science Monitor,* February 19, 1975.

Theatre Communications Group. *Theatre Profiles,* Vol. 1. New York. 1973.

"TCG Annual Fiscal Survey 1973–72." New York, 1975.

Theatre Development Fund. *Report 1: Last Minute Discounts of Unsold Tickets, A Study of TKTS*. New York, 1974.

"A Progress Report 1974–75."

"Off-Off Broadway: Finances, Funding and the TDF Voucher." Unpublished paper, 1975.

"Trinity's New Stage." *The Rhode Islander: The Providence Sunday Journal Magazine,* October 7, 1973.

The Washington Drama Society, Inc. "Financial Report, June 30, 1974."

Zeigler, Joseph Wesley. *Regional Theatre: The Revolutionary Stage*. Minneapolis: University of Minnesota Press, 1973.

Government, Economics, and Public Support of the Arts

The American Film Institute. "Summary of Curriculum and Conservatory Programs, Center for Advanced Film Studies – The American Film Institute"; "Analysis of Growth of AFI Self-Generated Revenue"; "Comparison of NEA Appropriations and American Film Institute General Grant Funding"; and "Comparison of Public Media Program funds with total NEA Grants and Contracts Awarded to AFI." Unpublished reports, 1975.

Associated Councils of the Arts. *Cultural Directory Guide to Federal Funds and Services for Cultural Activities*. New York, 1975.

Brustein, Robert. "The Coming Crisis for the Arts: Who's Going to Foot the Bill?" *The New York Times,* September 15, 1974.

The Corporation for Public Broadcasting. "Annual Report 1973"; "Public Broadcasting and Education"; "Policy for Public Radio Station Assistance" (January 1975); "Public Broadcasting and Long Range Funding: The Anatomy of a Bill"; "Public Broadcasting and Financing: Where the Money Comes From", "Public Television"; and "Annual Report: 1974." Washington, D.C.

Dempsey, David. "An enormous infusion of Federal funds into culture: Uncle Sam, the angel". *The New York Times Magazine,* March 24, 1974.

Epstein, Noel. "Politics and the Arts." *The Washington Post: Outlook,* August 25, 1974.

Galbraith, John Kenneth. *Economics and the Public Purpose.* New York: New American Library, 1973.

Glass, Andrew. "She's an Artist at Getting Money for the Arts." *The New York Times,* December 14, 1975.

Harris, John S. "The Government and Arts Patronage." *Public Administration Review,* No. 5, September/October 1973, pp. 407–14.

"The Politics of Government Patronage of the Arts in the United States." *Parliamentary Affairs,* Vol. 20, No. 4, 1967, pp. 315–28.

Kadis, Phillip M. "An Arts Funding 'Scandal'?" *The Washington Star,* November 13, 1975.

Lichtenstein, Grace. "Why Congress Said No to the Film Institute." *The New York Times,* January 26, 1975.

McDonald, William F. *Federal Relief Administration and the Arts.* Columbus: Ohio State University Press, 1973.

McKinzie, Richard D. *The New Deal for Artists.* Princeton: Princeton University Press, 1973.

Mark, Charles C. *A Study of Cultural Policy in the United States.* Paris: U.N.E.S.C.O. Press, 1969.

Marlin, William. "Ford, Nixon and Arts Policy." *The Christian Science Monitor,* August 23, 1974.

Martin, Judith. "Arts Funding Hearings: The Rhetoric Soared." *The Washington Post,* September 25, 1975.

National Endowment for the Arts. "The First Five Years: Fiscal 1966 through Fiscal 1970"; "Annual Report: 1969"; "Annual Report: 1970"; "New Dimensions for the Arts: 1971–72"; "Annual Report: 1973"; and "Annual Report: 1974." Washington, D.C.

"Guide to programs, 1974"; and "Guide to Programs 1975–76," Washington, D.C.

Program guidelines for: Architecture and Environmental Arts, 1976; Crafts Program 1975–76; "City Spirit Program"; Dance Touring (Sponsor) 1976; Dance Program 1976; Dance Touring 1977; Education – Artists in Schools 1976; Expansion Arts Program 1976–77; Federal-State Partnership 1975–76; Literature Program 1976; Assistance to Small Presses 1976; Museum Program 1976; Music Program 1976 – Orchestra, Composers/Librettist/Translators, Jazz/Folk/Ethnic, Opera; Public Media 1976; Theatre Program 1976; and Visual Arts 1976. Washington, D.C.

"Catalogue and Exhibition Grants," Fiscal Year 1974 Museum Program grants. Washington, D.C., March 1975.

"City Options," a list and description of each of the 148 grants approved by the endowment during FY 1974.

The Cultural Post, March 1975, June 1975, September 1975, March 1976, and May/June 1976.

"Resolution on Line-Itemming," passed by the National Council on the Arts, February 9–11, 1973.

"Resolution on Set Aside," passed by the National Council on the Arts, July 25–27, 1975.

"Fellowship Programs for Individuals: Some Comparisons," presented to the National Council on the Arts, July 1975.

"State Legislative Appropriations for the Arts, 1966–1975."

National Endowment for the Humanities. "Annual Report: 1970"; "Annual Report: 1971"; "Annual Report: 1972"; "Annual Report: 1973"; and "Annual Report: 1974." Washington, D.C.

"Program Announcement: 1974–75." Washington, D.C.

"The Endowment and the Bicentennial"; and "The Establishing of State Humanities Agencies: Examination of a Proposed Amendment to the Authorizing Legislation of the National Foundation on the Arts and Humanities: a Briefing Paper." September 1975.

National Foundation on the Arts and Humanities. *Estimates of the Appropriations for the Fiscal Year 1976.*

Netzer, Dick. "In Defense of Public Squalor." *New York Affairs,* Vol. 2, No. 4, Summer 1975.

"Large-Scale Public Support for the Arts." *New York Affairs,* Vol. 2, No. 1, Fall 1974.

"Property Tax Exemptions and Their Effects: A Dissenting View." *Proceedings of the Sixty-Fifth Annual Conference on Taxation,* October 1972.

Straight, Michael. "A New Artistic Era (If the Money Lasts)." *The New York Times,* October 20, 1974.

"Government's Contribution to Creative Expression" *The New Republic,* November 16, 1974, pp. 17–9.

"Tax Money for Arts: What it is buying." *U.S. News and World Report,* February 5, 1973.

U.S., Congress, House, Committee on Education, Select Subcommittee on Education. Discussion on H.R. 1118. Washington, D.C., November 12, 1975: Written testimony of Nancy Hanks.

Discussion on H.R. 7216, a bill to extend the authorization for the National Foundation on the Arts and Humanities. Washington, D.C., September 24–26, 1975: Written testimony of Thomas Fichandler, Louis Harris, Ramona Boughan, Anthony Bliss, John Crosby, the Minnesota Opera Company, Opera America, Cornell MacNeill, and John Blair Mitchell.

Discussion on H.R. 7216, Part B, the arts and artifacts indemnity act. New York, July 14, 1975: Written testimony of Joseph Veach Noble, Thomas Messer, and Thomas Hoving. New York, November 10, 1975: Written testimony of Douglas Dillon, Thomas Nicholson, Jean M. Weber, Joseph Veach Noble, Joel N. Bloom, Nancy Fessenden, and Dr. Emmanuel R. Piore.

U.S., Congress, House, Committee on Appropriations, Subcommittee of the Interior and Related Agencies. Hearings. Washington, D.C., March 26, 1974: Written testimony of Nancy Hanks. Washington, D.C., April 14, 1975: Written testimony of Nancy Hanks.

U.S., Congress, Senate, Committee on Labor and Public Welfare, Special Subcommittee on the Arts and Humanities; and House, Committee on Education and Labor, Select Subcommittee on Education and Labor. Joint Hearings; Discussion on S. 795, S. 916, H.R. 3926, and H.R. 4288. Washington, D.C., March 6, 1973: Written testimony of Nancy Hanks.

Joint Hearings; Discussion on S. 1800, S. 1809, H.R. 9657, and H.R. 7490. Washington, D.C., November 12–14, 1975: Written testimony of Nancy Hanks, Louise Tester, Richard Hastings, Ronald S. Berman, Fred Richmond, Amyas Ames, Robert Brustein, George Stevens, Charlton Heston, Suzanne Sheppard, and Douglas Davis.

U.S., Congress (94th Congress, 1st Session), Senate. S. 1809, "The National Foundation on the Arts and Humanities Amendments of 1975," a bill introduced by Senators Jacob K. Javits of New York. May 22, 1975.

S. 1800, a bill to amend and extend the National Foundation on the Arts and Humanities Act of 1965 to provide for the improvements of museum services, and to provide indemnities for exhibitions of artistic and humanistic endeavors and for other purposes, introduced by Senator Claiborne Pell of Rhode Island. May 21, 1975.

U.S. Department of Commerce. *Survey of Current Business,* Washington, D.C., July 1974.

U.S. Department of Commerce, Bureau of the Census. *Census of Population, 1970: Subject Reports, Final Report PC(2)-7A, Occupational Characteristics.* Washington, D.C.

Census of the Population, 1970: Subject Reports, Final Report PC(2)-7C, Occupation by Industry. Washington, D.C.

County Business Patterns, 1972, U.S. Summary, CBP-72-1. Washington, D.C.

Census of Selected Service Industries, 1972: Area Series, United States, SC72-A-52. Washington, D.C.

Census of Selected Service Industries, 1972: Miscellaneous Subjects, SC72-S-8. Washington, D.C.

Census of Manufactures, 1972: Vol. I, Summary and Subject Statistics. Washington, D.C.

Census of Retail Trade, 1972: Vol. I, Retail Trade – Summary Statistics. Washington, D.C.

University of Texas at Austin, Lyndon B. Johnson Library. "The Arts: Years of Development, Time of Decision." Symposium program, with written addresses by Beverly Sills and Hubert Humphrey, September 29–30, 1975.

Washington International Arts Letter. "Special NFAH Issue", Eighty-Seventh Letter, Vol. 10, No. 4, April 1971.
   "Expanding the Arts", Ninety-Eighth Letter, Vol. 11, No. 5, May 1972.

State Support of the Arts

The Economist, August 23, 1975.
Massachusetts Governor's Task Force on the Arts and Humanities. *The Arts: A Priority for Investment,* May 1973.
Mid-America Arts Alliance. *Focus,* Vol. 1, No. 1, January 1975.
National Assembly of State Arts Agencies. *Cultural Inquiries,* Vol. 1, No. 1.
National Research Center of the Arts, Inc. *Arts and the People: A Survey of Public Attitudes and Participation in the Arts and Culture in New York State.* New York: American Council for the Arts in Education, 1973.
   A Study of the Non-Profit Arts and Cultural Industry of New York State. New York: Performing Arts Association of New York State and New York State Association of Museums, 1972.
   "The Non-Profit Arts Industry in California: Highlights of Survey." 1974.
   "Californians and the Arts: Highlights of Survey." 1974.
New York State Commission on Cultural Resources. *Cultural Resource Development: Preliminary Planning Survey and Analysis.* Albany, New York: March 1973.
   State Financial Assistance for Cultural Resources. Albany, New York: 1971.
New York State Council on the Arts – Ad Hoc Committee of the Council. "A Report to the Chairman and Members of the New York State Council on the Arts." Unpublished report, January 17, 1975.
Scott, Mel. *The States and the Arts: The California Arts Commission and the Emerging Federal-State Partnership.* Berkeley, California: Institute of Governmental Studies, 1971.
Weber, Nathan. "County Funding of the Arts in New York State." Unpublished in-house report for the New York State Council on the Arts, July 1974.
White, Leslie C., and Helen M. Thompson, eds. "Survey of Arts Councils." American Symphony Orchestra League, 1959.

State Arts Councils Annual Reports and Program Guidelines

Alabama State Council on the Arts and Humanities. *Biennial Report: 1970–72;* "1972–73 Arts Activities"; "Publicity – Your Move: A Handbook for Community Arts Councils"; and *Alabama Arts,* Fall/Winter 1973; Summer 1974, and Spring 1975.

Alaska State Council on the Arts. *The Arts in Alaska,* September 15, 1974. Newsletter containing grant allocations for 1974–75.

Arizona Commission on the Arts and Humanities. *Annual Report to the Governor: 1974.*

Arkansas State Arts and Humanities Office. "Programs 1973–74"; "Arkansas Artists in Schools 1974–75"; and "Arkansas Arts: An Inventory of Cultural Programs, Organizations and Facilities of Arkansas," 1973.

California Arts Commission. *Annual Fiscal Report 1974–75;* "Grant Application Package"; and "1975 Performing Arts Organizations Grant Awards."

Connecticut Commission on the Arts. *Annual Report 1974.*

Delaware State Arts Council. *Annual Report 1973.*

Fine Arts Council of Florida. "Florida Division of Cultural Affairs and Fine Arts Council: Annual Report for 1973–74."

Georgia Council for the Arts. "A Search for Georgia Folk Art"; and "Grants Made During FY 1974."

Hawaii State Foundation on Culture and the Arts. *The Annual Report 1972–73.*

Idaho State Commission on the Arts and Humanities. *Annual Report 1973–74.*

Illinois Arts Council. *Seven Year Report: 1965–72.*

Indiana Arts Commission. *The Arts in Indiana: 1973–74 Annual Report.*

Iowa Arts Council. *Biennium Report: 1972–74;* and "Arts Council Programs 1974–75."

Kansas Cultural Arts Commission. *Annual Report 1973–74.*

Kentucky Arts Commission. *Annual Report 1973–74;* "Programs"; and "1975 Calendar."

Louisiana State Arts Council. "Louisiana Council for Music and Performing Arts, Inc.: Highlights of Programs and Projects 1973–74."

Maine State Commission on the Arts and Humanities. *Biennial Report: July 1972–June 1974.*

Maryland Arts Council. *Annual Report 1973–74.*

Massachusetts Council on the Arts and Humanities. *Annual Report 1974.*

Michigan Council for the Arts. "Report to State Legislature, March 1975," *Newsletter,* Winter, 1974–75.

Minnesota State Arts Council. *Annual Report 1973–74.*

Missouri State Council on the Arts. *Newsletter,* Vol. 1, No. 1, Winter, January 1975.

Nebraska Arts Council. "Guidelines for Nebraska Arts Council Project Assistance"; and "What is the Nebraska Arts Council?"

Nevada State Council on the Arts. "List of Grants for Fiscal Year 1975."

New Jersey State Council on the Arts. "Serving the Garden State – An Eighth Year Report." 1973.

New Mexico Arts Commission. *Ninth Annual Report Fiscal Year 1962 (1973–74).*

New York Council on the Arts. *Annual Report: 1969–70; Annual Report: 1970–71; Annual Report: 1971–72; Annual Report: 1972–73; Annual Report: 1973–74;* "The NYSCA, What it is and does," June 1974; "Program Information: 1975–75"; and "A List of NYSCA 1974–75 Grants."

North Carolina Arts Council. *The Third Biennium 1971–73.*

North Dakota Council on the Arts and Humanities. *Annual Report: 1973–74.*

Ohio Arts Council. "Guideline Booklet and Ninth Annual Report." 1975.

Oklahoma Arts and Humanities Council. "Guidelines for Project Assistance and Grant-Making Procedures and Deadlines."

Oregon Arts Commission. *Report 1974.*

Rhode Island State Council on the Arts. "Projected Budget: 1975–76"; and *1973–74 Report.*

South Carolina Arts Commission. *Annual Report 1971–73.*

Tennessee Arts Commission. "Directory of Services." 1974.

Texas Commission on the Arts and Humanities. *Annual Report 1974;* and "Report to the Governor: Fiscal Year 1974."

Utah State Division of Fine Arts. *Annual Report 1973–74.*

Vermont Council on the Arts. *1974 Annual Report;* "Writers in the Schools"; "Touring Artists Register"; and "Program Brochure."

Washington State Arts Commission. *Annual Report 1973–74.*

Municipal and Community Support

Associated Councils of the Arts. *A Guide to Community Arts Agencies.* New York, 1974.

The Bronx Council on the Arts. *Annual Report: June 12, 1974;* and "What We're All About."

Brooklyn Arts and Culture Association. "This is BACA."

Brooklyn Institute of Arts and Sciences. *Annual Report 1973–74.*

Easton, Allan, ed. *Community Support of the Performing Arts – Selected Problems of Local and National Interest. Hofstra University Yearbook of Business,* Series 7, Vol. 5, 1970.

Greater Philadelphia Cultural Alliance. "An Introduction to the Economics of Philadelphia's Cultural Organizations." February 1975.

Mayor's Committee on Cultural Policy. *Report of Committee.* New York, 1974.

New York City Cultural Council. *New York City Resources for the Arts and Artists.* New York: Cultural Council Foundation, 1973.

Visual Arts, Museums, Film, and Television

American Association of Museums. *America's Museums: The Belmont Report.* Washington, D.C., 1969.

Andre, Carl, et al. "The Role of the Artist in Today's Society." *The Art Journal,* Vol. 34, No. 4, Summer 1975, pp. 327–31.

Arts Development Service, Inc. "ADS Market Survey Study 1975: A Summary Report."

Association of College Unions, International Committee on the Arts. "Art Exhibitions: Sources and Resources 1972."

Brown, Les. "The $1.5 Million Adams Saga Overrun Shakes WNET." *The New York Times,* November 13, 1975.

Charlton, Linda. "The Humanities Endowment: Ballast on the ship of culture?" *ARTnews,* January 1976, pp. 37–40.

Clark, Bill. "Bleak Times Ahead for Artist." *The Villager,* September 4, 1975, p. 5.

The College Art Association. "Statistical Analysis of the Applicants and Positions listed by CAA's Placement Bureau: 1975." *The Art Journal,* Vol. 34, No. 4, Summer 1975, pp. 342–4.

Counts, Charles. "Encouraging American Craftsmen: Report of the Inter-agency Crafts Committee." Washington, D.C.: U.S. Government Printing Office, 1971.

The Gallery Association of New York State, Inc. "Second Annual Report January 1973–September 1973"; and "First One-Half, Third Annual Report, October 1973–March 1974."

Grace, Trudie. "Artists' Space." *The Art Journal,* Vol. 34, No. 4, Summer 1975, pp. 323–6.

Hubert, Dick. "A New Way to Fund Public TV." *The New York Times,* June 15, 1975.

Kisselgoff, Anna. "$3-million Dance Series on WNET." *The New York Times,* June 13, 1975.

Mandl, Cynthia, and Robert Kerr. "Museum Sponsorship of Performing Arts." Management Center for Arts Administration, Graduate School of Business, University of Wisconsin, January 1975.

National Endowment for the Arts. *Museums U.S.A.: Art, History, Science and Others.* Washington, D.C.: U.S. Government Printing Office, 1974.

"Museums U.S.A.: Highlights." 1973.

O'Doherty, Brian. "Public Art and the Government: A Progress Report." *Art in America,* May–June 1974.

O'Hare, Michael. "Should Museums Invest in Art, or is Speculation Immoral, Illegal, and Insufficiently Fattening?" *Museum News,* May 1975.

"Institutional Strategies for an Uncertain Future." Unpublished paper for MCA Financial Management Seminar, Massachusetts Institute of Technology, February 14–15, 1975.

"Arts Policy and Cultural Planning, Research Problems." Unpublished draft, May 11, 1974.

Skiles, Jacqueline. "The National Art Workers' Community: Still Struggling" *The Art Journal,* Vol. 34, No. 4, Summer 1975, pp. 320–2.

Welles, Chris. "Creeping Commercialism in Public TV." *The Village Voice,* May 12, 1975.

Young Filmakers Foundation. "Financial Report for the Fiscal Year Ended June 30, 1975."

Index